Nelson V Hutchinson

History of the Seventh Massachusetts Volunteer Infantry

In the War of the Rebellion of the Southern States Against....

Nelson V Hutchinson

History of the Seventh Massachusetts Volunteer Infantry
In the War of the Rebellion of the Southern States Against....

ISBN/EAN: 9783337116170

Printed in Europe, USA, Canada, Australia, Japan

Cover: Foto ©ninafisch / pixelio.de

More available books at **www.hansebooks.com**

HISTORY

OF THE

Seventh Massachusetts Volunteer Infantry

IN THE WAR OF THE

REBELLION OF THE SOUTHERN STATES

AGAINST CONSTITUTIONAL AUTHORITY.

1861-1865.

WITH

DESCRIPTION OF BATTLES, ARMY MOVEMENTS, HOSPITAL
LIFE, AND INCIDENTS OF THE CAMP, BY
OFFICERS AND PRIVATES;

AND A

COMPREHENSIVE INTRODUCTION OF THE MORAL AND POLITICAL
FORCES WHICH PRECIPITATED THE WAR OF SECESSION
UPON THE PEOPLE OF THE UNITED STATES.

BY THE AUTHOR,

NELSON V. HUTCHINSON.

TAUNTON, MASS.:
PUBLISHED BY AUTHORITY OF THE REGIMENTAL ASSOCIATION.
1890.

To the Brave Men

WHO GAVE UP THEIR OPPORTUNITIES IN CIVIL LIFE;

TO THE SICK AND WOUNDED

WHO DIED IN FIELD AND GENERAL HOSPITALS;

TO THOSE WHO DIED UPON THE FIELD OF HONOR

TO SUSTAIN THE INTEGRITY OF THE UNION;

IS THIS WORK

Lovingly Dedicated

BY THE AUTHOR.

ERRATA.

Page 7, and elsewhere, read "Z. Boylston Adams" instead of "Z. Bogelston Adams."

Page 8, read "Tillson" for "Tillston," and "Whiting" for "Whitney."

Page 12, first line, read "Sergts. Gurney and Whiting," instead of "Sergt. Gurney Whitney."

Page 16, line 21, read "*light* artillery" for "*heavy* artillery."

Page 129, read "Whiting" for "Whitney" also "Lieut. John C. Bosworth, Company A."

Page 130, read "Co. F—Killed—Lloyd W. Pratt" for "Loyal W. Pratt."

Page 131, read "and as all were worthy of record" instead of "and also all were daring of record."

Page 158, last paragraph, read, "We were now on same line of advance that McClellan made—under one of his most trusted lieutenants."

Page 171, line 17, for "piece" read "victory"; line 19, for "laugh" read "carp"; line 32, read, "*as* the right and left hand of Mars."

Page 175, line 32, read "enemy" for "army."

Page 176, next to last line, read, "on the right *flank* of the army."

Page 179, line 10, read "ensanguined" for "ensanguine."

Page 208, read, "Major-General Newton retired from the command of a *division* in the Sixth Corps."

Page 223, next to last line, read "*anti-septic*" for "*anti-septis*."

APOLOGY.

IN presenting the History of the Seventh Massachusetts Volunteer Infantry to the public, the author makes no pretension or claim to literary ability, but has essayed to give, in a plain and concise manner, the history of the Regiment, to record its sacrifices, its hardships, and the valor and endurance of its men who participated in the work of saving the Union as a Confederation of States, and establishing the principles of national unity, and also as a memorial of them, that their children and the generations to come who know not of their sacrifices by personal experience, may be taught the great lessons of patriotism which swelled the hearts of their fathers, the volunteers of 1861.

Shortly after the formation of the Regimental Association an effort was made to secure a Regimental History, and as it was a much more propitious time then than at the present, (it being in the seventies, shortly after the regiment left the service,) it is to be much regretted that it was not carried to a successful issue at that time. A committee was appointed, of which Capt. George Reed, of Co. K, was president; but shortly after its formation Capt. Reed was seized with a very severe sickness, from which he has never fully recovered.

At the seventeenth annual reunion of the Regimental Association a paper was read by the author, setting forth the advantages of a Regimental History, and after an animated discussion the following committee was chosen to collect and forward data to the historian, who had been chosen at the aforesaid meeting. That committee consisted of one member from each Company, with Col. F. P. Harlow as an additional committeeman at large. The following is the committee as appointed at the annual reunion: Company A, Walter S. Goss; Company B, James G. Church; Company C, Charles Staples; Company D, Henry H. Codding; Company E, Henry Tollman; Company F, Lieut. Harrie A. Cushman; Company G, Lieut. A. W. Lothrop; Company H, Hiram B. Reed; Company I, Lieut. William Wade; Company K, Nelson V. Hutchinson; Band, William M. Bowles.

Under the labors of this committee and the historian, the subject matter was collected and revised, and edited by the historian. It slowly grew into shape, and after being authorized by the Regimental Association, a contract was closed with Rand, Avery & Co., of Boston; but they subsequently suffered a perfect collapse, and were petitioned into insolvency, after having completed about one hundred and fifty pages of manuscript for five hundred volumes.

In closing up the affairs of the firm under the assignee appointed by the court for Suffolk county, the greater part of the manuscript was lost, necessitating the re-writing of that portion of the history. When the historian had completed that task, he entered into communication with Lieut. Charles B. Hathaway, of Taunton, Mass., formerly of Co. F, Seventh Massachusetts, and secured a very favorable contract from him for the completion of the history, he having sub-let the printing to the old and reliable printer, Ezra Davol, of Taunton, under whose contract the book was completed in every way the equal of the first contract,—Mr. Davol as printer and Mr. Hathaway as binder being among the oldest and most reliable firms of the state or country.

The historian is under very great and lasting obligations to the following named gentlemen, who very kindly did all in their power to aid him in obtaining the necessary data and material: Maj.-Gen. D. N. Couch, the former commander of the regiment; Maj.-Gen.

Schofield, commanding the Atlantic Division; the Hon. William Endicott, Secretary of War: Lieut.-Gen. Sheridan; Brig.-Gen. Nelson H. Davis (retired); Maj.-Gen. Don Carlos Buell; Maj.-Gen. Charles Devens; ex-Gov. John D. Long; the Hon. Secretary of State, Henry B. Peirce, who very kindly forwarded documents from Washington, obtained at the War Department and at the State House, Boston, (Mr. Peirce assisting by his own personal labor in looking up facts); Lieut.-Col. F. P. Harlow; Capt. Zeba F. Bliss; Capt. Gurney; William G. Litchfield and Corp. William Litchfield; Alfred Seaverns of Co. E; Harrie A. Cushman of Co. F. The historian would extend his heartfelt thanks to one and all for the very material assistance he has received in the compilation of this history.   N. V. H.

SEVENTH MASSACHUSETTS VOLUNTEER INFANTRY.

1861.

CHAPTER I.

CAUSES OF THE REBELLION OF STATES FROM CONSTITUTIONAL AUTHORITY.

IN presenting the history of the Seventh Massachusetts Volunteer Infantry to the public, it may be well to state the moral and political reasons and principles of civil polity held by the different sections of the country, the agitation of which led to the secession of States, whereby one of the greatest wars of modern or ancient times was precipitated upon the people of the different sections. The Slave States, so called, were inhabited by an agricultural people principally, who were hampered by the institution of slavery, handed down to them as a legacy by their ancestors; while the North-Eastern and North-Western States were peopled by a commercial, manufacturing, and agricultural people, in the older sections of which slave labor had been found unprofitable, and had therefore been abolished on or about the beginning of the present century. The slave question is, in the minds of many, the cause of the great Rebellion; but to the moral philosopher other and deeper reasons appear to the mind as the controlling power which forced this most unhappy strife upon the people of the United States so called. And, to state the question fairly, it may be said it was the clashing of two great and distinct civilizations, — one the advanced Christian mind, the other the pagan and Mosaic. The first, in its onward sweep of progress and moral enlightenment of the human race, found no law or place for their enslavement; while the pagan and Mosaic civilizations in their civil politics upheld and defended the principles of slavery. And to-day in pagan and semi-civilized countries only is it permitted for one people to enslave another people or nation.

The South, blessed by fertile plains, and valleys rich in all natural products, with cotton as king, waxed strong and haughty; and, as she increased in wealth, her white people became very aristocratic and overbearing, — the legitimate results of a moneyed aristocracy, be it North or South. And as wealth grew upon them, the greed of gold ate up the greater moral principles of the declaration of the confederative Constitution, "That all men are born free and equal, and possessed of certain inalienable rights; that among these are life, liberty, and the pursuit of happiness;" and they soon grew to brook no interference by legislative enactments by federal power in its efforts to confine the institution of slavery to the original Colonies or States.

Contrariwise the North had grown great in science, literature, and the arts; her villages, the products of her civilization, crowned a thousand hills; free labor was respected, education was upheld and supported by State and people; and a noble educational and Christian civilization had crowned the efforts of Pilgrim and Puritan to found a nation of freemen. And as the people of the North became more and more enlightened under the onward march of her civilization, the hideousness of slavery became more and more apparent; and by the agitation of the anti-slavery polity by her great moral statesmen, her people determined that it should not be allowed with its blighting influences to encroach any farther upon the principles of democratic government.

And the South, seeing the inevitable results of the progress of the Northern mind towards the true meaning of the confederative principles embodied in the Constitution, became alarmed, and by the machination of her leading men was forced to raise the red hand of rebellion against the Federal Union, and sought by the wage of internecine strife to disrupt the union of States, and to establish an empire whose corner-stone should be slavery. But ere the first shot had hurled the brick from Sumter's walls, a million of freemen stood ready to fight, and die if need be, for the perpetuity of the Union and Constitution. There were many makeshifts and compromises enacted to pacify the South; but as her power grew, she became more and more arrogant. The South had enough allies at the North previous to the opening of the Rebellion to enact the following laws to pacify and lull both North and South until she was ready for separation. First I will mention the Wilmot Proviso, Mason and Dixon's Line enactment, Dred Scott decision, Supreme Court, and others, *pro* and *con*.

The *animus* of this Southern cabal had shown itself as early as 1832, at the time of Jackson's administration, in the nullification schemes of South Carolina, led by that father of traitors, John C. Calhoun, who was also the father of the Southern Rebellion; for, by his treasonable construction and interpretation of the Constitution in its relation to the separate States, he laid the seed of the greatest rebellion the world ever knew, and one for which the historian can find the fewest excuses. The several agitations by the different contendants led to the border warfare in Kansas, and the John Brown *émeute* at Harper's Ferry in the year 1859, and finally took the form of secession of the Southern States when Abraham Lincoln, the nominee of the Republican party, was elected President in 1860. The Democratic party had become hopelessly divided, and the key of power was wrested from them, to return only after more than a quarter of a century had passed away.

Soon from threats the seceders proceeded to overt acts of treason. Sumter was assaulted and fell. Lincoln then issued his call for 75,000 three-months' troops: then 43,000 (3d of May), and very soon again for 300,000. Bull Run had been fought, and the Great Rebellion was opened, which was only to close when the shackles had been struck from 4,000,000 of slaves, and the armies of the North had traversed a continent in their victorious advance, after rivers of blood had been shed, and countless treasure lost and expended, which results were inevitable from the moral and progressive strides of modern civilization.

But the South was smitten not to die, but to be purified; and she has risen from her furnace of affliction, a noble sister in the strife for a higher civilization, and is now hand in hand with the onward march of the nineteenth century,— a noble people in a beautiful land,—

> "A land of supernatural powers,—
> Their lakes adorned with flowers;
> Like seas their rivers run;"

and will soon be the home of a people noted for their education and loyalty,— a people of kindness and wealth, the results of a great moral and civil revolution.

And the North can find many lessons of instruction, and much to profit by, as we look back and review the causes of the great rebellion: the same principles of revolution being found in the huge corporations and monopolies raised up since the rebellion, and which corrupt the halls of legislation.

Thus I have set as a frontispiece to the opening page of the Regimental History these preliminary remarks on the great moral, political, and revolutionary causes which have made such a history possible: the fruitage of which will be found in the succeeding pages a monument to the Volunteers of 1861.

DARIUS N. COUCH,
Colonel.

CHAPTER II.

ORGANIZATION AND MOVEMENT TO WASHINGTON.

THE SEVENTH MASSACHUSETTS VOLUNTEER INFANTRY was recruited and organized at Taunton. Mass., by Col., now Major-Gen., Couch, and was a Bristol-County regiment: "all except E and K Companies" having been recruited in that county. It was sworn into the United-States service, June 15, 1861. Eight companies were recruited in Fall River, Taunton, Raynham, Easton, Mansfield, Attleborough, Dighton; while Companies E and K were recruited in Abington and Dorchester. It remained in camp at Taunton until the twelfth day of July, when it proceeded to Washington by order of Secretary of War. While at Taunton it was prepared for active service in field by Col. Couch, aided by a corps of able and zealous officers.

On the fourth day of July, 1861, the regiment paraded, and marched to Taunton, and there took part in the celebration of the Declaration of Independence by the citizens of Taunton; Col. Couch, Hon. Samuel Crocker, the mayor of the city, and others, making very powerful and eloquent speeches in favor of the suppression of the rebellion, and in support of the Constitution and laws of the land. After a bountiful collation had been partaken of, the regiment returned to camp, where they were engaged in drilling and guard-duty, until they were ordered to Washington. On the morning of July 12, the regiment was ordered to break camp, and form line in heavy marching order, to take the cars to proceed to Washington. The day was most beautiful, a strong breeze relieving the heat of a July sun. Shortly after noon we filed aboard the cars waiting for us, and amid the waving of handkerchiefs, and tearful adieus, we moved off on our way to Washington. Oh, how many of that regiment, who in the full pride of youthful manhood went forth to battle for their country's life, never more returned to gladden the friends of their once happy homes, or ever more kissed a fond mother's careworn brow, — the mothers of our Northern homes, zealous and faithful through much sorrow and gloom, and death of many a husband and son! Many, many, sleep the sleep that knows no waking. They rest in death's peaceful slumbers on many a field and plain, — some beside the placid waters of Old Potomac's gently moving tides; others beneath the murky heights of Fredericksburg; some on the James's fever-laden banks; others still beneath the tangled thickets of the Wilderness, and in the bloody lines of Spotsylvania; and others yet on Cold Harbor's battle-stained plains, — never more to live, only in the tender remembrance of friends and comrades, until God, the Giver of life, shall call all men to life eternal on the resurrection morn. They died for their country in manhood's early days, and offered their lives a sacrifice on the altar of their country, that the Union and Constitution might be preserved, and our national life rescued from the clutch of traitors' hands, and that our noble land might be restored to its pristine vigor and life, the home of free men, and a pledge of progressive civilization to all mankind.

Major-Gen. Couch, the first commander of the regiment, graduated from West Point in 1846, when he was promoted to brevet second lieutenant, Fourth Artillery; served in the war with Mexico, 1846-48, being engaged in the battle of Buena Vista, Mex., as second lieutenant of Capt. Washington's Battery Light Artillery, and was brevetted first lieutenant for gallant and meritorious conduct; was in the Seminole war in Florida, 1850-51. He married, in 1854, a daughter of the Hon. Samuel S. Crocker of Taunton, Mass. At the breaking out of the Rebellion he was in Taunton, Mass., where he recruited and organized the Seventh Massachusetts Volunteer Infantry; was promoted brigadier-general in August following, the brigades of Couch, Graham, and Peck forming a division commanded by Gen. Don Carlos Buell, then by Gen. Keys, commander of Fourth Corps on the Peninsula, then by Couch who succeeded him. He held the line on the left at the siege of Yorktown, and bore a very honorable part in all the battles of that campaign; was promoted to command of the Second Corps after the battle of Antietam; was a very gallant and meritorious officer, whose history is so interwoven with all that appertains to the great strife and campaigns of the Army of the Potomac, that it is needless to further recite his achievements in that army. He now resides in Norwalk, Conn., enjoying a restful ease after a life of great activity and honor, in both a civil and military capacity, beloved by all the men he ever commanded, a true soldier, a noble citizen, an educated gentleman, a noble product of the energy and educational influences of the Christian civilization of the nineteenth century.

He had as his staff, while in command of the Seventh Massachusetts Volunteer Regiment, — as adjutant, Othniel Gilmore; quartermaster, Daniel Edson; surgeon, S. Atherton Holman; assistant surgeon, Z. Bogleston Adams; as field-officers, Chester W. Green of Fall River; David E. Holman, Attleborough. He had as line-officers the following able and efficient captains, who proved themselves to be men of the right mould in the right place: —

Company A of Fall River, Commanded by Capt. David H. Dyer.
" B " " " " John Cushing.
" C " Raynham, " " Charles T. Robinson.
" D " Taunton. " " Joseph B. Leonard.
" E " Dorchester, " " Horace Fox.
" F " Taunton, " " Ziba F. Bliss.
" G " Easton, " " Ward L. Foster.
" H " Mansfield, " " John R. Whitcomb.
" I " Attleborough, " " John F. Ashley.
" K " Abington, " " Franklin P. Harlow.

Many lieutenants rose to grade of captain, and bore an honorable part in all the achievements of the regiment, who will be more especially mentioned as the History proceeds. They were men who were in earnest in the cause of constitutional liberty, and gave up their positions in civil life that the nation's life might be preserved. Bullock and Tillston and Mitchell and Whitney yielded up their lives in the fore-front of battle, zealous patriots, loyal and true, the pride of the companies which they commanded, beloved by all.

After the regiment had filed aboard the cars, and were seated, we moved off on the Mansfield branch through to main line of Providence Railroad, thence through to Providence, thence to Stonington in Connecticut, where we took the steamer "Commonwealth" up the Sound to New York. Arrived in New York about five o'clock, July 13, 1861. As we passed down East River on that early summer morning, we were greeted by a sight given to a very few men to see in a lifetime. The wharves and piers of East and North Rivers were literally packed with shipping. As far as the eye could see, huge three-masted square-riggers lined the wharves, — some from India and Europe, some from China, Japan, and the far-off isles of the sea, loading and unloading; for at that time the United States was mistress of the carrying-trade of the world; but when the regiment returned, after three years of service, the whole scene was changed. England had usurped the carrying-trade, helped by her own privateers under Confederate colors, and the piers and wharves were largely deserted. We lay at the wharf some six or eight hours, and while there many friends of the regiment visited the men and officers. I remember well George Beal, the principal of Scituate High School, visited his old acquaintances and scholars from Scituate, who were enlisted in Company K. While lying at the wharf, one of Company K's men (Darling by name) received a severe bayonet-wound in the arm, the first serious casualty of the campaign thus far. In the early part of the afternoon we steamed quickly down New-York Harbor to take the cars at Elizabethport on the New-Jersey Central Railroad. The train was soon made up; and here we first beheld the beautiful red clay so difficult of extraction from the heel of one's stocking after a brisk rain has set its liquid properties in motion. To the men of Massachusetts the engines of this road were a marvel, being two story, and four driving-wheels on a side, built expressly to draw heavy loads of coal; the seacoast terminal of which road is Elizabethport, a great coal-trade centre. At about three o'clock we were safely ensconced in our box-cars, and moved off on the road to Harrisburg through the centre of the State of New Jersey. And such beautiful scenery! fields of wheat as far as the eye could see, and immense peach-orchards interspersed with hill and dale, gave to the scenery under the glowing sun a fulness and beauty seldom seen, and which, with many remarks from officers and men, gave to the trip a varied and exciting zest, which old soldiers can fully enjoy in reminiscence to-day. Without any serious accident, only the separation of the train in the mountain grades, we steamed into Harrisburg about eleven o'clock at night. The scenery on this part of the road through the Alleghany Mountains is magnificent beyond conception, and, to be fully appreciated, should be seen in a palace-car, rather than in a box-car running thirty miles an hour, while one is packed like sardines in a box. We were obliged to run at an exceedingly fast rate of speed to clear the track for an express-train which would have the right of way. The train was very long and heavily laden: every company having a team consisting of four horses, an army-wagon, and driver. but which luxury became sadly depleted after the Peninsula campaign. We lay quietly side-tracked in Harrisburg that night and part of next day, when we steamed down the road to Baltimore. When we had arrived to within about five miles from Baltimore we filed out of the cars, and loaded our rifles; Col. Couch having no idea of being caught napping, as was the "Old Sixth" when they passed through Baltimore in the April preceding. And well do we remember how the old regiment looked as we marched through Baltimore, one thousand and ten strong, led by our gallant commander. Col. (now Major-Gen.) Couch. Company K was the leading company, its captain being the senior captain of the regiment, which position was held by military usage. After a quiet march led by the mayor of the city, we arrived at the depot of the Baltimore and Washington Railroad. After being ordered aboard train, we had not long to wait, but proceeded very slowly, as the bridges were not in the best of repair. We arrived in Washington July 15, 1861. We had a very brisk welcome all along the route from the troops of Butler's command. We reached Washington about half-past six o'clock P.M. As we had prepared rations, we were not long in taking a lunch, after which we were ordered to fall in, and march to the Capitol, in which magnificent building we were quartered until we took up our march to Kalorama.

Hon. JAMES BUFFINTON,
Private Co. "A."

CHAPTER III.

CAMP KALORAMA AND CAMP BRIGHTWOOD. — MOVEMENT AROUND WASHINGTON.

THE regiment was much indebted to the Hon. James Buffington, "the able Representative of the Fifth Representative District in Congress from Fall River, Mass., a refined and genial man," for much of its comforts while encamped in Washington. The streets of Washington at that time (early in 1861) were very wide, without pavements, and were used as runs for cattle and pigs, and were very muddy and in very poor repair. We soon marched to Kalorama Heights, where we encamped. The camp lay upon the left side of Rock Creek, a babbling, noisy brook, whose banks were fringed with growth of woods and briers, blackberry bushes and brambles. This camp was high and healthy. We were soon in good order, our tents having been pitched, and camp-kitchens erected. As soon as the camp had been properly established, we were set to drilling, and fitting ourselves for the duties of a soldier's life; Col. Couch being a very strict disciplinarian, firm and just. On Sunday, the 21st of July, 1861, as a large number of the regiment were attending divine service under our worthy chaplain, Joseph Carver, in the grove to right rear of camp, there came to the ears of the men who had not forgotten the religious principles of their home life, the sullen boom of field-artillery from across the river. Prominent among the worshippers on that eventful day were our gallant colonel, Capt. Harlow, Capt. Bliss, Capt. Dyer, Lieut. Reed, Lieut.

Mayhew, and Sergeant Gurney Whitney of Company I, and others too numerous to mention. We doubt if the words of the chaplain, after the first half-hour of the cannonade, reached many hearts or ears, for all was suppressed excitement. After the chaplain had closed the services, the officers drew around the colonel; and soon all were at their quarters waiting for the *long roll*, — that tap of drum which has called so many soldiers to a speedy death. They had not long to wait. Soon its ominous sounds were heard reverberating through the camp, and the stern order "Fall in!" was given from company officers by command of Col. Couch. After standing in line an hour or more, we were dismissed, and sent to quarters under orders to be ready to fall in again at a moment's notice.

But no call came. The regimental ambulances were sent across the river to help bring in from the roadsides and fields the wounded and exhausted of that wild retreat, caused by the sinister influences of political carpers, who had broken down even Scott's great moral force of mind, and induced him to order an advance before the troops were fitted for such a movement, and who still later caused untold misery and distress to the army by their Satanic meddling. The regiment remained in camp at Kalorama until we were removed to Camp Brightwood, at junction of Seventh and Fourteenth Streets, some five miles from Washington. Company K had been detailed to serve as guard to *tête-de-pont* on the Virginia side of Long Bridge, but was ordered back to camp, it having been a mistake by some staff-officers. We lay here in camp trying to keep comfortable, — it being very hot and sultry, — drill being almost dispensed with on account of extreme heat ; guard-mounting and dress-parade being the principal military work. While lying at this camp, President Lincoln, accompanied by Gen. Scott, reviewed the regiment. Charles Sumner visited us at this camp. But Gov. Andrew found no time, as his Suffolk-county regiments absorbed all his attention while visiting the Capitol, — a

slight the men of the Seventh Massachusetts never forgot
nor forgave; and whenever they speak of Gov. Andrew,
"some may think him near perfection; but the men of Bristol and other counties think he was very *human*, and could
show preference to a marked degree in his official intercourse
with people."

Aug. 6, 1861, we were moved to Camp Brightwood, — a
high and healthy location on the left of Fourteenth Street,
leading from the city, where we had an abundance of pure
water, and ample scope for drill and military manœuvring.
The day was very hot; and many men were prostrated from
the heat, and from the effects of loading themselves down
with a huge knapsack, generally stuffed with a family Bible,
shaving-kit, and extra shirts, blankets, Hardee's "Tactics,"
and several mementos of the campaign thus far, — some
stone work, or iron work, or other heavy material, which
served to make the load almost unendurable, — a freak of
greenness we paid a high penalty for in our first marches,
and for which ignorance the officers were to be held accountable in a degree, as well as the privates.

We marched up towards Brightwood some four miles,
and filed into a field upon the right of the road, where we
encamped a few days, when we moved into the permanent
camp of Brightwood. While in this camp, Lieut.-Col. Green
held command; and we were inspected by Gen. Don Carlos
Buell, that splendid and efficient officer. We were very
highly complimented by him. Previous to this inspection,
we had been reviewed by Major-Gen. McClellan. And to
this day he has a warm place in the hearts of all his old
soldiers, — so soldierly, so gallant, so considerate of all. He
was the idol of the old Army of the Potomac; and the
feeling only changed in a degree when Halleck's Western
Napoleons and Stanton's "On to Richmond," never-mind-the-cost generals took command of the soldiers who were
recruited later, and who never knew his greatness or
goodness.

While at this camp, the following letter was sent to the paper herein mentioned; and as it is quite amusing, we insert it.

[*Written for The Fall-River Journal.*]

1861.

WAR CORRESPONDENCE.

CHRONICLES I.

BY PETER THE PATRIOTIC.

Now it came to pass, that when Abraham was made chief ruler of the land, there arose a great tumult among the Southern brethren. And all of that part of the land gathered together, and murmured among themselves, saying, What manner of man is this who would rule over us? Surely, he may be great among flat-boatmen, and a mighty splitter of rails ; but we verily believe that he cannot keep a hotel. And they chose unto themselves a chief, even Jeff Davis, the bosom-friend of one Floyd, who was noted for his pickings from the public crib, and forthwith declared war against Abraham and his people. When Abraham heard of these things, he was sorely vexed, and sent unto all the rulers of the loyal States, saying, Gather together all thy valorous men of war, even the patriotic, and come down and help us to defend the stars and stripes; for the Philistines are upon us, and surely will lay waste the great city of the rulers, and swallow us up with a gulf, if the fighting-men come not. And it came to pass that when John, who ruled over that part of the land inherited by the Pilgrim stock, heard of these things, he was greatly exercised in mind, and bestirred himself corporally. And he sent unto all his chief men of war, even unto one Darius, who dwelt in the land which lieth on the river called Taunton. Now it was said of Darius that he was a mighty man in battle, having fought valiantly under one Zachary, who slew the Mexicans with exceeding great slaughter.

And John, the ruler, spoke unto Darius, the man of war, saying, Get thee together a regiment, even one thousand strong; and I will make thee ruler over them. And Darius did as he was bid. And he tarried a short time in the land of the Puritans; and when spring was nearly ended, he and his valorous men of war journeyed toward the South; and when they were come nigh, even unto the great city of the rulers, they pitched their tents, and encamped nigh unto the gates thereof.

And as they encamped on the borders of the city, Darius found great favor in the eyes of the ruler; and they spake unto him, saying, Thou hast

EDWARD T. MARVEL,
Private Co. "A."

been faithful over a thousand, therefore thou shalt be made ruler over four thousand. Darius departed to take command of the four thousand; and the second ruler, one Chester, a dweller in the city of spindles, commanded in his stead. Now, Chester was a man of peace, and not skilful in the cunning tactics of warfare; but whatsoever he lacketh in knowledge, he essayeth to amend with great zeal. When he would utter words of wisdom, his tongue cleaveth to the roof of his mouth. He openeth his mouth, and wisdom bubbleth not forth.

After sojourning a few days nigh unto the great city, Chester, the ruler, commandeth to remove from thence farther into the wilderness, and nigh unto the borders of Maryland, there to meet the enemy, who dwelleth in the land of Jeff. They tarried long in the land of Brightwood, where none appeared to molest or make afraid.

They builded unto themselves hillocks of sand, and called them forts, and mounted thereon ordnances of iron, which burneth much powder, and maketh a mighty noise, like unto the rushing of many waters. After this they rested from their labors, and grew very fat by devouring much rations. And they made unto themselves a commandment that they might dwell together in peace, respect their rulers, and depart not from the paths of rectitude. These commandments are written in these chronicles, and are as follows: —

1st, Thou shalt have no other man to rule over thee, save Old Abe, and such of his friends as he chooses, to carry out his ordinances. Thou shalt not cast thine eye wishfully toward the land of Jeff, nor sigh for the flesh-pots of thy Northern brethren. Thou shalt bow submissively to those appointed over thee; for they are vigilant rulers, visiting the iniquities of your shortcomings with guard-house visions, even unto bucking all them that hate them.

2d, Thou shalt not make use of intemperate language, nor "cuss" excessively in the officers' presence; for the wages of thy sin is a shilling a swear.

3d, Remember the sabbath day and the inspection thereon, that thy brasses may shine with great lustre, and every thing about thy person rejoice in cleanliness.

4th, Six days shalt thou drill, and do whatsoever thou art commanded.

5th, Honor them that rule over thee, that thy days may pass pleasantly in the land of "Secesh."

6th, Thou shalt not slay thy friends, but thine enemies slay with great slaughter, even with a two-edged sword, as it is written in the articles of war, sect. 9990.

7th, Thou shalt not adulterate thy water with whiskey; for it will surely bring thee to the horizontal pole, even unto the straddling thereof; for it might cause a soreness in the regions of thy vertebrae.

8th, Thou shalt not, under any mistake, seize or take thy neighbor's blanket, nor his knapsack, nor any thing contained therein; for on a long march, it might exceedingly weary thee.

9th. Thou shalt not bear false witness against thy fellow-soldier, for it appertaineth not unto patriotism.

10th. Thou shalt not covet thy corporal's stripes; thou shalt not covet thy neighbor's "salt junks," his "hard-tack," nor his "soft-tack," nor his knife, nor his spoon, nor his fork, nor his cup; for if thou hast neither, thou canst get a quill.

NELSON H. DAVIS,
Colonel.

CHAPTER IV.

THE REGIMENT UNDER COL. DAVIS, CAMP BRIGHTWOOD.

SEPT. 4. 1861, Col. Couch having been promoted brigadier-general of volunteers, Col. Nelson H. Davis took command of the regiment. His services, told in the succeeding pages, fitly portray the character and influence of this sound and efficient commander. He came to us unknown; but soon his great military knowledge left its imprint on officers and men.

In an extract from Cullum's "West-Point Biography," I find the following recorded in relation to Col. Davis's connection with the army of the United States: —

"Col. Nelson H. Davis was a graduate of West-Point Military Academy; was born in Massachusetts, and appointed a cadet United-States Military Academy, July 1, 1841, to July 1, 1846, when he graduated; promoted in army brevet second lieutenant Third Infantry from July 1, 1846; served in the war with Mexico, 1846 to 1848, being engaged in siege of Vera Cruz, battle of Cerro Gordo, at Contreras and Churubusco; also in the assault and capture of city of Mexico; brevetted first lieutenant for gallant and meritorious conduct in the battles of Contreras and Churubusco; on duty in various portions of the United States, and acting against the Indians in the West; captain Second Regular Infantry from 1853 to 1855; served during the Rebellion; battle of Bull Run; appointed colonel Seventh Massachusetts Volunteer Infantry, Sept. 4, 1861; served in that capacity until Nov. 12, 1861; major and assistant inspector-general, Nov. 12,

1861; served in the Peninsular campaigns in several battles; in campaign of Army Potomac in Maryland, 1862; Rappahannock campaign, battles of Chancellorsville and Gettysburg; brevet lieutenant-colonel, July 3, for gallant and meritorious services July 3, 1863, at the battle of Gettysburg; commander of Department of New Mexico, 1863 and 1865; brevet colonel for gallant and meritorious services in action with Apache Indians, Arizona, May 29, 1864; is now retired, having become inspector-general of the United-States Army."

Col. Davis was a very firm and strict disciplinarian, and soon the effects of his work became apparent in the better knowledge of officers and men in their respective military duties. Battalion and company drills came thick and fast, guard-duty and inspections being required in regular army style. To this thorough training was due much of the steadiness of the men in action, and the regiment felt the benefit of their colonel's early discipline in its later hours of need and trial. Reviews by brigade and division were in order. Brigade and division drills through the fall were often ordered at Meridian Hill, near Washington, under Don Carlos Buell and Gen. Keys. The Seventh Massachusetts obtained the right of the brigade, and the brigade the right of the division, from the superior proficiency shown by the regiment while on battalion and brigade drill. Gen. McClellan reviewed the division several times, and was much pleased with the ability shown by the Seventh Massachusetts; and the regiment received his compliments for its excellent marching and soldierly bearing. We were drilled almost constantly in battalion, skirmish, and brigade drill.

Col. Green having resigned Nov. 22, Lieut.-Col. Charles Raymond, of Plymouth, Mass., was appointed to be lieutenant-colonel of the regiment. It was with many misgivings we saw a man from civil life appointed over our faithful Major F. P. Harlow, especially as there were officers in the

CHESTER W. GREENE,
Lieutenant Colonel.

regiment who were well qualified to hold the position. But
we were ever loyal to orders and the best interests of our
State, and were bound to obey no matter who commanded,
provided he had the proper authority. Lieut.-Col. Raymond
was a fine man personally, and obtained the respect and love
of the officers and men; and this did much to cover his shortcomings in military life. He was a very fine man in civil
life, but not competent to handle masses of men in action;
he was highly esteemed as a citizen, but we never appreciated
him as a soldier, he having been selected by Gov. Andrew
through political influence.

While Col. Couch, Lieut.-Cols. Green and Raymond, held
command, Forts Stevens and Slocum were built, which was
hard and laborious work; certain companies being detailed
from the regiment, and others of the brigade, to work certain hours in a day. It was hard digging, and the weather
was extremely hot. Many of the boys were suffering from
climatic changes, and consequently were weak, and easily
exhausted by any unusual work.

And so the summer wore away. Rock Creek and Seventh
and Fourteenth Streets were picketed, and a very close scru-
tiny exercised over all passing; a good school for both officers
and men, although nothing serious occurred except the arrest
of a few suspicious characters, and the wounding of a melon-
patch or two, or the capture of contraband whiskey while it
was being conveyed through the lines. The boys constructed
very comfortable booths, in which the guards were quartered.
It was more discomfort to stand the heat and mosquitoes
than the work of guard-duty.

Nov. 24, 1861, Col. Davis left us, having been promoted, as
herein stated; and Joseph Wheelock took command. He was
a West-Point graduate, having entered that institution from
Massachusetts, July 1, 1846, and graduating July 1, 1850.
He was brevetted second lieutenant of artillery, July 1,
1850; served in the Seminole war in Florida; on sick leave

during the year 1856; assistant professor Military Academy, 1851 to 1855; first lieutenant Fourth Artillery. Jan. 13, 1856; resigned March 1, 1857; his civil history unknown; served in the war of the Rebellion; appointed colonel of Seventh Massachusetts Volunteer Infantry. Nov. 20, 1861; resigned Jan. 31, 1862; died at Washington, D.C., aged thirty-three years. A very fine man mentally, but whose habits were not of the best; one of Gov. Andrew's selections without personal knowledge of the man.

The weather had begun to change, and "Frosty weather" became the by-word. Some of the citizens would come and stand by our fires, if allowed through the lines, and say, "It's right smart cold, — it's right smart frosty," and shiver as though a cyclone had struck them. We would often ask, "How far is it to Frederick City, up to the north-west?" and then they would reply, "One look, two looks, and a right smart distance;" or, "How far to a certain place?" — "Oh, right smart distance!" — a fair sample of the majority of the rank and file of the Southern army coerced into rebellion by their political leaders.

The evenings of early fall were spent in whiling the time away in various ways, some playing checkers or chess, some playing bluff straight, five-cent *chips*, or ten-cent *straddle*, and as much higher as the skill and wishes of the players required; while others studied tactics and army regulations, endeavoring to perfect themselves for the duties of higher positions in the service. Such fond hopes in many cases blossomed, but never bore fruit. So the early fall wore away; and "All quiet on the Potomac" being the battle-cry, preparations for winter-quarters were begun. Details were made from each company to go into the woods to fell the trees with which to build the log houses that were to shelter us through the winter. Cottonwood was the timber largely used, which is easily riven or split. The quarters were about twenty-five feet long, and about ten feet wide, with three tiers of bunks on sides and end. The head of the company faced the west, and the wisdom of the first platoon were on the westerly end of the houses. They were very comfortable, and were mentioned in the Adjutant-General's Report for Massachusetts as such, on his return from the Army of the Potomac in fall of 1861.

CHAPTER V.

REGIMENT UNDER COL. RUSSELL. — CAMP BRIGHTWOOD. AND MOVEMENT TO MANASSAS JUNCTION. — SIEGE OF YORKTOWN. AND BATTLE OF WILLIAMSBURG.

COL. WHEELOCK having resigned Jan. 31, 1862, Capt. David A. Russell, Fourth Regiment of Infantry, took command of the regiment. Would that my feeble pen could give an adequate description of that sterling officer and man! It is given to but few organizations to have the good fortune to be commanded by such an efficient officer. Firm, just, and temperate, he ruled his men more by the weight of his character than by the stern requirements of military law, impressing upon his officers and men that duty fully performed is the quickest way to fame and glory. He soon commanded the unbounded love and respect of both men and officers, who felt that their colonel would never needlessly sacrifice them. Being ever careful and prudent, he proved himself a very superior officer, who never risked a man's life that he might be promoted for the gallantry displayed in shedding other men's blood, but rather husbanded the strength of his command to await the supreme moment in action, when the science of his blows was irresistible.

His bravery and efficiency in battle were well shown at Rappahannock Station, Spottsylvania, Cold Harbor, and the sad but ever memorable field of Opequan, where he fell at the head of his division in the hour of his glory and victory. Having previously been wounded in the side by a minie

DAVID A. RUSSELL,
Colonel.

ball, he still kept his saddle, and urged on his troops, though suffering terribly. As he saw the battle trembling in the balance, and victory was almost assured, a piece of shell pierced his heart, and he fell, one of nature's noblemen, to rise no more. He died upon the field of honor, Sept. 19, 1864; and his fall left a vacancy in the Sixth Corps never to be filled. It has been said of him, that, as a colonel, he had no equal; as a leader of a brigade, he was superb; and, as a division commander, brilliant and almost unequalled. He met his death at the early age of forty-two. Beloved by all, his memory is revered as a *chevalier pur et sans reproche.* — *Requiescat in pace.*

In Gen. Sheridan's report of that battle, we find the following testimony to the faithful and efficient services of David A. Russell: —

"At this juncture, Russell's division of the Sixth Corps splendidly improved a golden opportunity. [See Valley Campaign Reports, by Sheridan.] Ordered at once to move up into the front line now needing re-enforcements, this change brought it into the gap created by the Confederate charge, and, continuing its advance, it struck the flank of the hostile force which was sweeping away the Union right, and aided by the Fifth Maine Battery, which enfiladed the enemy's line with canister, at once turned the tide. The enemy retreated, but Russell had fallen." "His death," said Sheridan, "brought sadness to every heart in the army." For further eulogies, the reader is referred to the reports of the Valley Campaign.

During the winter, guard-duty, drill, and Sunday-morning inspections, formed the principal work of the regiment.

March 11, 1862, the regiment marched to Prospect Hill, Va., on the Manassas campaign; and a more muddy and dreary march could not be had. Rain, rain, rain, a good precursor of the campaign soon to follow. After camping out some three days, we took up our return march back to Camp Brightwood. After staying in our old camp something like a week, marched to embark on the steamer "Daniel Webster," for Fortress Monroe, Va. After being four days on the steamer, we disembarked on the 29th, and marched seven miles, and went into camp at Camp W. F. Smith, Va.; and now the grand old Army of the Potomac was launched upon that historic campaign, which, from inexperience of the commanding officers, and lack of moral and material support at Washington, was destined to defeat from the first, and, while rich in deeds of heroism and valor, was to end in the tactical defeat of the Union forces, although it inflicted upon the enemy great slaughter, from which they never fully recovered. The Seventh Massachusetts bore a very conspicuous and honorable part in the Peninsular campaign. Always in front, sometimes so far that it was often taken for the enemy, it held a very prominent position with the rest of Gen. Devens's brigade, he having been promoted from the Fifteenth Massachusetts to take command of Couch's old brigade. April 4 the regiment marched eight miles, and encamped ; April 5 marched ten miles, and encamped near Warwick Court-House, Va., at Camp Winfield Scott, where the regiment did its full share of work in the siege of Yorktown. After the fall of Yorktown, it marched, May 4, eight miles towards Williamsburg, and encamped for the night. On the 5th of May, the regiment marched on to the field of Williamsburg at half-past two o'clock P.M., much exhausted and fatigued, after floundering through seas of mud and thousands of troops. The regiment was subjected to a very severe artillery-fire; but, under the leadership of Col. Russell, they stood their first baptism of fire like veterans, and marched with steady ranks and proud bearing to the support of Gen. Peck's exhausted troops. At nightfall the regiment relieved the One Hundred and Second Pennsylvania Volunteers of Peck's brigade, and, without blankets or fires, stood by their arms in a drenching storm of wind and rain. Company K, having been detailed as skirmishers, advanced, under Capt. Reed, with a detachment of Gen. Davidson's brigade, and occupied Fort Magruder at daylight. The casualties were, one killed (Andrew S. Lawton, a private of Company A, killed by a projectile from Fort Magruder), and two wounded. While the boys were marching on to the battle-field, a regiment broke, and ran through the ranks; but the Old Seventh discipline held them firm with the knowledge that the eyes of Massachusetts were upon them to uphold the honor of the Old Bay State. Military readers will know how trying to new troops is the breaking of the front lines, and the rush to the rear is generally very demoralizing; but Col. Russell was there, a born leader; and the regiment marched steadily to the front under a very heavy fire, and bore a most honorable part in this its first engagement.

The next day the regiment commenced its toilsome march up the muddy road that led to Richmond as its terminal, and which many a poor boy of the Old Seventh was destined to never see, except as prisoner of war, or as a visitor after the city had capitulated to the last general who attempted to take it. The sun came out hot and muggy after the battle, mud was knee-deep about all the way on the line of march, and many were the jokes cast off in army lore about the condition of all Rebeldom if this was a fair sample of their would-be confederacy. Capts. Reed, Foster, and others were rather fleshy for such tramping; and Lieut. Mayhew of Company K kept up a string of jokes characteristic of himself, being a warm-hearted, whole-souled fellow, possessed of a fund of humor which the technical part of a soldier's life could not subdue. After floundering through the mud for about nine miles, we were ordered to halt, and rest for the night, and find, if possible, a dry spot to build our little fires, and make the soldier's sterling cup of good cheer, — a full pint of good old Government coffee, — which used to so warm the tired and weary soldier while in active service. The next day, 10th of May, marched seven miles, and camped near Roper's Church, one of the gospel hospitals, where the good divines

of the Old Dominion poured into willing ears the story of
the Bible bondmen and the holy sacredness of their dear
institution, which furnished them and their families bread at
the expense of the sweat from other men's brows.

HAVING received from Sergeant Walter S. Goss of Company A the following communication written by him for "The Woonsocket Patriot," on the battle of Williamsburg, I here insert it as a very valuable contribution to this History in relation to the Peninsular campaign.

"When it was discovered that Yorktown was evacuated by the enemy, Gen. Stoneman with his cavalry and artillery followed them up. The Confederates had strong earthworks in front of Williamsburg, thirteen in all, Fort Magruder being the central and strongest, an earthwork with bastion front. It was a good half-mile in extent, and surrounded by a deep, wide ditch, full of water. The other earthworks were open redoubts. These works were nearly two miles from Williamsburg. When Stoneman approached their lines, he was met by the enemy's cavalry; and then the heavy guns of Fort Magruder opened upon him. So he called a halt, and then fell back four miles, and waited for the infantry to come up and do the fighting. The most the cavalry did on the Peninsula was to fall back; 'it was their best hold.' Hooker, who then commanded a division in Heintzelman's Third Corps, was anxious for a fight. He found the road ahead of him blocked by the troops of Smith's division, so he obtained permission to push over from the Yorktown road to the Lee's-Mill road. He marched until midnight, when he bivouacked. Rain was falling, and the roads were so muddy they were nearly impassable. But at early dawn Hooker's men were up again and away, pushing for the front. At half-past seven he ordered an attack, sending in four regiments as skirmishers. In a short time Hooker had planned out a pretty stiff fight. Gen. Johnston, who had left only a rear guard here, while the bulk of his army was pressing on towards the Chickahominy, deemed it expedient to recall them; so that, by eleven o'clock, Hooker had all his reserves in the front lines, and was calling upon Sumner and Heintzelman for re-enforcements without getting a response from either. The troops were out of ammunition, and had to rely on that taken from the cartridge-boxes of the dead and wounded.

"Patterson's New-Jersey brigade, the Sixth, Seventh, and Eighth, probably did some of the heaviest fighting of the day, and at times it was most desperate. Their dead literally covered the ground, which they stubbornly held against massed Confederates. Hooker fought nearly nine consecutive hours, with no help except Peck's and Devens's brigades of Couch's division, who arrived early in the afternoon, and took a position on his right, and held back the enemy at that point. Thirty thousand troops lay within an hour's march of the battle-field. Why Sumner, who was in command of the advance, allowed Hooker to fight this battle unaided, is to this day unexplained. To be sure, he detached Hancock, and sent him to the extreme right, where he took possession of two detached redoubts, thereby calling Johnston's attention to them, as he did not know before of their existence. After Hancock had secured his flank position, he failed to hold it for lack of re-enforcements, which he called for with great earnestness, as he saw it was the key to the whole battle-field. At the break of day the division of Phil Kearney is at Yorktown, twelve miles away, while Hooker is struggling against heavy odds. Kearney's men are pushing for the front, struggling with the mud which besets them wherever they set their feet. At a little past four they began to arrive on the field, where they take the front, while Hooker's men fall back as reserves. The fighting, which had languished and nearly petered out, now began to crackle and roar under the direction of the gallant and tempestuous Phil, who immediately took the offensive, and began to push the enemy from their rifle-pits. The two other brigades of Couch's division are now on the field; and in the mean time McClellan has come up to the front, and ordered Hancock to be re-enforced. The Confederates are hard pressed, and seek shelter behind their main line of works, when darkness settles down upon the bloody tragedy, and its sable mantle wraps in its foggy embrace the silent dead who are scattered through the woodland and glen on this field of fratricidal strife.

"I have here given a brief account of the leading points of the battle, and will now fall back and bring up the troops in which I am most interested.

"We lay during the night in an old wheat-field, and many of us managed to make our beds in the old dead furrows. During the night there was a copious downfall of water, and a flooded field was the result. Then, in the morning, there was a general wringing out of blankets and overcoats, which were thoroughly soaked with *aqua*. It was nearly nine o'clock when we received the orders to fall in, and then the tug of war commenced. The roads of Virginia are bad enough at the best; but when an army has passed over them, with its ponderous artillery and heavy trains, there are not enough hard words in the English language to emphasize their condition. Horses and mules appear to swim in their pasty depths, while the cannons' mouths drink in their fill of mud. But we give very little attention to the roads this day, for away ahead we hear the suppressed thud and roar of the bull-dogs of war; and with our sodden packs weighing us down, and driving us under like pile-drivers, we are racing for the front. But it is a slow race, hurry it as we may, for the roads are blocked with bemired artillery and sloughed-in trains; drivers are lashing and cursing their poor beasts with very little apparent effect; while the troops take to the fields, on through newly ploughed ground, slough-holes, and stubble, over ravines, raging torrents, and swollen brooks. How the mud sticks in those 'little gunboat' brogans! It is a question of time whether the mud will take off the 'brogans,' or the 'brogans' will take off the mud. The brogan usually takes the mud, and our pedal extremities are assuming gigantic proportions under the adhesive qualities of the sacred soil of Old Virginia. Ike Plunkins said, that, 'Betwixt the knapsack and the mud, I am loaded at both ends. But I'll be hanged if I am going off very fast.' Lossing, in his 'Pictorial Field-Book,' says the whole Army of the Potomac was but four-hours' march away from the Williamsburg battle-field, which statement would be true were the roads and weather in fine condition; but with the rain and mud combined, as it was at that time, it is one of his many historical romances. Several thousand troops were pushed forward that day for all they were worth; and none made the distance in less than six hours, nor was it possible for a loaded man or mule to make it in less time. It is easy to march and fight battles in the abstract; but, when we come down to the concrete, the racy historian, who fights his battles with type metals, might find that his metal was of that type which lags behind in the race. At that time we were not experienced in road-marches; and this was a long stretch for men new at the business, even had the roads been in good condition. A collection of men marching under orders, and carrying a load of seventy pounds or more, as we did at the time, cannot be compared to a pedestrian who goes alone and at his own will. A regiment may meet an obstruction, and undouble files to single file, which will retard the rear so that they are strung out half a mile; and, when the closing-up process is to be gone through with, there is a long run to be made to double up again; and none know what that means except old soldiers.

"In my struggle with the mud on that forced march, it seemed as though I should have to give it up, and nothing but the sullen boom of the big guns ahead held me up to the work; so we pulled wearily along, and yet the gunnery appeared as far off in sound as it had five hours before. I finally became demoralized, and sat down. Seeing a comrade straggling along in another company, I called upon him to come, and sit upon the log with me, remarking I wasn't going another inch until I had got a rest; whereupon the captain of that company, who was in light marching order, shouted, 'Cowards, cowards, come on! no skulking!' to which I replied, 'Oh! you carry my knapsack, and I'll go with you.' The captain was brave, but he couldn't screw his courage up to the bigness of that knapsack, and he passed.

"Shortly after, one of the general's orderlies came riding back from the direction of the battle-field; and I asked him how far it was to where the fighting was, to which he replied, 'About a mile,' and then asked what regiment we belonged to. Our reply brought out the remark that it was going right into the fight. 'Well,' said I, 'this won't do, for we have got to be there.' And we got up, and trotted — yes, we just trotted — past the brave captain who, a few moments before, had pronounced us cowards; and we saluted him as we passed by.

"The regiment was coming in on right by file into line, and we are 'there' on the nick of time to file into our places by regimental front. We go forward, and the sight that greets us is two men with a stretcher, bearing off the field a wounded man who was gory. He raised his head as they passed, and yelled, 'Give them hell!' We go forward to a rail-fence, halt, unsling knapsacks, and pile them in a stack. 'Load at will' is the next order, and it begins to look like business. Col. Russell climbs the fence to go into the woods ahead, when he is met by Capt. Titus, a staff-officer, who remarked with numerous oaths, 'For God's sake, colonel, don't go in there! the woods are chock full of rebels.' — 'Oh, well! I've got a little wood-lot in there I want to look over;' and he disappeared in the woods, while the captain sat on the fence indulging in a profusion of profanity to keep up his reputation as the champion swearer of the army. The

NATHANIEL S. GERRY,
Private Co. "A."

captain was afterwards the colonel of the One Hundred and Twenty-second Pennsylvania Volunteers, who joined our division at Antietam. His nickname among the men was 'Dare-Devil Dick.'

"The colonel soon returned, and told us not to fire, as the First Massachusetts were in ahead of us as skirmishers. We did not hold this position long, as it was too tame; so we climbed the fence, and, by the right flank, skirted the roads, then came to a front behind a gun stationed on the Yorktown road.

"My company, A, rests across the road immediately behind the field-piece. I am near the left, on the side of the road, and standing on the butt of a log apparently pulled out of the road where it was placed to obstruct. I observe that a man is at the muzzle of the cannon, in the act of loading, while another stands with a rammer in position to ram home the cartridge, when there comes a shell tearing its way through the woods. It is so near the ground that it almost seems to roll. I see it coming, and it is a big spheroid. How slowly it seems to move compared to my thoughts, which are working with electric speed! Just before it reached the piece, it exploded with a bang, scattering deadly missiles in our ranks. The man with the cartridge is killed, the one with the rammer is picked up with both feet hanging limp, and I find myself dreamily wondering what has become of his shoes, when I am aroused by being jerked backwards off the log, and an excited voice exclaiming, 'You son of a gun, come and help me take Lawton to the rear!' My reply, so I was told, was, 'To —— with Lawton! Where are the stretcher-bearers?' I look about me, and see two men of my company borne to the rear. Both were mortally wounded. Lawton lived but a few moments, and died regretting that he could not have been spared long enough to have got just one shot at the enemy before he died; while the other, genial Nathaniel S. Gerry, lingered a week or more. But the shells are howling; and, as I turn again to the front, not an artillery-man is in sight, or to be seen, except a major, who is excitedly begging and imploring some one 'for God's sake' to man his artillery. We give him little heed, as the colonel gives the order, 'By the right flank, march;' then, 'By the front, march.' The shells are still coming for us; and the colonel cries out, 'Spread out, men! don't let one of these shells take a dozen of you.' We spread apart like a heavy skirmishing line, and it was a pretty good shell that could take more than two of us at a time. We are moving slowly to the front by flank, and then by front. Gen. Couch is riding close on our rear, smoking a cigar, and switching a little riding-whip which he was hardly ever without; and I found myself wishing that I felt as cool and comfortable as Couch appeared to be, but I wasn't. I had filled my pipe, and lighted it as soon as I had loaded my rifle, resolved to take the thing coolly, calmly, and collectedly; but the first shell stupefied me. I obeyed orders in a benumbed and struck kind of way. My pipe was gone: where and when it went, was more than I could tell. I found it afterwards in my pocket, where I had mechanically put it. I found myself continually getting ahead of the line, and had hard work to hold myself back. Others were like me in that respect, and, out of curiosity, I asked one of them what was his hurry. He replied, with a ghastly smile that would befit a ghost, 'I want to get where them thundering things come from!' That was what I felt like, and it is the uppermost thought in all soldiers' minds when under a destructive artillery-fire; and they will charge into their very mouths, fighting like devils, actuated by the idea that they want to stop the thundering things. Any thing is better than taking it passively as it comes.

"Brig.-Gen. Devens rode by the side of Couch; and he remarked in a loud voice, — no doubt for encouragement, — 'See how these men go in like regulars.' — 'Of course they do,' replied Couch, in a matter-of-fact way. Of course we did what we were there for. What had we been drilling for all these months if it was not to be as steady under fire as any regulars that walked the earth? The volunteers were not the kind to run away under the first fire, if they had a head they could depend upon. And we had one in Russell, under whom we never flinched; for we believed in him and his judgments, which is more than we could say of some of the generals. Here we are under the shadow of Fort Magruder, which, with its heavy guns, is sending its compliments over us. In front of us, and separating us from the fort, is a 'slashing,' a perfect whirl and tangle of trees, felled with a view to obstruct travel; it looks like a chaotic jumble, but there is a method and system to it. Here we bivouac for the night, tired, wet, worn, weary, and hungry. Our knapsacks are to the rear; and we lie as we drop, rifles in hand, ready for immediate use. I crawled in behind a supposed log, where I lay with chattering teeth, whether from cold or fear I couldn't tell, but probably a little of both mixed. My log, I found in the morning, was simply punk, and was no shelter at all, except to my mind, and it answered that purpose as well as a log. During the night I was called up, and posted out as a watch to keep track of the rebel movements. I leaned against a tree, and soon became interested in the movements within the fort. The officers of the fort are turning out their men, and falling them in; hammers are going, knocking things to pieces, or boxing them up; little fires are blazing, lighting up the interior of the fort. I have my doubts about giving any alarm, and am studying the situation intently, when a heavy hand fell upon my shoulder from the rear, and gave me a sudden start. 'Well, my man, how are things at the fort?' I recognize the colonel's voice, and reply, that, in my opinion, the rebs are vacating. 'Don't get that idea in your head, for we have got to do some hard fighting in the morning,' said Russell. Then I explained to him all I had heard, and told him, that, if the enemy were not leaving, we were in for a fight before morning, for they were surely moving. He staid by me a quarter of an hour or more,

listening to the signs, when he remarked that he thought I
was right, but to keep a sharp lookout, and give the alarm
at the least sign of danger. He then disappeared. Shortly
after, things became quiet at the fort; and, when I was
relieved, I lay down with the consciousness that the morrow
would not bring forth a fight. I was willing the enemy
should leave, as I had no particular use for them. We had
but struck the ragged edge of the battle of Williamsburg,
and my curiosity had been appeased. I had seen all the
shells I cared to see, and, although I had not had a very big
taste of fighting, I was satisfied to let my war record end
right here: for between the mud and rain, the discouraging
march, the human gore, patriotism had fled, and a supreme
disgust for the heroics of battle had filled the void."

CHAPTER VI.

ON THE CHICKAHOMINY.

WE remained two days in camp at Roper's Church. The regiment drew rations, had regimental inspection, and, on the 13th, marched thirteen miles to New Kent Court-House, where we remained two days more in camp, it raining almost constantly. Having had occasion to speak of the condition of the "*terreian*" upon which the Army of the Potomac was called to move, and fight its battles, it will be well to give a slight description of the same.

The Peninsula of Virginia, as it is called by geographers, is a tongue of land commencing at the city of Richmond on the James, and at West Point on the Pamunkey, — a tributary of the York, — and runs in a south-easterly direction, constantly narrowing until it comes to a point in the tide-waters of Chesapeake Bay and James River confluence. At its extreme point is Fortress Monroe.

At the time of which we write, this was the largest and strongest fortress in the United States, mounting some one thousand guns when fully armed and equipped. The immediate vicinity of the fort is sandy, the waters of the bay and river laving its foundations.

As you progress up the peninsula, it widens; and there are fine plantations, producing peaches, corn, and wheat, which, under slave-workmen, were in a good state of cultivation before the war.

Passing Warwick Court-House, the river of that name takes its run to the north and west of Yorktown, and was the first real obstacle the army encountered, except the weather. The river runs through a sluggish morass, and empties into the James, giving to an enemy holding a position bound by its lines a formidable defence, if his flanks are protected by proper works, strengthened by gunboats in the James and York; otherwise he is liable to be turned on both flanks.

As you press on farther, this strip of country widens, and is interspersed with dense forests, and a few open places where houses are built and plantations are operated by slave-workers. The soil is a spongy clay, stiff as common mortar when once worked up by the tramp of men and rush of artillery and wagons. Truly, a slough of despondency and fear; and many a poor soldier-boy has had to make an extra requisition on the quartermaster for shoes or boots, having left his own in its loving infoldment. As you strike the Chickahominy River, it is lined with morasses and timber-lands, whose bottoms are subject to sudden overflows in the spring of the year from the waters of the adjoining tributaries and the table-lands in the direction of Richmond.

The regiment on the 16th of May made an armed reconnoissance, and succeeded in driving the rebel cavalry back towards the Chickahominy, encamping at Baltimore Cross-Roads for the night. The 17th we made a reconnoissance of six miles, and encamped three miles from Bottom's Bridge. We threw out a strong cordon of pickets towards the river, so as to be prepared against a sudden dash of rebel cavalry or infantry, of which there was a very strong force in the immediate vicinity. After roll-call the boys turned in, it being rainy, and all around one sea of mud.

On the morning of the 18th our pickets and the Eighth Pennsylvania Cavalry took possession of the Richmond and West-Point Railroad to within about one mile of the bridge crossing the Chickahominy River. The 19th we marched one mile, and encamped on the bank of the river near the railroad, being well secured on our flank, and secreted from rebel observation. A detachment of those sterling companies. B and G, made a move up to the bridge, and found the left bank of the river evacuated.

On the 20th a detachment of Company C, under command of Major Harlow and Capt. Holman, were engaged in an examination of the bridge, and had a very brisk skirmish before Bottom's Bridge. On the 21st, Company F (Capt. Bliss) and Company A — the one at the railroad-bridge, the other at the plank road crossing the river — had a very lively skirmish, and succeeded in driving away the rebels, and crossing the river, the regiment losing two men wounded, and one sergeant taken prisoner. After crossing, a detachment from the remainder of the regiment made a reconnoissance of over two miles in the direction of Richmond, but found no heavy force of rebels. Gen. Johnston having taken up a position well under the fortifications of the city. Johnston's object was to entice McClellan to divide and separate his several corps, so that he could fall upon them in detail, and destroy such portions as had crossed the river and become detached from the right wing of the Union army. Encamped on the banks of the river.

The following interesting account was written by Walter S. Goss, and published in " The Woonsocket Patriot," April 30, 1886: —

" We have made our camp on the high land overlooking the Chickahominy River. The Chickahominy is a sluggish stream, margined by swamps and low, marshy land. It has a disposition to overflow its banks at the slightest apology for a shower. The regiment is an outpost on this line, as the rest of the troops are three or four miles at the rear of us. On our left front, about a quarter of a mile away, is Bottom's Bridge ; and on our front equidistant stand the piers of a destroyed railroad-bridge. Half a mile at the rear on the railroad, is a saw-mill with its piles of boards. Col. Russell confidentially informed our orderly that there was a flat car on the brink of the bridge, and a half-dozen men might steal it quietly away under cover of the night. The hint is taken :

and at early evening that car is trundled down the track, and the boards were soon on the move campward. It was a lazy man who did not have his tent floored before another sun had set.

"For nearly a week the river barrier was the scene of skirmish, picket, and exchange of shot. There were very few casualties, however. I remember one night another man and myself were lying behind a fence near the margin of the water, when a bullet struck the rail near our heads, and the other fellow told me he believed his eye was shot out; so he went crawling to the rear, up to a house near by where the captain had his quarters. He came back later with the soothing intelligence that his eye was not out, but that the ball threw rotten wood into it. Poor fellow! he afterwards laid down his young life on an ensanguined battle-field.

"The Sunday evening following our encampment here, a farmer-looking citizen might have been seen strolling along by the river's side in an apparently languid, leisurely manner, leading by the hand a small girl. That old farmer was our Col. Russell. He had borrowed a suit of clothes and the little child for that special occasion, and was studying the condition of things on the other side. He arrived at a conclusion, and decided to try the bridge. During the evening he visited the captain of Company A, who are on the picket-line, and told him to make an attempt to cross over Bottom's Bridge at daylight in the morning. He thought that there was but a small force there; yet there might be a large one 'playing possum.' We get the news, and have time to think it over. The bridge had been partially destroyed; but the stringers were left, and were passable for pedestrians. There were two men to a picket-post, and about forty posts of our men strung along the river. Toward morning, 'Toodles,' who was on duty near the bridge, conceives the brilliant idea that it is the better part of strategy to surprise the bridge, the rebs, and the regimental commanders, by effecting a crossing before daylight. He came down to my post, which was next to his, loaded with his important decision, and we immediately agreed to it. Then each post was visited, and a signal adopted for a grand rally, near the bridge, on double-quick time.

"The eastern horizon begins to show signs of approaching day while we await the signal to start on what may be a perilous adventure.

"Hark! There goes the signal, a low whistle, which is sent down the line; a few moments of breathless suspense, and then there is heard a subdued tramp of hurried feet. Away we go in a long, trailing line for the bridge, — yes, and right over it with our acquired momentum, where we rally in line, and are ready to fight any foe who dare to put in an appearance. The boys are in the humor for a free fight, for their enthusiasm is at fever-heat. There are no officers to interfere with them, and each man is his own captain and commander-in-chief. On the rising ground a few rods beyond us is a house; and in the dusky morning light, forms are seen flitting about.

"'Toodles,' who hardly ever opened his mouth without putting his foot into it, hailed with, 'What regiment is that?' And the reply came back, 'The Tenth.' — 'The Tenth, hey!' says Toodles. 'I didn't know that you got over here ahead of us.' He had addled his brain over the Tenth Massachusetts. 'What regiment is that?' now came from the whole rebel side. 'The 199th,' the answer. '199th what?' — 'The 199th Massachusetts.' — 'Ha, ha! just the condemned sons of dogs we are after!' and with the exclamation came a pattering volley from rebeldom, shot wildly into the thin air, and about as random a volley was returned; that is, our guns were pointed somewhere in their direction.

"This shooting in the dark, squinting over invisible sights, is not conducive to good marksmanship. After emptying our 'pieces' a gallant charge was made with a rush for the Johnnies; but there was 'mounting in hot haste,' a clatter of hoofs, and the foe is up and away for Richmond to spread the news that the 'Yanks' have crossed the Chickahominy in heavy force. The discharge of musketry on the resonant morning atmosphere has stirred up the captain; and he comes over, rubbing his eyes in a bewildered manner, more surprised at our temerity than the rebs themselves. When he became thoroughly awake, and had recovered from his astonishment, he sent a man to apprise the colonel of the doings of the privates of Company A. Russell soon put in an appearance, and there was not a sleepy indication about his person. There was not a more pleased man in the whole Army of the Potomac. He immediately sent for the regimental colors, and planted them on the position we had so nobly taken in a bloodless charge; then he made a speech to us, complimenting us upon our bravery and dash. I have often wondered since what he would have said to the survivors had we run our noses into a snag, or fell into a trap, and had suffered a terrible loss, as we were liable to do had there been a large body of the enemy lurking in the vicinity. No doubt, the brilliancy of the foolhardy movement would have been dimmed by blood, and nothing gained thereby. But in war it is the foolhardy movements, when successful, that win the applause of men, and another laurel is added to the science of so-called military strategy. But if failure stamps it with its iron hoof of fate, the fool in it bulges into such prominence that there are none so low but feel above its contempt. Russell's triumph was of but a few hours' duration; for at about noon of that day, May 24, Naglee's brigade of Casey's division crossed over the river, and made a movement toward Fair Oaks, met the enemy's outpost, and had a little skirmish. Russell was in a towering passion at having the front, won by his men, so ruthlessly wrested from his grasp; and he sought the headquarters of Gen. Keyes. After an hour's absence he came back, all smiles again.

"He said, 'They tried to take the front away from us after we had earned the position, but they didn't do it, and Gen. Naglee is ordered back to the rear; so we have the front again, the position of honor, which we may well feel proud of.'

"Well, we were not the 'leastest' mite proud; and honors get mighty thin and easy by the time they are filtered through to the privates, so we were not very enthusiastic in spirit, or great sticklers over the proprieties of military etiquette: but in order to be in harmony with the commander, the boys strove to look pleased, and essayed a feeble cheer. Men learn fast in the fires of battle; and they had already learned that the road to military honor was crimsoned with blood, and paved with dead and mutilated humanity. I have given in full the particulars of what is called the 'battle of Bottom's Bridge.' There was no battle about it, and it can scarcely be lifted to the dignity of a skirmish.

"After the crossing of Bottom's Bridge had become an established fact, the troops of the army were pushed over the Chickahominy to establish their lines. Casey's division, the greenest troops of Keyes's corps, were given the front. They were given a position a half a mile or more in advance of what was called the Seven Pines, while Couch's division lay within supporting distance at Seven Pines. Heintzelman's corps were still farther to the rear; Kearney's division was near Savage Station, and Hooker's guarding White-Oak Swamp.

"We were in camp on the Williamsburg road in an open field surrounded by woods. Each company was allowed but two camp-kettles wherein to cook their coffee, beans, or rice, so that our courses were few and far between. Every morning teams came over and brought a day's ration of grub, and then hurried away as though they were expected to be lit upon and gobbled up by the enemy. Near where we were located, the rebs had an encampment of board shanties; and when we arrived, there was a grabbing of boards for flooring of tents; and the men who had grabbed the most boards, grabbed with them a prize that was destined to thrive and stick to him through his entire term of service in the army.

"I give the readers fair warning, that if they are inclined to be squeamish, or have fastidious tastes, they had better not go any farther with me in this paper. No picture of army life would be complete without giving a hasty touch, at least, on this subject. I have had them; and the remembrance of them inclines me even now, to stop scratching with the pen, and use the finger-tips as assiduously as of yore. The graybacks, as the soldiers on both sides came to call them, first made themselves felt in Couch's division at Seven Pines. It was there they introduced themselves to us, with the understanding that they had come to stay. Victory or defeat, rain or shine, did not deter them from doing what they had marked out as their duty; and they did it nobly, if there was anything noble in sticking to a fellow who didn't want their attentions.

My first experience with the 'critters' was humiliating. I was the happy possessor of two 'brand new' warranted all-wool shirts; but there came a time when one of them appeared to have become possessed of devils, and 'I felt the awful sense of something crawling 'round me.' Shame overcame me; and a lonely guilt so bore me down that I crept into my tent, and surreptitiously tucked my other shirt under my blouse, and skulked away into the woods, into its innermost recess; and there I exchanged the garments, and cast the inhabited one into the solitude of the bushes, to multiply and replenish at other expense than mine. When I returned to the camp, I found that the profound secret which each man had locked within his own breast, and carried around in his shirt, had become an open one; and it had leaked out that every man, from general to private, was guilty of secretly supporting a body-guard. Gen. Couch's headquarters were placarded with a legend which read, 'All persons carrying uncles or aunts about their person are requested to keep away from this tent.'

"The colonel was inquiring for the whereabouts of a sutler. He wanted to buy a shirt, as he had thrown his away; and he said it wasn't ragged nor dirty either. After hearing all this, I concluded that I had been hasty in my action; and so I rushed into the woods in search of the discarded garment, but could not find it. Some one less squeamish than I had picked it up, or it had crawled away beyond my find. All manner of schemes and devices were resorted to in order to get the better of the pests. In camp, where time and opportunity gave a man an even show in the war of extermination, a camp-kettle and boiling water was all-sufficient. But some 'shiftless cuss' managed to retain a stock that on a campaign would spread and multiply beyond the needs of practical utility. Ike Plunkins said, 'The best way to fix the varmints is to turn your shirt wrong side out, and it gives them a day's march to outflank the position.' Another way that was in common use was the singeing process: a man would hold his shirt over a fire, and singe it as people do poultry. Whether it amounted to any thing, is more than any one could tell; but there was satisfaction in it, at least, when in imagination you pictured the tortures of the writhing victim; and the thoughts of the good old doctrine preached from home-pulpits, that once wrung our youthful hearts with woe, would well up in our minds, and we were happy as parsons who roast and toast sinners over their fervid theological coals.

"Soap was my hobby; and I kept the seams of all my garments well supplied with the requisite every day (if the rush of business did not interpose), and thereby thought that I retarded the multiplication of the ever present reminder that man was not born to walk the earth alone. But why dwell longer on the subject? Every old soldier knows how it is himself, while those who have never stood in line at rigid attention can never know what a blood-curdling sensation tingles the very fibres of the soul as marshalled hosts creep insidiously over their flesh. Ugh! with army life a cruel dream where nightmare lurked fading out of life's horizon, let us bid the puny pests of the past a lasting farewell, I hope forever."

DAVID H. DYER,
Captain Co. "A."

CHAPTER VII.

BATTLE OF FAIR OAKS.

ON the 24th marched five miles towards Richmond, and encamped; and on the 25th marched three miles, and encamped near Fair Oaks, where we were engaged with the rest of the brigade in building rifle-pits, which were so useful in the battle soon after fought. The battle of Fair Oaks was fought under great disadvantages on the part of the Fourth Corps, its poorest and weakest division being in the advance under a superannuated general, whose personal magnetism and bearing amounted to but very little as a factor in holding green and undisciplined troops up to the work in severe action. On Saturday and Sunday the Fourth Corps was in position as indicated by the accompanying diagram of that battle, Gen. Casey's division being in front, with Couch's division in rear as support about one mile off, and Hooker and Kearney's division being in support on the left rear.

About two o'clock on May 31 the rebels moved up to the attack in overwhelming numbers, brushing away the skirmishers of Casey's division as a broom sweeps cobwebs from a ceiling, and soon struck Naglee's brigade, which, after a brisk fire, was forced back upon the reserves. On came the rebels in magnificent style; and soon Casey's division, or the largest portion of it, was routed by superior numbers, some parts of it doing excellent fighting, while others were altogether too active in getting away from the roaring shot and shell, and whistling *ping* of the minie. Presently portions of Couch's division were ordered up to stay the on-rushing line of rebels, but to little purpose; and as Gen. Couch took his old brigade in hand to ward off an impending blow upon the right flank of the corps, he was forced into a position to the extreme right, and separated from the rest of his division. He found it a useless task to try to cut his way through the rebel lines, and withdrew towards Fair-Oaks Station on the York-river Railroad, and nine-mile road to Richmond, where he secured a very strong position, to which he clung with great tenacity, until relieved by the welcome troops of Sumner's Second Corps. This corps had come up as fast as legs could carry them through the seas of mud and water; and by their timely assistance, Couch's remnant was saved from destruction.

The Seventh Massachusetts, with the rest of the brigade under Gen. Devens, was actively engaged in this battle; but our casualties were few in number, owing to Col. Russell keeping his men under cover, — and when did this commander ever commit an error in saving the lives of his men? — our loss being four men wounded, the regiment having been used as a support to a battery of heavy artillery.

The following description of the battle of Fair Oaks, written by Comrade Goss for "The Woonsocket Patriot," is here inserted as being of interest to the readers of this history: —

"The Army of the Potomac is in a bad situation. Four divisions of it are across the Chickahominy widely scattered, while their nearest support is Sumner's corps, separated from them by a river that was flooded by a freshet. Gen. Sumner's troops arrived at the river on the 24th of May. In view of the situation of the advance of the army on the Richmond side, he came to the conclusion that his services might be needed across the river at any moment. On the 25th he sent for Col. E. E. Cross of the Fifth New Hampshire, and requested him to construct a bridge over the stream. The New-Hampshire boys, with the aid of a small detail from the Sixty-fourth and Sixty-ninth New-York regiments, built a bridge eighty rods in length, through a swamp and over the river, in a little over four days, having it all completed on the night of the 30th. This bridge was composed of good solid logs, many of them cut half a mile up the stream, and floated down by wading and swimming men. It was bound together and anchored with grapevines, from which it took its name of the 'Grapevine Bridge.' The work was well done by the hardy sons of the 'Granite State,' who shortly after proved their fighting qualities on the Fair-Oaks battle-field; and at the end of the war their record was second to none, and equalled only by a select few. Col. Cross, who laid down his life at Gettysburg, is one of the few names of his rank that will live in our nation's history as a grateful remembrance of heroic service rendered in its hour of peril.

"When the bridge was finished, Col. Cross rode over it and back on a gallop, to show its compactness. The 'Grapevine Bridge' proved an important factor in the Fair-Oaks battles, and one that was overlooked by the rebel general, Johnson, as he thought to crush and annihilate the forces of Keyes and Heintzelman before re-enforcements could reach them. It is an easy task to plan a battle if the enemy will only do as is expected of them, which they 'most always don't.' A battle-plan supposes that every part of the army will work like a perfect machine, and will be in its place in the nick of time, which hardly ever comes to pass in the best disciplined army. In Johnson's plan, Sumner's troops were left out of his calculations; and Huger's, whom he had sent around White-Oak swamp to flank our left, he had counted in, which was quite a balance in our favor; and we were in need of the whole balance in order to hold our lines.

"Gen. Johnson intended to made us an early call; but on account of the heavy roads, he did not get along until near noon. On the morning of May 31, the teams came up, and donated us a ration of beans; and I was detailed to cook the

company's dinner. The two kettles of beans were over a
fire, boiling, and anxious men were calling around at times to
see if 'them are beans were done.' I see that all the historians of the battle fix the time of its opening after the
dinner-hour ; either they are mistaken in the time, or we were
late with dinner that day, which, I think, we were not. At
about half-past eleven, as I remember the time, from the
front was heard a spluttering, scattering fire of musketry
detonated by a bass-drum-like chorus from a piece of artillery. There was an immediate getting on of equipments by
all the men, and a falling into company lines without an
order being uttered. I fell in with the rest of the boys, leaving the beans to go it alone. The lieutenant in command
ordered me out of the ranks, telling me that it was nothing
but a skirmish, and that I must stay to look after the camp,
and have dinner ready for them when they came back ; so I
fell back on the support of the beans, and looked, and listened
to the fight. I watched the regimental line form, and saw it
depart for the front on the 'double quick,' urged on by
a general's aid. The spluttering fire of skirmishers has
increased to volleys, then to a sullen, continuous roar, above
which could be heard the pounding of the cannon. Gen.
Naglee has, with his brigade, advanced, and met the enemy;
but he is outflanked and brushed aside, yet he makes a valiant
fight against fearful odds. Casey is flanked by the enemy
on his left, and falls back upon Couch, who now stubbornly
contests the ground inch by inch, but is outnumbered three
to one. The division is broken up, and regiments sent in
different directions to strive to hold the line. Casey's troops,
many of them, fight on with fearful loss ; while others break
up, and go to the rear like sheep struck with a panic. From
my post of observation I watch the procession ; first come
trailing to the rear coatless men by twenties and by fifties,
with picks and shovels ; they had been disobeying Gen. Mc-
Clellan's order, which specified that each man working on
intrenchments should wear his full equipments, while a com-

rade should stand near and hold his gun while he worked. After the trenchers had passed, the men who were holding guns came trooping by; at any rate, they had guns, and were not putting them to a very good use in this hour of need. This being in the rear of a battle is enough to drive out all the faith one has in the heroic devotion of man to his country. If you ask one of these skedaddlers where his regiment is, he will pull down his chin, and mournfully swear that ' it is all cut to pieces,' and he is the only survivor. The plot thickens: the wounded are being brought along; a captain of the Tenth Massachusetts, very badly wounded, is lying under cover of the hill that makes my cook-stand a place of safety. Shells begin to shriek out their warning cry that death is carried within them; and the leaden bullets are beginning to buzz about our ears, admonishing us that our rear position is getting well up towards the front. The wounded were taken farther to the rear, and soon 'Sampy' — my aid — and I are left alone. The right of our line has crumbled and gone to pieces under the heavy pressure of the rebels' flanking movement. The Tenth Massachusetts, after the breaking up of Casey's troops, endeavored to stem the storm of battle on the right, and were broken up and re-formed three times on a new rear line, only to be outflanked again on their new line; but in spite of their defeats and terrible losses, they struggled heroically, like old veterans of a hundred battles. Other regiments were doing the same heroic duty as the Tenth, which was only a specimen of the tenacious grip of the Northern soldier when his fighting blood was up. Col. Russell and his regiment stood by the Tenth in the earlier part of the fight, but were, with the Sixty-second New York, 'Anderson's Zouaves,' and another regiment, — the Fifty-fifth New York, I think, — ordered off to the extreme right, near Fair Oaks, to check a movement of rebel troops under the command of Gen. Gustavus W. Smith, who was striving to wedge in between the river and our line of retreat towards Bottom's Bridge. This movement transferred the final battle-field from Seven Pines on the Williamsburg road to a point a mile farther north and across the railroad below Fair-Oaks station. My narrative, by a devious route, will convey me there also. As I before remarked, 'Sampy' and I appeared to be left alone. 'Sampy' was anxious to leave, and kept saying, 'Let's go.' Sampy was the nickname of a young fellow of about twenty years, who was any thing rather than a soldier: he would forage, steal, bum, beat, or cook better than he could fight. I was in no hurry to leave a position apparently free from danger, and so hung on, crawling up the little eminence at times to get an observation of the surroundings. At last I discovered a rebel line of battle in the edge of the woods on the opposite side of the camp, looking for some one or more to shoot at. I held up my cap invitingly, while I lay low, and the bullets began to whistle, and whisper 'zip.' So I 'skun' down the hill, dumped the beans, packed up, and prepared to toddle. But which way? was now the question for us to solve. Shells were screaming over us, and bursting in the swamp in our rear; and our only path of retreat appeared to be in that direction, but we were a 'little bit' afraid of those shells. Sampy was, at any rate, so there is no need of giving myself away; and to please him, I concluded we had better try the Williamsburg road. We had gone but a short distance in that direction when we met a wounded man, who told us not to go there, as the shot was coming like hail down the road. The wounded man had a broken-handle shovel in his hand, which he had held against his head in his retreat, to ward off the leaden hail.

"This young man chanced to have been a schoolmate of mine in days gone by; and here we meet on the battle-field, after years of separation, and here we renew old acquaintance amid the rattle of musketry and the artillery's thunderous roar. He had become a carpenter, and had drifted down into the State of Mississippi to ply his trade. When the war had become a foregone conclusion, he hurried Northward. On arriving in Pennsylvania, he saw a chance to enlist; and his loyalty for the old flag was so intense, that he was afraid, if he went back to his old home, the fighting positions would all be filled, and that he would be left out in the cold; so he enlisted in a Pennsylvania regiment, and again set his face Southward without visiting his relatives and friends. Here is a specimen of patriotism for croakers to chew upon. The army was well supplied with such men in the ranks, and the word 'fail' never appeared upon *their* banners. The generals often got whipped, but the army never.

"We concluded to try the swamp route. I carried a gun with a full set of equipments, a knapsack, an axe, and one end of a pole, whereon were strung the camp-kettles. Never did cooks make a more orderly or leisurely retreat. Leisurely, because, in the promiscuous fighting, it was a question as to which way the rear was. There was a rebel line near the Williamsburg road; and they were banging away for all they were worth, apparently to hear themselves make a noise, as there were no troops to oppose them within a mile, except a few stragglers like myself; for by this time Casey's and most of Couch's men had pulled out of range of the rebel fire. A few regiments of Couch's division were down below Fair-Oaks station, cut off from the main body, and they were hard pressed. The rebel lines about Seven Pines seemed to be satisfied with their victory, as they made no attempt to advance farther, but contented themselves with random shots in the woods on their front. When we reached the open ground, after playing hide and seek in the woods, dodging the range of shells, we joined forces with a colonel, who was leading his horse to the rear. Whether he had left his command, or his command had left him, was more than I was able to find out, as he was not in a talking mood. He appeared to be willing to be guided by my judgment as to the safest line of retreat; but I finally lost sight of him in a belt of woods which the rebs were so intent upon shelling that I backed out of them, and made tracks for the railroad. When we found the railroad, we also found Gen. Berry with his brigade, which was part of Kearny's division, his advance guard in fact. Gen. Berry was fooling around there, marching and countermarching his regiments for a long time, and he personally refused to let us pass to the rear of him; so we sat on the bank, and watched what I should call his red-tape manœuvres. While we are waiting for Berry to move on, I will describe a battle-field scene which is inscribed so vividly upon the tablets of my memory that it will never be erased therefrom. About an eighth of a mile to the rear of our camp, within a clear space in the surrounding woods, was a little white cottage embowered in a mass of roses of all the hues ever assumed by that queen of flowers. Its occupants were apparently mother and daughter, of about twenty and forty years of age. In my retreat, either solicitude or curiosity prompted me to look in upon them, and see how they were getting along. The older lady was a consumptive, and confined to her bed. The picture that greeted me was worthy of a master, to be preserved on canvas. The daughter sat by the bedside, her countenance calm and unmoved by the terrible din of battle which raged all around them. Hurtling shot and shell hissed and shrieked about them, while volleys roared, and cannon thundered; yet there she sat, with not a tremor of fear apparent, clasping the hand of the mother, who lay with closed eyes, overshadowed by a pallid, death-like hue. I seemed to hear the flutter of the wings of the death-angel; so I turned, closed the door softly, and stole away. The participants in the raging tumult of war outside were intruders in that room of quiet peace.

"But Berry has solved his problem to his satisfaction, and has moved on; so we take to the road, but in order to push to the rear; but a guard is stationed there, and we are ordered off, with the information that the rebs have planted a battery, and are going to sweep the road clean; so we compromise by keeping the bank, and reach a point near Savage Station in safety. Here I leave Sampy in charge of the camp property, and begin to look for the regiment. One of the Tenth men told me that it was all cut into pieces, and scattered, as he saw them go in where the firing was hot, and the fighting terrible. I finally find the surgeon, and he gives me a back-handed blessing for skulking at the rear; and I retort in about the same strain. He condescends at last to give me the desired information, — that they are up the railroad, and on the right of it: then I depart for the front like a little hero, leaving the doctor in a frame of mind that seemed to intimate that he would like to saw my leg off. The doctor and I never came together without a brush; for there was no love between us, and all on account of my refusal to swallow his dirty drugs when I was under the weather, and he pronounced me sick, and then he swore I wasn't sick. He was a very irritable man, anyway, and suffered from dyspepsia very severely.

CHAPTER VIII.

MOVEMENT TO THE JAMES.

WALTER S. GOSS thus describes the movement to the James in "The Woonsocket Patriot" of June 4, 1886: —

"We are now entering upon a season of blood-letting that gave the fighting-men of the army their fill. Gen. Robert E. Lee had taken the command of the Confederate army; and while Gen. McClellan was felicitating himself and the Washington authorities with despatches, that he had his army just where he wanted them, Lee was forging a thunderbolt to be launched upon him, that would send him and his army, that 'was never checked' in the vigor of a fighting flight, to the sheltering banks of the River James. Jackson had cut loose from Gens. Shields and Banks, and had re-enforced Lee. The initiatory movement was made on the 25th of June on Hooker's front, which was a line a little in advance of Casey's old position prior to the battle of Seven Pines.

"I remember that on the morning of the 25th that I had charge of the first relief of the regimental camp-guard. My guard had not been posted over fifteen minutes when orders came to me to double-quick around the camp, and order the guard to report to their companies immediately, and then pack up, and fall into my own company. I made a flying run around that camp; and before I got back to my quarters, the regiment was off on a run. To pack up the few duds in my possession was not a hard task; and that done, I headed up the Williamsburg pike, trailing after the guard, which looked

AUGUSTUS W. LOTHROP,
1st Lieutenant Co. "G."

like the tail to the regimental kite. Ha! that was a hard run of two miles. The weather was hot, and the perspiration streamed from every pore.

"We hove to in front of a redoubt, and stood there in line long enough to have walked slowly over the track: we had come under the pressure of a hasty call. We had thought that the fate of the Republic was hanging on our being there; but it wasn't — it was only a military spasm of some one in authority, who told us to 'git up and git,' and that is why we dusted in such a hurry. The fort was located on the crest of a gentle declivity.

"The artillery stationed at the fort was throwing case-shot and shell over our heads into the woods beyond. It is not a comfortable position to stand in front of shooting artillerymen, even if they do belong to the friendly side. Experience had taught us that missiles were not to be depended on to reach the enemy's lives at all times, and this time was not an exception; for a flying fragment from one of the guns struck the first lieutenant of Company B in the side, and killed him instantly. My ambition was not to die for my country, and, least of all, by the friendly hands of a gunner. It was an act of careless murder, and hundreds of men lost their lives during the war by the reckless carelessness of those whose business it was to waste all such ammunition on the enemy.

"We soon leave the dangerous rear behind, and, with regimental front, go plunging into the thick brush. Here we walk over a recumbent line of men, and the order came to halt. Russell, who always appeared to be more afraid of the troops in his rear than those on his front, sent in his usual challenge of, 'What regiment is that?' A stout, florid man, with whiskers of a sunset hue, assumed the perpendicular, and promptly announced that it was the New-York Excelsior Brigade, commanded by Gen. Sickles. 'This regiment,' said he, 'is the Second Excelsior, and I am Gen. Sickles.' The information did not appear to weigh very heavily on the mind of our valiant colonel, as he replied, 'Well, I want you to remember that I am in front of you; and if your men fire into my regiment, I will about face, and fight you, dem ya!'

"It was the first time that I had seen the much-noted man; but several months later, when he had but one leg, I acted as his orderly a few hours, when he was on a tour of inspection, and was not feeling very proud over it either, as I had to take the place of his minus leg every time he moved, and felt more than relieved when I helped him into his carriage, and saw him ride away.

"After the colonel had relieved his pent-up thoughts on the valiant, robust general, he gave the order to forward; and as we advanced, the enemy fell back. It was not a part of their programme to make or bring on a fight at this point, and the probabilities were that the line on our front were the only troops there; at any rate, they were willing to keep quiet if we would let them. This battle-field is known by the name of Oak Grove; but I saw no grove, unless the scrub-oaks, that were not high enough to hide a man's head from the reb sharpshooters, can be termed a grove, by applying the Cape-Cod theory that 'two huckleberry bushes and a mullein-stalk make a grove.' The fighting is not very ferocious along our part of the line, as we are simply watching each other; now and then volleys of musketry thunder along the line, and the enemy's sharpshooters keep up a continual sputtering; for wherever they see a head, they are bound to hit it. They became so troublesome that the colonel called for two volunteers to creep up and pick them off. I was a volunteer, but was told that my services were not wanted. The colonel picked out his men, two of the worst ones in the company, and they crept away to the rear; if they got any nearer to the enemy than they were when they started, it was a mistake on their part. They are now both borne on the regimental rolls as deserters.

"Those sharpshooters soon taught us to keep our heads

down if we wished to keep them intact. The day wore slowly away, as we lay there upon our bellies, and munched hard-tack, with eyes and ears open to catch the first signs of hostilities. We were so near Richmond that the city-clocks could be heard announcing the time of day during the intervals of oppressive silence.

"On a quiet summer's day, there are lulls in the most hardly contested battles where the silence becomes oppressive, from the fact that every combatant is in momentary expectancy; for like a thunderbolt from a cloudless sky, comes the shock of battle; it rolls along the line, and dies away like pattering raindrops after a shower; then suddenly, like a flash of blinding light, it leaps forth with a maddening tumultuous crash that seems to make the earth quake; while weak, sensitive humanity shrivels, and shrinklingly crawls into its boots. There is no doubt that the fellow who wanted swords beaten into ploughshares, and the spears into pruning-hooks, had been there. But if he had been so unfortunate as to have lived in the days of gunpowder detonation, he would have prayed that the thundering cannon might be ground into G. A. R. badges and sewing-machines, and placed under the peaceful footing of blessed, non-combatant women.

"As the sun dips below the western horizon, the reb plucks up courage under the conviction that our quiet demeanor proves that we have left the field clear for him to post his pickets near where our lines had been; so he advances with two pieces of artillery, one throwing shells, the other shrapnel. They kept advancing and firing until they came so near our lines that we could distinctly hear the orders to load and fire, and hear the percussion snap before the explosion of the piece. We had orders to keep quiet and hold our ground at all hazards; and as they trimmed the scrub-oaks over us, I did my share of holding that ground down; for I pressed the bosom of old mother earth with all the avoirdupois of my weightiness. I really believe that the impression of my body can be found in that scrub-oak, even unto this day. One of the hardest things in war is to lie quiescent, and let the other fellows do all the shooting. I never felt so much like going for any thing — no, not even a square meal — as I did for those guns; but we must obey orders if it took a leg.

"The big guns had met with no response from our side, so we heard the Johnnies coming in to establish their picket line. Somehow the idea had become impressed upon my mind that the average reb did not know what fear was; but we soon learned that the fear principle was as deeply graven on the rebel heart as it was on ours, and that fact aided our courage materially. The Johnnies on our front were very reluctant to advance, and needed a large amount of urging to get them along; we could hear their officers tell them to 'Come along! what are you afraid of? The Yanks have all gone.' The men didn't appear to believe their officers; and we knew they lied, although we did not tell them so — from motives of policy. They commenced to put out their picket-posts; and so near were they to our lines, that a lieutenant with three men nearly stumbled over us; as we raise up with bayonets charged, he softly remarked, 'Put those guns down, boys; I am afraid of them.' He and his men stepped over us as coolly as though they were on dress-parade, and they were taken to the rear.

"That was a long, sleepless night for us; it was dark; the mist settled down upon that low ground, and made every thing miserable, except the blackness of night. Our lines are so near together, that the breaking of a twig or dry stick would elicit a sheet of flame all along our line. One who has never experienced a fight in the dark can have no idea of the lurid sight; suddenly, like a lightning flash, a dazzling sheet of flame leaps out of the inky darkness, and roaring volleys pierce the midnight silence; then its echoes die away, and silence reigns supreme, while aching, overstrained ears in imagination hear the advancing tramp of hostile feet; and again the ruddy flame lights up the scene, leaving behind a black pall that can be felt as well as seen.

"Russell does not appear to like his position: the other troops have fallen back to the intrenchments, and we are in an exposed situation. To the rear of us, probably twenty rods away, is a road; and back of this road the colonel orders his regiment, a company at a time. The company to which I belong has the right of the line: next us is Company G. As that company starts to fall back, the rebs catch on to them, and open up a sprightly little fire. Both sides are getting panicky, and the shooting is lively: our men, at the rear, are having a hack with the rebs in musketry duelling, while we lay between the two fires quietly, wishing they would stop that kind of fun. When the shooting at one another's flashes subsides, we also go out to the road. Some one has been sent to the rear, and a shovel or two for each company has been procured. A rail-fence was pulled down, and the rails packed atop one another, and mud was thrown over them, so that we had a shelter to lay behind; and yet we keep the shovels busy until we have quite a respectable breastworks.

"My job was an order to keep two men out a rod in advance of the rifle-pit. I think it was the hardest task that I ever undertook. In the first place, it was almost impossible to induce a man to go out across the road; and then, when the shooting opened, in would run my brave men. Persuasion and threats were thrown away on such men: the unseen was more than their brains were able to cope with. It was useless to try to beat it into their heads that the rebs were as scared as they were; that they could not be hired to advance an inch. No, it appeared impossible to them that a reb could get as cowardly as they felt just at that time. They did not say as much, but they acted it. Men who were brave to rashness in daylight were completely unnerved by this night's fitful blaze. They did not think or reason on the matter. Had they, the coming morn would have haunted them more than the present darkness; for all the danger of the situation lay in the movements of the enemy when the sun got up to throw his light upon the subject.

"But when the day peeped out of the night, the demonstrations of our rebel neighbors ceased; and as their (and our) courage increased, gentle peace settled down upon our banners. Then we got out of the wilderness of a night of panic (not of the running kind), and steered straight back to our camp.

"A fifteen hours' mental strain makes sad inroads upon a man's nervous system. When the excitement that has held him up has passed away, then the whole man relaxes, and tumbles to pieces physically, and he becomes as limp as a wet dish-rag: at least, that is the way I felt the next day, and I was not alone in that way of feeling."

CHAPTER IX.

FROM FAIR OAKS TO HARRISON'S LANDING.

AFTER the battle, details were sent out to bury the dead, and to burn the dead horses. The regiment was sent, June 2, to Golding's Farm, two miles to right front, where they intrenched. On the 5th supported a battery at the farm, lying in line of battle for two days; were then ordered to Savage Station, where we remained performing picket duty until the forced reconnoissance of parts of the First and Fourth Corps. In the advance ordered by Gen. McClellan preparatory to the attack ordered to be made on the Nine-mile Road, he says, in his general orders, "for the advance of the army, and attack on Richmond." This attack of June 25 was for the purpose of securing additional ground, so as to deploy and advance sufficient force for a determined attack upon the fortifications of Richmond. The resistance was very stubborn, and the Union forces suffered severely. The Seventh Massachusetts was engaged, losing quite a number of brave men, sixteen being killed and wounded. It was the severest engagement the regiment had been in, as related to direct casualties.

Gen. McClellan says, in his report of the Army of the Potomac in the Peninsula, —

"On the 25th of June, our bridges and intrenchments being at last completed, an advance of our picket-line on the left was ordered, preparatory to a general forward movement. Immediately in front of the most advanced redoubt on the Williamsburg road was a large, open field; beyond that, a swampy belt of timber some five hundred yards wide, which had been disputed ground for many days. Farther in advance was an open field crossed by the Williamsburg road and the railroad, and commanded by a redoubt and rifle-pits of the enemy. It was decided to push our lines to the other side of these woods in order to enable us to ascertain the nature of the ground, and to place Gens. Heintzelman and Sumner in position to support the attack intended to be made on the Old Tavern on the 26th or 27th by Gen. Franklin assaulting that position in the rear. Between eight and nine o'clock on the morning of the 25th, the advance was begun by Gen. Heintzelman's corps. The enemy was found to be in strong force all along the line, and contested the advance stubbornly; but by sunset our object was accomplished. The troops engaged in this affair were the whole of Heintzelman's corps, Palmer's brigade of Couch's division of Keyes's corps, and a part of Richardson's division of Sumner's corps."

Also the Seventh Massachusetts of Couch's division, Devens's brigade, Keyes's corps, but which is omitted by Gen. McClellan in his report. But the Seventh was in that fight, losing sixteen men, all told, out of the five hundred and sixteen lost by the troops engaged, supposed to be some twenty-five thousand in all. Quite a respectable number for the smallest organization to lose!

On the 26th and 27th, Lee and Jackson commenced the historical movement around McClellan's right flank, which necessitated the raising of the siege of Richmond, and his retreat, or change of base, to the James River, — a movement which was only accomplished after rivers of blood had been shed, and an immense amount of material destroyed.

The Seventh Massachusetts and Couch's division on the 27th marched eight miles towards Malvern Hill, and camped for the night on the Charles-city Road. Gen. Keyes's corps having been ordered to cross White-Oak Swamp to cover the reserve artillery and baggage-train in advance of the grand move towards the James River.

On the 28th marched five miles and encamped, and on the 29th had a skirmish with the enemy's cavalry. This cavalry force belonged to Gen. Holmes's division on the river-road, and were roughly handled a day or two afterwards by Taylor's reserve artillery from the heights of Malvern and Turkey-Island Bridge. When we halted for the night, we had marched ten miles towards the James River.

Sergeant Walter S. Goss, in "The Woonsocket Patriot" of June 11, speaks of the situation as follows: —

"Gen. McClellan was crying aloud to the powers in Washington for heavy re-enforcements; and on the supposition that he was to receive them, he had stretched the right of his line to Mechanicsville in order to form a junction with the corps of McDowell. But he received only the small division of McCall's Pennsylvania reserves. The Northern army which was occupying Virginia was peculiarly situated. Fremont had an army in the mountainous regions; Banks occupied, or tried to, the Shenandoah Valley; and McDowell held the line of the Rappahannock, while McClellan was thundering at the gates of Richmond, and each was acting independently of the other commands, and each at last resolved themselves into forces of observation and defence, in place of "pooling their issues" by the concentration of their armies, and hurling them upon the enemy's front and flanks to crush him by the weight of their superior numbers. The armies for the defence of Washington had not even interested themselves in the whereabouts of Stonewall Jackson, the only army confronting them and menacing the capital, but re-enacted the part of Patterson, of Bull-Run notoriety, by loosing him from their grasp, that he might throw his force upon the long-drawn-out and thin lines of McClellan's right flank.

"On the 26th of June, Confederates from the Richmond side of the Chickahominy crossed the river above Meadow Bridge, and at noon of that day attacked and drove in the Union pickets. The engagement is known as the battle of Mechanicsville, although it was fought on the left bank of the Beaver Dam Creek, the left of the line resting upon the Chickahominy, while the right was inclined to be "in the air," and was in thick woods beyond a road that lay between Mechanicsville and Cold Harbor.

"The position was naturally a strong one for defence, and had been rendered more so by the careful preparation of the rifle-pits and filled timber. It was impracticable for the advancement of offensive artillery, except by two roads — the upper and lower — where at different times the severest struggles raged. McCall's troops held the front lines, and were supported by the brigades of Martindale and Griffin of Morrill's division. The massed troops of the evening assailed the position savagely, and were repulsed, only to re-form, and like dashing waves to again break and shatter against the serial lines of the determined defenders who held the outposts of the position. The attack was made by A. P. Hill's division, which, according to the Richmond papers, got a severe pummelling and sustained heavy losses, particularly among the officers : the Forty-fourth Georgia and the First North Carolina were nearly annihilated in their first charge. At 9 P.M. the firing ceased, the enemy fell back, and the little sanguinary battle of Beaver-Dam Creek was at an end after six hours struggle.

"McClellan had decided to abandon his exposed base of supplies, and remove it to the James River; and Gen. Lee was an important factor in deciding him on that course, although Lee did not intend to let him go undisturbed, neither did he mean to let him get there.

"In order to save his army, its heavy trains, and provide for his line of retreat, it was a necessity that McClellan should hold the left of the Chickahominy until he could gain time to provide and secure a new base of supplies upon the James.

"For this purpose the Fifth Corps was withdrawn from its extended right position, and concentrated in and about the vicinity of Gaines's Mills, holding within its embrace the bridges over the River Chickahominy and within supporting distance of the army on the Richmond side. Before daylight of the morning of the 27th, Porter had removed his trains and most of the heavy guns across the river, also performed the delicate task of extricating the force at Beaver-Dam Creek from its perilous position, and was ready for the developments of the enemy's progress for the day.

"The Confederate forces began to show themselves about noon, and at two o'clock P.M. the ball opened lively. At three o'clock the fighting had become so terrific that Porter had merged his supporting lines and all his reserves into the foremost line of battle, and called for re-enforcements. Never in the history of strife was more desperate, long-sustained fighting done. Porter's army of about twenty-five thousand men were holding in check the troops of Hill, Longstreet, and Jackson, who were assaulting them in front and in flank with an army of sixty thousand men.

"Slocum's division arrived on the ground at half-past three, and were immediately broken into fragments, and sent to the weak spots in the line by brigades and regiments. For a season victory appeared to perch upon the Union banners. Porter's men had repulsed the assaults of the enemy all along their line. The fighting grows fierce and desperate as the day wanes. The Confederates bring up their reserves, and hurl them with crushing force against the weak points of the Union line; every available man is now brought forward by the rebs, and massed columns are thrown with tremendous force in rapid and successive charges against the wavering Federal lines. Jackson finally gathers up the divisions of Whiting and Jackson, and throws them upon the Union left with furious assault, when Butterfield's brigade, which has for over an hour been gallantly holding back the enemy's furious onslaught, gives way before the heavy attack on front and flank, and goes scudding to the rear. The line begins to crumble and dissolve into fragments, and the day appears to have been lost by crushing defeat. Porter has again called for help, and the brigades of Meagher and

French are on the way to re-enforce him. Meantime chaos reigns all along his line: his men are discouraged, and are giving up the fight. The troops are breaking to the rear in confused masses, when two horsemen appear on the scene. Their steeds are white with foam as they furiously ride upon the field, brandishing their swords, and calling upon the men to form a line: they ride forward, and make a stand. Like magic the war-worn, disheartened men gather new courage under the leadership of these two officers, Gen. Porter and Col. Berdan, and form a defensive line half a mile or more at the rear of their old position. The men fell into line without regard to organization, as there was a curious mixture of States. Massachusetts men fought that day by the side of the heroic men of Michigan: it was a question of national importance, above all doctrines of State rights. Those men who that night rallied on the line with the heroic Porter and gallant Berdan deserve to go down to history as heroes, the example of which it would have been well for several well-known generals to have followed. I have written ‘heroic Porter’ with a vivid understanding of the meaning of the term. I care nothing for the verdict of a packed court-martial to create a scapegoat that the tottering fortunes of others might be propped up thereby. As an interested participant in that bloody seven-days' fray, I write ‘heroic’ above the names of Porter, Berdan, and that rallying band of warriors who formed their lines in the face of an humiliating defeat; that long, straggling line that sent up cheer upon cheer, and stayed with palsied fear the onward course of that rebel horde, who believed that that little band were re-enforcements from over the river; and when, shortly, after the famous Irish brigade combined with French's sailed into their midst with dashing charge, they were confirmed in that opinion, and fell back with discretion to bivouac for the night, while Porter with all his re-enforcements pulled himself together, and crossed over the Chickahominy, after which the bridges were destroyed.

'The rebels in Richmond were jubilant that night, but there was a particle of alloy mixed with their exhilaration. The pulverizing process was not quite so thorough as they had hoped or anticipated. Their loss had been terrible, if we can believe their own accounts. Again, they expected that McClellan would pull up stakes, re-cross the river, and strike a bee-line for Fortress Monroe; but his movements did not point in that direction, and they were a little puzzled over their programme for the future.

"On our side of the river we were not idle that day. The rebs on our front were uneasy, and given to getting up demonstrations. They did not care to fight; but it would have been better for us, had we forced them into one on a grand scale. Their apparent uneasiness had its desired effect; for our generals were anxious to retain their men, and leave Porter to go it alone, and that was what Lee was playing for.

"In the forenoon of the 27th, we were ordered down to Savage Station; what for, is more than I was able to fathom, as we did nothing except stand around, and try to steal something; but the guard was too much for us in that line. The army stores at White-House Landing were being transported by rail to Savage Station; and there were heaps and stacks of grub and ammunition there, — yes, and whiskey by the cask, and the boys tried all manner of strategy in order to get a seductive nip.

"The red tape of war is something wonderful to behold. A pile of eatables larger than a dozen Virginia court-houses was stacked up, and finally consumed by the devouring fire, while a guard presided over it; and hungry soldiers with empty haversacks, and bellies to match, trudged, fought, bled, died, during those weary days and gloomy nights, suffering the tortures of the damned in heroic endeavor to uphold the integrity of the Federal Government.

"We are again ordered back to camp from the station, and spend the rest of the day in packing up for a move in the early morning. We hear the sullen roar of battle upon the right; and anxiety is depicted upon the countenances of all, as the rumors fly through the camp that Porter is in a critical position. The movement of army supplies to our side of the river, and the sudden stoppage of the same, tell us that a storm is brewing, and that a forced move of the army may become a necessity.

"The morning of the 28th of June finds us on the move in the direction of the White-Oak Swamp, to cover the retreat of the army. At noon we have crossed the bridge over the stream that flows through the swamp, and takes its name therefrom, and have taken a position upon the higher lands beyond. Here we hold our position until relieved by Slocum's division, when we again move on to new scenes of action."

The 30th of June marched two miles, and encamped near Turkey-Island Bend. July 1, 1862, we marched about one mile to the woods near Malvern Hill, and went on picket. On the 2d marched nine miles, and encamped near Harrison's Landing. The 3d marched out on the front lines about three miles, and encamped. The casualties of the Seventh Massachusetts in this movement were very small, but this was none of their choosing; and only the lucky chances of war saved them from the mortality usually attending so dangerous a movement.

While Couch's division, of which his old brigade was an integral part, was earning imperishable renown, and by great good fortune as a part of that brigade the Tenth Massachusetts, and that gallant and efficient regiment, the Thirty-sixth New York, were winning honors never to fade as long as history lasts, the Seventh Massachusetts and Second Rhode Island, a part of the same brigade, were ordered to a certain part of the field, which the general commanding was in fear would be forced, and told to hold it at all hazards. But by the fortunes of war these regiments were not called upon to make the heroic sacrifices which the Tenth and Thirty-sixth were so nobly making on the heights of Malvern.

Gen. Couch, in his eloquent address delivered at the reunion of his old brigade at Oakland Garden in the summer of 1884, in speaking of the work of his old command at Malvern, said, —

"While the Tenth and Thirty-sixth were earning immortal renown on the heights, where were you of the Second Rhode Island and Seventh Massachusetts? Early in the day I received an order to detach two of my most efficient regiments to hold a certain point in our line of battle, upon which was expected an overwhelming attack of the enemy. And who could I send to their deaths better than the Seventh Massachusetts and the Second Rhode Island? and only by the fickle chances of war were you saved from a glorious death or heroic sacrifice."

In the "Woonsocket Patriot" of July 2, was the following letter from Sergeant Walter S. Goss, and which I take pleasure in presenting to my readers : —

"Harrison's Landing was the centre of gravitation for the Army of the Potomac. We had found a lodgement in what had been, the year before, a field of corn; but mud is now the chief product of that soil. Around us in every direction, so far as the eye could view, were garnered wheat-sheaves in shocks or stooks. But I was not thinking of wheat-straw just at that time, but on coffee was intent. I had taken a look at the river, and that was running yellow with mud: the puddles were severely afflicted with earthy matter; but near was a grass-plat, over which mules had travelled and left the impression of their cloven hoofs. I followed their footsteps, and dipped water and hayseed from their tracks, a spoonful at a time, until a full ration was gathered. Then I went at the wet corn stubble, and tried to coax a blaze out of them; and while I was wiping my weeping eyes, I caught a glimpse of travelling wheat-bundles, and for fear of being left out in the wet mud over night, I forsook all, and struck out on a brisk walk for my share of straw.

"The whole army appeared to be after straw, and to have

got the start of me, as the wheat-shocks became disrupted and travelled away faster than I could walk: so I quickened my pace to a lively run. But it was like chasing a mirage; when I got where the straw was, it wasn't there. I had to give up the chase. It was the most curious sight I ever saw; the stooks disappeared like magic, and they resolved themselves into a tangled mass of moving sheaves of straw. My mind reverted to the moving green of 'great Birnam wood to high Dunsinane hill.' But I got a bundle of straw; for my tent-mate Tom, who rushed with the first crowd, had such a game of scrabbling and dodging from one shock to another before securing the coveted prize, he concluded to gobble two sheaves, and wait for my coming; and I found him sitting on them, patiently waiting.

"During the evening Hill, the champion coffee-kicker, who was among the missing, turned up; and he had a doleful story to tell. It appeared that he crawled off into the bushes for an undisturbed night's sleep, and when we came away he was not found to be awakened, so he slept 'like a warrior taking his rest,' until the ponderous rain-drops baptized him into a fresh morning start; then he shook himself like a big dog, rubbed his eyes with amazed stupidity, turned around a few times to add to his confusion, then started to look up his regiment. He had not proceeded far before he was confronted by a challenge to halt, from the rebel picket-line. He politely invited them to go to a region notorious for its theological torridity, and about-faced, leaving tracks with his heels toward the enemy, while a shower of bullets whistled harmless about his ears. The rebel cavalry followed him up, when he took to the woods, running and stumbling for miles, and struck our picket-lines, when he was ordered to halt, and was again fired upon because he told them to join the rebs he had consigned to Hades.

"He was taken a prisoner, and passed along to his regiment to be identified. In telling his adventure, he remarked that he would never try that exploit over again, as it was the hardest job he ever did. Hill was one of the best soldiers in the army; he knew no fear, and was always anxious to charge, knowing that his heavy weight would carry him through, while his dimensions made a good target for bullets. Fifty thousand men like Hill, with his charging proclivities, would have proved a terror to any enemy. But the valiant Hill, with many another good man, went down in death in the blind and bloody tangles of the Wilderness.

"In the morning we moved out again to get our new lines of defence. A little incident illustrates the ease with which troops assume to be veterans. While moving out, we halted opposite a Pennsylvania regiment, of high numbers, who were marching in. They wore their blankets in rolls swung over their shoulders, while we had hung to our knapsacks, thinking them much better than rolls. Members of the Pennsylvania battalion asked what regiment we were, and were answered, 'A Down East regiment, by golly.'—'Just out, are you?'—'Yes,' was the reply. 'Well, I thought so: you won't carry them knapsacks when you have been out here as long as we have.' Some one asked the State and number of our regiment, and, when told, turned to the spokesman of his party, and said, 'Shut up, you fool: that regiment was out here before you thought of enlisting, they were the ones that passed through Baltimore.' He was mistaken. We passed through that city, but Gen. B. F. Butler was there at the time: it was the Sixth militia the men had mixed up with us.

"Our company was pushed out well at the front again; and then the colonel was not satisfied, as there was a long gap in the picket-line, and he wanted three good men placed out as a post of observation, and the lot fell upon the three men on the left of the company; that meant Sergeant Brightman, another man, and myself. We took orders from the colonel, and went to our duty. We pulled through the woods, and came to a high fence, beyond which was a rod-wide streak of scrubby oaks, and then an open field a quarter of a mile long, in the centre of which was a house with outbuildings. On our right, at the extreme end of the field, was a line of Confederate cavalry, while confronting them on our left were our horsemen: they were watching one another's movements.

"Brightman instructed me to skirt along the fence at the right, and find our pickets, while the other man went to the left on a like errand.

"I followed along the fence cautiously, listening for friend or foe; as Russell had told us to be careful, as the woods were full of rebs. I heard men talking at last, and crept over the fence, and crawled up until I saw that they wore the blue, when I confronted them with the query, 'What regiment do you belong to?' They all three grasped their guns, and came to an aim, and demanded my business, which I explained so they were satisfied. They told me they belonged to the Forty-ninth New-York Infantry. On my way back I started up an old sow with a litter of little pigs, and one of those little fellows appeared to be just the size to 'fill a long-felt want' that raged within: so, heedless of all things else, I gave chase to infantile pork.

"Well, we rushed like a whirlwind, through the bushes, until I saw Brightman — who had 'clomb' the fence, and come to the front — fleeing before our charge like a startled pig, as he leaped the fence like a frightened deer, and then he about-faced, and pointed his shooting-iron square at me; then I yelled for him to stop it. We came to a mutual understanding; but the pork had slipped my greedy grasp, and its economic scarcity value had gone up a peg. Brightman declared, when I asked him what made him run so, that we made such a noise rushing through the bushes, that the rebel cavalry, he thought, were charging down upon him, but he didn't intend to investigate until he was safely over the fence.

"We established our post, and watched the horsemen on either side of our front. I was very anxious to see a cavalry charge right on that field in front; but there appeared to be no fight in either crowd, and they did not deem it expedient to give an exhibition of their valor to appease the morbid curiosity of us lonely footmen. In an hour or so the rebs quietly withdrew within the shadow of the woods, and shortly after our men retired beneath the cooling shade of the adjoining foliage. Then Col. Russell boldly took the road, and rode across towards the opposite woodland; but he soon came cantering back with two rebel horsemen trailing at his rear. They showed no disposition to shoot at him, although they were within pistol-shot of him; and the brave officer appeared to be in no hurry, as he was simply trying to draw them in, and they to capture him. They came near enough our post to make an easy shot for us; but Russell made no motion to indicate any such a desire, and we were too well trained to interfere with the business; but the pickets away down on the left opened upon them, so they relinquished their chase, turned tail, and got. Then Russell was mad. He drew his sword, and rode down to that picket front; and, judging by his motions, he poured out the vials of his choice pulpit invectives upon them for their well-meant simplicity.

"I was left alone by the other men of the post, and a cannonading at the rear of me made me nervously inclined. The colonel came up to visit me, to see what was going on at the front; and I saluted him with the question, 'What does all this shooting at the rear mean? Have the rebs got there?' Laconically he answered, 'Fourth of July damphools.' I hadn't thought of it. The glorious day of independence might have passed by unremembered by me, had the patriots at the rear been satisfied with the gunpowder explosions of the past few days. But they were not. There is an intensely patriotic streak in the average Northerner; and it runs to noise, from the small boy with his toy pistol up to the grown-up old boy with his booming cannon. We heard, nor heard of, no noise from the other side; for they saved their powder to prop up an institution dearer to them than any Fourth of July. In spite of her Washington, Jefferson,

Patrick Henry, and her old-time Lees, Virginia was worshipping at the shrine of a traitor to whom the shibboleth of liberty was a continual menace to the fabric of his would-be government.

"During the day Gen. Couch came up to the post to get an observation. I was standing at the edge of the bush when he came up; and he pulled me in, and told me to be careful and not show myself, or I would get shot. I thought differently, and pointed out a man at the house in front, who appeared to have on a red shirt without a coat: he was running about like one possessed of seventeen devils, but was so far away that I couldn't make out what he was up to, only by a rough estimate. 'Well, who is he?' said the general. 'One of our cavalry, I think, as there is a squadron of them over in that wood on the left.' — 'Well, what takes him there?' — 'His appetite, I reckon.' was my reply, as I began to think that my appetite would take me ten miles if there was only a square meal at the end of it. 'What do you mean by that?' asked Couch. And I told him that it looked to me as though the man were racing after pigs or poultry on an empty stomach.

"The gallant general brought the focus of his field-glass to bear upon him, uttered an emphatic 'Humph!' and walked away. Now, what made me discover, with unaided vision, what the general could not see through without the aid of his field-glass? Simply this: Observation had taught me that no soldier ever exercised himself so vigorously, of his own volition, as that man was doing, unless there was something to eat in the concluding exercises."

July 12 the writer of this History joined his regiment, in company with some ten or twelve others who had been sick in hospitals at Washington. I found the boys encamped on the outer line, worn out with marching, and ragged and dirty from their terrible labors for the past two months. I was welcomed back most cordially by Capt. Reed, Lieuts. Mayhew and Gurney, and all the boys: but I never, to this day, really knew whether or not it was for the reason that picket and guard duty would come a little easier; 'twould be hard to say. I am sure, however, that the razor I brought with me did much to smooth my reception; for it was in constant demand for a week, by which time the boys had cleaned up, and recovered their old-time elasticity of spirits, which had been considerably lowered by the terrible strain of the last week of battles.

I made my home with some Scituate boys, — Charles, Hosea D., Nott, and Joseph O. Marsh, — good boys, every one of them, whole-hearted and true. The tent was pitched over four crotched sticks, two at each end, with long ones running lengthwise, and resting on the short ones at head and foot. At this time of the year, at that particular place in Old Virginia, a bed raised from off the ground was very essential to comfort, as we were subjected to very severe thunder-storms, the water from the skies coming not only in drops, but in sheets; and soon every thing was afloat. The gulches became roaring torrents, which had only to be disturbed to become a rushing stream of mud.

The weather was intensely hot, and good drinking-water scarce, unless we went to the river-springs, or outside the lines about a mile and a half, or three miles to the river. The surface-water which collected upon the sub-stratum of marl was very fatal to the men who were too feeble to go to the springs, and were obliged to drink this "lime-water," thus laying the foundation for chronic diarrhœa, from which many never recovered. Corp. Benjamin F. Hutchinson contracted the disease here, and died in Craney-Island Hospital off Norfolk, Va. I may also mention Frederick Cook of Company K, who was taken ill with the disease at this camp, and died while we were encamped at Downsville, Md.; also, Richardson of Company I, who died in hospital at Washington.

CHAPTER X.

LETTER BY CAPT. REED.

HAVING received a very interesting narrative from Capt. George Reed, formerly commander of Company K, of the regiment's participation in the Seven Days' Fight, and of his own company's part in that engagement, which was published in "The Abington Standard" at Abington, Mass., Sept. 6, 1862, I take the liberty of inserting it as a part of this history : —

"On Wednesday, June 25, early in the morning, a smart firing commenced on our right from Hooker's pickets. It soon increased ; and in a little while the heavy boom of cannon broke upon our ears, which showed it was something more serious than mere picket skirmishing. I had hardly reached camp when I received orders to have my company in readiness to march at a moment's notice. Cartridges were issued, haversacks filled, canteens replenished, and shortly the order came to " Fall in ; " and in a very few moments the Seventh were marching with full ranks in the direction of the firing. We proceeded to the front of our lines, stacked arms, and waited some three hours, while the firing sensibly slackened.

"Gens. Couch, Kearny, Hooker, Keyes, Palmer, Grover, and others were in consultation on our left, and our brigade finally received orders to advance. We proceeded at the double-quick some two miles, and were posted in front of De Russy's battery as a support. The batteries were firing shell very rapidly ; and we had been in position but a few moments when the casing of one of the shells hit Lieut. Bullock of Fall River on the left hip, cutting his sword in two, and inflicting an awful and mortal wound. We then moved about a hundred yards to the right, and were ordered to advance, which we did, passing over dead horses, broken gun-carriages, and cut-up roads, to the extreme front of the line. We were posted across an open field, some eight hundred yards from thick woods where the rebels were stationed, with the right and left of our regiment under cover of a swamp.

"My company being in the centre of the regiment, we were in a very exposed position, and soon were made aware of the presence of sharpshooters by the whistling of bullets in very uncomfortable proximity to our ears. Major Harlow was selected by them as a mark; but though they shot all around him, they did not succeed in hitting him. We were ordered to lie down when we took our position, and this made it extremely difficult to hit us. But one rebel in a large oak fired very accurately, and, selecting Capt. Bliss of Company F as his mark, sent a ball crashing through the brain of John White, who was lying by the captain's side. The rebel did not exult long in his deed, as one of our skirmishers, who had been watching for him, shot him as he exposed himself to fire; and he came rushing down into the fork of the tree ere the report of his rifle had ceased to echo in the surrounding woods.

"At this time word was passed down the line for our men to lie close as possible, as the rebels were moving artillery to the front. In a few minutes they opened upon us with a sharp fire of shell, which was exceedingly well directed, and in good range, the shell bursting over in front and in rear of us; and it seemed as if half of the regiment would be disabled; but, singular to relate, not a man of our regiment was injured, while the Second Rhode Island, which lay right in our rear, lost a good many. They then commenced a terrible fire of grape and canister, which swept over us in a fearful manner some fifteen minutes, cutting shrubs as clean as with a scythe, and striking all around us without injuring a man. At dusk their firing ceased, and their artillery limbered up and retired. We seized the opportunity given us in the darkness to eat a few hard bread (or, as the men say, reduce a few squares), as we had eaten nothing since morning, and were getting faint and exhausted from our uncomfortable position.

"The enemy had been driven about a mile, and we were an advance picket with orders to hold the position. As the evening advanced, it became evident that we should have great odds to encounter, as we could hear regiment after regiment march up in front of us; hear the word of command of the officers to halt, right dress, order arms, and even heard old Magruder order one Capt. Nolen to have their dead near the old oak-tree removed for burial, our skirmishers having piled them up there to some purpose.

"About nine in the evening. Adjt. Packard came along the line with orders from the colonel to have the men in readiness to move in good order, and in perfect silence, a short distance to the rear. The men were formed in line, faced by the rear rank, and were moving silently away, when Company C got into some disorder, and the colonel halted the line. Some of Company K halted before I heard the order, while the rest of the company were some two rods in advance. I had just gone to the left to move them up into line, when a most severe and galling fire of musketry was opened within two hundred yards of our line from, I should think, a whole brigade. The suddenness of the attack, and the men being out of their accustomed places, threw them into some confusion; and some of the men who were in the advance faced about and fired right into our faces. The Second Rhode Island upon our right also commenced firing, without waiting to see whether they were firing upon friend or foe. Company K was in the centre of this converging fire; and never before was it my fortune to stand where the bullets flew so thick and fast as they did for some ten minutes on this eventful night. The night was very dark; and nothing could look so pretty, and at the same time so fearful, as the sheet of fire which blazed from the unseen foe in our front. Company K soon got into order, and returned the fire with interest; and nothing was heard for a time but the short, sharp commands of the officers, and the rapid crack of the rifles of the combatants.

"In the height of the fire, Private Augustine Fullerton — a braver and a better soldier I have not got in my company — came up to me, and said, 'Captain, I am shot badly.' — 'Where?' I asked him. 'Right through here,' he said, placing his hand upon his right breast; and the poor boy's voice quivered with emotion as he thought of his home and friends. I sent him to the rear in charge of Private J. E. Josselyn; and he had hardly started, when Private Sylvester Edmund of Scituate came up with, 'Captain, they have hit me right here in the shoulder.' I sent him to the rear also. These two, with Private T. H. Cook who had accidentally shot himself in the foot in the afternoon, were all the casualties I had in my company.

"In a short time we had the satisfaction of finding the fire of the enemy slackening, and soon it had ceased. Our men were then ordered to go to work digging rifle-pits; and though weak and exhausted, they set to work with a right good will, and in the hardest digging ever seen. They had worked about three hours when another fierce attack was made by the rebels; but the men laid down their shovels, grasped their rifles without the slightest confusion, and poured a steady and well-directed fire into the flash of the enemy's rifles till they retired. The men then fell to work again, and labored until about three o'clock A.M.: the colonel moving along the lines, and encouraging the troops, exhorting them, telling them their salvation depended upon their labors.

"We were indeed in a fearful position, having been

ordered to hold it at all hazards, — and Col. Russell was not the man to draw back without an order, — while the rebels could bring heavy odds against us. The Rhode-Island regiment had been withdrawn; and the New-York regiment on our left was completely demoralized, their colonel being intemperate, their lieutenant-colonel being too timid to take command, and most of their officers having left, together with several hundred of the men. We had certainly a brigade to contend with, and probably a larger force was being concentrated on the rebel side. Daylight was looked for with deep anxiety; but we had determined to give a good account of the Seventh, and defend our position to the last. Just before daylight we had an order to fall back to the rifle-pits, a little more than a mile in our rear; and the men were quietly withdrawn.

"In the whole affair the bearing of Company K was very gratifying to me; and I think it was owing to the coolness and example of Lieuts. Mayhew and Gurney, who rendered me valuable assistance, as indeed they have on all occasions when we have been called upon to encounter the enemy.

"We now took our position in Casey's rifle-pits, and remained there until noon, or very near that time, when we returned to camp, and ate for the first time that day. It had been an exceedingly hard spell for us, as my company had been on picket-duty the night previous, so we had no sleep for two nights, with scarcely a mouthful to eat for over twenty-four hours, and at work all night — the second night — after a very fatiguing march during the day. We had hardly reached camp when a tremendous cannonading broke out on our extreme right, and continued without intermission until nine in the evening. We were ordered to be ready to march at any moment, but were not ordered out during the afternoon.

"The next morning, Friday, the cannonading was resumed with great fury, and soon we had orders to fall in and march; but, instead of moving to the right, we marched to the rear, past Savage Station, nearly to the Chickahominy, and then set our faces towards the James River. We rested after a very long and fatiguing march, 'mid the dust and heat of a sultry day, through the camp of Peck's division on the extreme left of our line.

"In the morning we were routed out at four, and ordered to fall in as soon as we had made our coffee; but before the order could be carried out, Company K was detailed for duty, and had to leave without breakfast. We were marched to White-Oak-Swamp Creek, and went to work to repair the road, and build a bridge across the creek. The men having had no breakfast, and nearly beaten out by the duties of the last few days, were employed some two hours in carrying huge logs and laying them across the stream.

"When our regiment came up, we were ordered to fall in, and proceeded on our march. We were now on a new route in the enemy's country, and leading the advance, a position which, while one of honor, is by no means one of ease. We marched a few miles, halted, and learned we were to remain there twenty-four hours as pickets. Our line was formed in an open piece of woods with a large field of wheat in our front. We stacked arms, masked them with green boughs, posted sentries, and lay down to obtain some rest. We could have no fires near the front, and the men who wanted coffee had to proceed some distance to the rear to make it. A battery of six-pound guns was placed at the fence between the wood and the wheat-field, and masked so that the most acute scout could not have told, at a distance of a hundred yards, whether it was any thing but underbrush. We had to be on the watch all night for fear of an attack, but the day dawned without any thing of moment occurring.

"The forenoon passed off very quietly, the men employing the time, as a general thing, in trying to sleep. Just after one P.M., I was lying near our stack of arms, almost asleep, when I was suddenly aroused by the tramp of horses and the yell of rebel cavalry right in our lines. Our men were lying in all shapes, without their equipments; but in an incredibly short time we were in line, and eager for the fight.

"It was a surprise to us, as they had driven in our cavalry scouts, and came in so mixed up with them, that our sentries dared not fire for fear of killing our own men. The rebs rushed up to the wood, and wheeled into line; but before they formed, we poured such a fire into them that they broke in confusion, with the loss of their major commanding, two captains, and nine men killed, and some twenty-five prisoners. As they were skedaddling down the road, our battery opened on them, overturning horses and men to their evident consternation. They supposed they were attacking a small cavalry picket, and, with their five companies of cavalry, rushed confidently on to a regiment of Massachusetts infantry. We took sabres of the United-States pattern, stolen by Floyd, Sharp's carbine rifles, double-barrelled guns, and some valuable horses. Indeed, their major, though mortally wounded, thought more about his horse than any thing else; for he said he had paid two hundred dollars for him only a few days before.

"In the afternoon we were relieved by the Sixth Maine, and received orders to cross White-Oak Swamp in advance, and in the night. This was regarded as rather tough, as we had no sleep the night previous, to speak of, had been exposed to a heavy rain, and had not got our blankets dry, which made knapsacks hang rather heavy. We had been on short allowance of food; had scarcely any chance to make coffee, — that sheet-anchor of the soldier, — and were nearly worn out by fatigue and exposure.

"Speaking of food, the officers are sometimes placed in very unpleasant circumstances with regard to rations. Not drawing any thing from Government, and the brigade commissary being miles in the rear, on protracted marches they frequently find themselves blessed with a good appetite, and nothing to eat. As this only happens when the men are nearly out, it becomes a grave question of ways and means as to the manner of supplying our internal economy. Lieut. Gurney and myself started on this march with half a hardbread between us, and with no knowledge as to how or when we should obtain more. However, orders must be obeyed, and we started in good spirits for our long and dangerous march.

"We reached the edge of the swamp at dark, when every man had orders to cap his piece, carry it at the shoulder, not to fire without orders, not to light a match, or suffer his dipper to rattle, to preserve the most perfect silence, and to keep closed up at all hazards. We then plunged into the recesses of the swamp, and so dark was it that I could not see the man before me, although my hand was on his knapsack. For eight long hours we were in this horrible hole; wading streams, stumbling over fallen trees, halting whenever we approached a more than ordinarily dangerous place, until the ground had been felt over before the main body of the regiment proceeded on their way. Durign one of these halts, I fell asleep standing at the head of my company, and did not wake until the leading file nearly stumbled over me. We had a battery with us of six rifled guns, two Parrotts, two three-inch rifled, and two brass twelve-pounders. Once we were halted, and the artillery ordered to the front. I concluded we were in for it; but at three A.M. we reached the James River, and the welcome words, 'Break ranks,' greeted our ears. At five A.M. we were aroused, and without any breakfast, put in motion over an exceedingly dusty road at a very quick pace; and some of the men grumbled, as they had no supper the night before.

"Think of it, you who live at home and think the soldier is more than paid for his services. Think of those who have endured such privations and hardships amid the swamps of the Old Dominion; and if any poor fellow gets his discharge from the service, do not pursue him with imputations of cowardice until you have been through a tithe of what he has. You can have no idea of what is sacrificed and endured by the volunteer who has left home and friends to fight his and your enemy, and restore the stars and stripes to their old position as the flag of a united and happy people.

"But to return. We were marched two or three miles, halted, and waited two hours in the hot sun for further orders. We then marched into a large wheat-field where the golden grain had just been harvested, and lay in huge stacks for acres and acres. Cherry-trees loaded with their tempting fruit were scattered around; and an orchard of apple-trees, with apples nearly ripe, was discovered by our boys. After we had stacked arms and been dismissed, away rushed the men, some for water, some for the fruit, some for straw, and some soon spied a field of potatoes, which were uprooted; and for a little while we revelled in all the luxuries of the season. Six hours after our entrance, there was a contrast in the appearance of the place to what it was when we arrived. The whole of Porter's division had entered the same field, and between their boys and ours every thing was stripped. The huge stacks of wheat had disappeared, fruit-trees were despoiled, the potatoes were all dug, and the men were sighing for new fields to conquer.

"In the afternoon the enemy attacked our left, and soon a furious cannonading was in progress. The 'Galena' and 'Monitor' were lying within a half-mile of us; and in a few minutes after the firing commenced, a signal-officer mounted the chimney of a large house in the field where we lay, and signalled to the boats. A thundering roar soon announced that the terrible gunboats had opened upon the rebel hordes. Their 155-pound shell flew with an unearthly scream over our heads; and we could hear them burst some two miles to the front, to the great terror of the rebels, and the corresponding joy of our forces. We were not ordered out that afternoon, but lay there watching the ceaseless stream of baggage-wagons and troops which continued to pour in till far into the night. The battle had ceased at dark; but once in a while the deep roar of a gun was heard, with an occasional report from a musket or rifle. Finally all was hushed save the continuous rattle of our baggage-train.

"Tuesday morning all was quiet until ten o'clock, when the ball again opened. We were soon called into line, and after standing a half-hour stacked arms, and were dismissed with orders to commanders of companies to keep their men ready for a call. In about an hour it came, and we moved once more for the field of battle. Choked with dust, the perspiration streaming down their faces, the men soon presented an uncouth and strange appearance; but they toiled on, lightening their way with jokes and sarcasms upon the appearance of the various regiments, or such general officers as they passed. We met the wounded by scores; some in ambulances, some on stretchers, and some on foot wending their way to the rear.

"When we reached the battle-field, a grand spectacle was spread out before us. Imagine a high ridge of land where we stood, falling off gradually to a stream of water some half-mile to the front, then rising as gradually on the other side of the stream to a thick wood where the rebels were posted. The length of this opening was three miles, and its width one mile. In this amphitheatre, line after line of our batteries could be seen with their supports of infantry extending for miles. Some two hundred pieces of artillery were thus disposed in various commanding positions from right to left, as far as the eye could discern.

"We entered upon the left centre, halted, formed line, and stacked arms, and the men given a chance to rest. While we were watching the scene, a puff of smoke, followed by the screaming of a shell, from the edge of the wood opposite, showed that the rebels were commencing fire again. In a few moments battery after battery on our side opened in reply, and the air was filled with shells, hissing and screaming; some bursting in mid-air, others falling among the dense masses of the enemy before they exploded, and still others plunging far over the wood, scattering their shower of fragments harmlessly around. In the midst of this terrific fire, an aid rode up to Col. Russell with, 'Is this the Massachusetts Seventh?'—'Yes,' said the colonel. 'You are ordered to report to Gen. Hancock on extreme right, as the enemy are concentrating troops there, and he must hold his position.'—'Fall in,' was the word; and we were again on the march, traversing the field of battle from left to right, through woods and wheat-fields and over creeks, till at dark we reached our position. Two companies were detailed for picket-duty, when there was found to be a misunderstanding of the line by the regiment posted on our left, and on the line being re-organized by Major Harlow of the Seventh, it threw my company out; and we returned to the regiment, getting lost in the thick woods, and floundering around in the dark for an hour before we found it. The men had permission to lie down with equipments on, ready to start at a moment's notice.

"In the middle of the night we were aroused; and I was ordered to have my company fall in silently and rapidly, and to move forward when the left of the regiment started. The first sound that struck my ear was the rumble of artillery in every direction, mingled with the roll of baggage-wagons, and the indescribable sound produced by the tread of many thousand men. I knew at once some very important movement was in progress. The men were soon in line, and we commenced our march; but it was difficult to move the regiment in a thick wood, with a dark night and no path, and it required all our attention not to get strayed from the main body. After groping among roots, brambles, and fallen trees, slipping into holes, and falling over prostrate timber, we emerged from the pathless wood, upon the main road, and joined the living stream that was flowing to the rear. Innumerable baggage-wagons mixed up with the artillery blocked the road for miles; while regiment after regiment passed, some at double-quick, others at rout-step.

"While we were halted, awaiting orders, the colonel had the quartermaster issue what rations he had on hand. Six hard-bread were given to each man, with the caution to be saving of them, as there was no knowing when we could obtain any more. After waiting for an hour, we received our orders. The colonel sent for the officers, and said our regiment had been detailed as the extreme rear-guard; that it was a position of great danger and responsibility, and he relied on their efforts to encourage the men, and hold the enemy in check; that they had better communicate the fact to the men, so that they could act understandingly. This was done; our pieces were loaded, and officers and men resigned themselves to the almost certain fact of death or a prison, which seemed inevitable under the circumstances.

"Thus we remained for an hour or more, watching the different regiments as they filed past, and commenting on the terrified appearance of the great majority of the wagoners, as with oaths and execrations, and frantic lashing of the mules, they urged their heavily loaded teams over the muddy road. They had been passing for eight hours when our men were ordered to fall in; and we proceeded at the double-quick over a road where deep mud was the best travelling, crowding by the enormous number of wagons that filled the way, until half of the men fell behind from sheer exhaustion. We at length reached our designated position, and formed in divisions on a large hill near the James River, covered with splendid wheat all ready for the harvest. We remained an hour or more at this place; but the rebels not appearing, the word was again 'Forward.' The men wallowed through the wheat, — or what was the wheat-field, for after the passage of an army over such a place it would take a shrewd man to guess or determine what green thing had ever grown there, — and rushed with their dippers to dip up the mingled clay and rain-water which ran down the gullies, and quench their raging thirst. I drank it repeatedly; and never water tasted sweeter, though it was liquid mud. After an exhausting march we reached James River at noon on Wednesday, July 2, 1862, making eight days of hardship, exposure, and fatigue, that will challenge comparison with any campaign of this most unhappy war. The men were thoroughly worn out. It had been the battle, march, and picket, for eight days, with scarcely any food, insufficient water, no rest, and harassed in mind and body. Friends were missing on every side, no one knowing whether they were numbered with the slain or held as prisoners by the enemy. Gloom and depression pervaded every countenance as we formed our line and stacked arms in a magnificent wheat-field on the bank of the river, and then came the welcome order to 'break ranks.' The field, soaked by the heavy rain, trodden by thousands of men and animals, and cut up by the artillery and wagons, was a deep bed of mud; but officers and men spread their blankets, and were soon wrapped in slumber, dreaming of their own happy firesides, the war and its attendant horrors forgotten."

JAMES P. GALLAGHER,
Private Co. "G."

CHAPTER XI.

OPERATIONS AT HARRISON'S LANDING. — MOVEMENT TO FAIRFAX COURT-HOUSE. — RETREAT DOWN THE PENINSULA. — MARCH TO ANTIETAM.

THE regiment made a reconnoissance to Turkey-Island Bend, Aug. 5, 1862. After marching all night, or at least moving a short distance at a time, the general found himself lost; and we returned to camp, a tired and disgusted set of men. On the 8th made another reconnoissance to Haxall's Station; also marched over Malvern Hill, where the battle of that name was fought.

It was on this move that Hospital Steward Gallagher was bitten by a copperhead snake. In a short time he was swollen almost beyond recognition; but by the use of good old commissary whiskey and gunpowder, under the direction of Surgeon Holman, his life was saved, although it incapacitated him for further duties in the army. He is remembered by all the regiment as a very faithful and competent nurse and steward, many a brave boy's life having been saved by his faithfulness rather than by the surgeons.

Soon rumors were rife that we were to be removed from the Peninsula, and march to support some of Pope and Halleck's unique schemes of defeating Lee in his aggressive movements, notwithstanding the earnest protest of McClellan, — the one great strategist of the war. So on the 16th we broke camp, and marched nineteen miles down the Peninsula to re-enforce Pope, and encamped near Charles City Court-House. It was dusty and fearful hot. On the 17th marched twenty-five miles, and crossed the Chickahominy

River, resting on its banks that night. It was a grand treat for the boys to bathe their blistered feet, and remove the dust and dirt in the cooling waters of the river, after such long and arduous marching under a broiling sun. On the 18th marched eighteen miles through the battle-field of Williamsburg, and bivouacked five miles beyond the city. Rested one day in camp here; and on the 20th we marched eight miles, passing through Yorktown, and encamped two miles from the town on the Big Bethel Road. We were located in an immense peach-orchard; and the men spent their time while here in fishing for oysters in the neighboring creeks and bayous, from whose beds of mud they took many of the succulent bivalves, thus materially lengthening their scanty rations.

In the mean time the regiment had been paid off; and on the twenty-ninth day of August we marched to Yorktown, and embarked on the bark "Texas" for Alexandria, where we arrived Aug. 31. We had a very fine sail up the Chesapeake Bay and Potomac River. On the 1st of September, disembarked, and marched fifteen miles towards Fairfax Court-House. The field-officers had left their horses at Alexandria; and, not being used to marching, it is said that some of them took to the transportation teams as a means of locomotion. After we had tramped the fifteen miles on the road towards Fairfax Court-House, we were ordered back to the fortifications of Washington, Pope having received a disastrous defeat on the old Bull Run battle-field. We returned to within four miles of Chain Bridge, formed line of battle, and encamped.

The previous night we had a very severe rain, the usual result of a hard battle. All was gloom and despondency; but, as soon as it was known that Gen. McClellan had been re-instated, the spirits and *morale* of the troops began to improve. The men never had any faith in Halleck or Stanton; for, as their orders would leak out, it was apparent to all, that, as commanders and strategists, they were most lamentable failures; and to them, and them alone, were attributed the most of our disasters.

But to return to the narrative. The 5th of September, crossed Chain Bridge, and marched through Tenallytown, about nine miles. We were now once more on loyal ground and among loyal people, and were marching through a very picturesque part of Maryland. Sixth of September, marched to Orfutt's Cross-Roads, Md. Here we halted, and rested two days. We were holding the left flank of the Army of the Potomac; Couch's division being the extreme left, and Gen. Devens's brigade being the left of the division. Sept. 9, marched eight miles, and bivouacked near Seneca Mills. While here, Companies K and H were detailed to guard the fords and river-front while the rest of the regiment proceeded towards the South-Mountain range. On the 10th, 12th, and 13th marched twenty-five miles over the mountains, through Jefferson, and bivouacked near Burkettsville. On the 14th marched through Burkettsville and South-Mountain Gap, or Crampton Pass, into Pleasant Valley. On the 17th marched eight miles up South Mountain through Rohrersville, and bivouacked for the night. On the 18th marched for the battle-field of Antietam; and, while passing through Turner's Gap in the South Mountain, Companies H and K, commanded by Capt. Whitcomb of Company H, rejoined the regiment. These companies had previously passed over Crampton's Gap, where Franklin had made his successful charge the day before, the *débris* of the fight being thickly strewn upon the declivity and the top of the mountain. By hard marching, they had come up with the regiment in hopes to be in time to engage in the battle impending. Arriving at the battle-field, we formed line of battle in rear of Porter's corps, where we rested a few hours, then crossed Antietam River, and were placed upon skirmish-line. About six o'clock P.M. a flag of truce was displayed upon the lines, and our wounded were brought in. There was active skirmishing all along the line, but the regiment was not severely engaged.

Early in the morning, Adjt. Dan Packard of the Seventh came along the reserve line, and awakened the men; for we were massed for a grand rush on Lee's lines. But the wily rebel had stolen away in the darkness of the night, his army crippled by the loss of more than thirty thousand men in killed, wounded, and stragglers. He was a defeated and out-generalled man; and by this battle, as Gen. Longstreet has well said in his articles in "The Century Magazine," published by Scribners. "The key-stone to the Confederate arch was sprung." By the loss of so many of his noble soldiers, Lee never recovered his former prestige or prowess. The South could ill afford the loss of so many men, while the North was as strong as ever by natural accessions.

CHAPTER XII.

FROM BULL RUN TO ANTIETAM.

THE following account of the events mentioned in the preceding chapter was written by Sergt. Walter S. Goss for "The Woonsocket Patriot," and is presented here as being of particular interest to the men of the Seventh Massachusetts:—

"After two or three hours' halt at Chantilly, we are up again and away. The whole army is getting back on the lines about Washington. Our field and staff are all afoot, and are getting a sample of foot-soldiering. The rank and file are well aware of that fact; and, when the head of the column is pointed Washingtonward, the word is passed down the line to march in close order, and stretch out for a home gait. Well, there was never better marching put on record. Without halt or straggle we make quick time over that fifteen miles or more of road, and rest when we get back on the knapsack base. About a half an hour after, the first dismounted officer comes limping feebly along, and is saluted by a volley from the ranks of 'Close up there! close up there!' which the valiant lieutenant-colonel took up and repeated. He saw the point; as he had often before, when the boys were trudging along weary and foot-sore, exasperated them with the infernal refrain of 'Close up there!' until forbearance seemed no longer a virtue. It was over an hour before all our stragglers — official ones — came in; and then we shouldered our little trunks, and went up over the hills and down into a little vale, and hid up. But the respite was not long; for shortly a mounted orderly came down upon the colonel with 'I have been looking for you over an hour, colonel.' — 'Well, you have found me, but I did not mean for you to,' responded Russell.

"Then we got orders to go to Chain Bridge. The colonel and staff were completely played out, so an old farmer was found with a rickety 'carryall' who for pelf took on the dismounted officials; and the line of march was now to follow the team. Either through ignorance of the road or a purpose mistake that old farmer carted his cargo of officers into our picket-line away up to Ball's Cross-Roads, and a straggling few of the foot-men had followed on, while the rest of the regiment had fallen out, and bivouacked by the wayside. The first question the colonel asked the picket was, 'Is there any water here?' — 'Yes, plenty.' — 'Then we'll stay here to-night.' In fact, it was so dark that we might have blundered about all night without getting any nearer our destination. Since leaving the ship, about thirty hours before, we had marched about fifty-two miles, — that is, the less than a hundred men who stacked arms that night as a regiment; and tired and sleepy would but weakly express our feelings.

"In the morning we made tracks for Chain Bridge, and found the better part of the regiment there. We encamped on nearly the same ground where we got such a taste of soldiering early in the spring. Since we left here, and have gained in experience and cheek, we are ready to play all manner of pranks on the newly recruited regiments, who set us down as roughs, and think themselves the *beau-ideal* soldiers because they sport paper collars and white gloves; but we are not on our parade just at this time, as we have passed that point.

"One little experience with new troops I will narrate before we push on to new fields. Lying near us here was a Pennsylvania regiment which had just come out. They kept a guard around their camp; and, although they allowed their men to go out and in at their pleasure, no outsiders were admitted within. But they had a sutler who had a good stock of tobacco and good things which we were anxious to purchase, but it was no go. I kept my eye on that campguard, and tried to study up a plan to get around them. Eureka! I have solved the problem! The scalding noon-day sun has knocked out the new recruits. A new relief has gone on, some without their coats, and others without equipments. I called together a few of my chums, and invited them to go with me to the sutler's, to which they agreed if I would do the bluffing. Well, we walked straight over the guarded line. The sentry ordered us to halt, and I asked him for his authority. He said he was a guard, and I told him that old soldiers did not recognize a man in his shirt-sleeves and without equipments as a general thing. That staggered him, and he cried lustily for the corporal of the guard; but he, luckily for us, came without a coat, and we refused to notice him. Well, we kicked up the Devil's own row in that regiment, and brought the officer of the day down on us. He pompously demanded what we meant by running over his guard, to which we replied that we hadn't seen any guard; that if he would consult the rules and regulations, he would find that his camp-guard must be armed and equipped and in uniform. We carried the point; and the sequel of the matter was, that the whole guard was taken off, and marched to their quarters; and, when they came back, they were in full dress, white gloves and all; but they had orders to let old soldiers pass to the sutler's, so he was made happy, and we lived fat the rest of the day. And I think the officers of that regiment will never forget how the old soldiers disciplined them for the poor privilege of patronizing their sutler.

"Our tarry near Chain Bridge is short, as the army is pushing into Maryland to look up and head off Lee. The columns spread over a large section of country, trying to cover Washington and the enemy at the same time. We take the river-road. Sept. 4 we stop near Tenallytown; on the 6th are at Offent's Cross-Road. The 9th finds us at the mouth of the Seneca. On the night of the 10th we arrive at Poolville, and stop there over the 11th. I remember Poolville, and a night's lodging which I tried to put in there, which narration will show how low the soldier fell in his estimate of comforts. We halted at Poolville near evening: the weather was lowery, and foreboded a rain. The orderly-sergeant came to me, and confidentially imparted the information that he had found a first-rate place to sleep: he told me to take my knapsack, and hurry up before the place was pre-empted. I hurried, and found the house with its ample yard was vacant. We crawled into the snug little house, and found it well littered with fine straw. We spread our blankets, and prepared to put in a good solid night's snooze, which we didn't; for in less than an hour every square inch of our bodies was tingling and quivering under the agony of ten thousand bites. It was no miracle when we took up our beds, and walked: it was fleas that drove us forth. 'The wicked flee when no man pursueth,' but it is a pretty good man who can pursue a flea with success. We carried away a young million of those fleas out into a pelting storm, where we chose to take our chances with those we had captured rather than with those we left behind. I had always thought that it was a hog's nature to rub and scratch, but I learned that his surroundings made the process an urgent necessity. Those wicked fleas clung to us, and made life miserable for three days, when one evening we went up into the shade of 'Sugarloaf' Mountain, disrobed, laid our clothes on the ground, and beat them with a bush until the last flea fled. Then we registered an oath to consort with hogs and their abiding-places no more.

" Our division threw off regiments all along the route to guard the crossing of the Potomac: also single companies were left. Then we would halt long enough for them to overtake us. The 12th, we are at Barnesville for the night; and the 13th, at Lickville. Here, I think it was, a detail was thrown out upon a road, with instructions to let no one

HENRY B. BENNETT,
Wagoner Co. "A."

pass without finding out all about their business. I was on post three from the outer one. About midnight there is a clatter of hoofs and a rattle of sabres, then the challenge, 'Halt!' On they come again, and are again halted; then the man on our post takes up the 'Halt,' to a dozen or so horsemen. 'Well, I'll be danged! what does all this mean?' inquired the leader; and when told what the orders were, he replied, 'You've got a d——d sweet time ahead! I am Gen. Stoneman, and I have ten thousand cavalrymen coming in.' We let them come without any more questioning.

"One night about an hour before sunset we were halted in a field enclosed with a high snake-fence on the outskirts of the aristocratic town of Jefferson. Col. Russell told us that we would stop here a short time, and march all night. 'So make your little fires, and cook your little coffee, men, but don't touch the rail-fence.' The fence was all the available wood in sight, so some of the men propounded the conundrum to the commander. 'Well,' said he, 'you can take the top rail.' When I got around to the fence, the top rails, and more, were gone; and while I was weighing the probabilities of getting snubbed if I filched another rail, a man stepped up, and took one off. 'Here! here!' said the colonel, who was standing near, 'didn't I tell you to take only the top rail?' With the utmost nonchalance the man put the rail back, then stepped away, and struck an attitude with both arms spread out, and exclaimed, 'There, colonel! isn't that the top rail?' The official was outflanked, and replied with a wavering voice, 'Oh, take it away, dem ye! you would take the bottom rail, and then swear it was the top one.' Then I took a ration of rail; and, when we got through with that fence, the bottom rails were the top ones.

"To show the bias of the upper classes who dwelt in 'my Maryland,' I give this little incident: I was detailed to take out a squad to fill the canteens of the company, and we picked out a brick mansion that supported a wooden pump in the yard. There was a bucket by the side of the pump, which we used to fill from. The woman of the house came to the door, and said to a negro, 'Sam, bring that pail in here.' We filled the pail, and gave it to Sam, when we were saluted with, 'Throw the water out, Sam. I don't want any Yankee slobberings.' Then I ordered Sam to bring the pail back, while she threatened him with dire calamity if he did not obey her; but I carried the day, as soldiers always did with darkeys. 'Madam, I suppose you would not let us have the water if you could stop us,' said I. 'You may be sure that I would not,' was her reply ; and she looked it.

"I bid her a polite good-evening, which she did not condescend to notice, then left her to enjoy her own company, if such a thing were possible.

"At nine o'clock we are again on the march, and swing off through the town to the tune of 'Old John Brown,' sung by five hundred voices. We trail on, up over the mountain road in a splendid moonlight night. On the side of this mountain, in a shanty, old John Brown had his first headquarters in Maryland, and that is why we gave the inhabitants of Jefferson City our parting shot; and they stood at their doors, and listened, while not a comment from them reached our ears.

"This part of the State through which the army passed on its way to Antietam is pastoral and beautiful, — mountain ridges with farms on their table-lands, and perfect gems of fruitful valleys. This is the impression which I brought away with me. The reason may be, that I was favorably impressed, because we got a plenty to eat, as bread was but ten cents for a big loaf, and butter ten cents a pound if we did not locate, which, if we did, the demand drove up the price. When we first got to Poolville, sugar could be bought for six cents per pound ; and before we left, the price went up to twenty-five cents. A trader is a sharper the world over; and there is no limit to his conscience or price, only the ability of his patrons to pay, and hold out in the race.

"We are passing on in support of Franklin, who is at

Burkettsville, and is fighting the battle of Crampton Pass. There is but one street passing through Burkettsville, as I remember it, and that goes straight over the mountain ridge. It was on the Burkettsville side of the mountain, and on the crest, where the enemy made their last stand behind a stone wall, that the fighting was done. The enemy were Howell Cobb's Georgia troops; and the best part of the fighting on our side was done by the First Jersey brigade, commanded by Gen. John Newton. They scaled the heights on the left of the road, or pass, and drove the enemy before them; and how they did such an act in the face of a heavy fire, was a clincher to me when I went over their tracks shortly after. The side of the mountain was so near to the perpendicular in places, that I had to pull myself up by the aid of the shrubbery which clothed its ledge sides. And they left their dead strewn to mark their tracks. To me it seemed hard to die in such a place, where bushes were all that held them in position, and kept them from rolling down to the valley below.

"About four hundred prisoners, from seventeen different organizations, were taken here; and I was there to witness the formalities of paroling the officers, and saw two of them nudging each other, and express their satisfaction that they were well out of the coming fight. They were intelligent-looking young men; but they did not love fighting, it appeared, any better than a fellow who stood near them that I could easily put my finger upon.

"There was but one church in the neat little village of Burkettsville, and it was filled with the wounded Union men. The inhabitants were intensely loyal, and were anxious to aid in the care of the suffering soldiers; and it was the only scene of that description that I saw during the war, for the women were trotting around with little dishes filled with dainties, hurrying and hovering about the church. It was a busy day for the people of that village, and everybody seemed to be on the tiptoe of excitement; while the soldiers, tough sinners, hardened and of sterner stuff, lolled around unconcerned of the present, knowing that this small fight was but the precursor of an event where the crimson tide from thousands will baptize the soil of Maryland.

"On the same day, Sept. 14, that the battle of Crampton Gap was fought, there were two more distinct engagements farther up the South-Mountain range for the purpose of turning or forcing the passage of Turner's Gap, which was defended by the Confederate general, D. H. Hill, who bore the brunt of the fighting. Gen. Hooker with the First, and Gen. Reno with the Ninth Corps, did the fighting here. Reno was on the old Sharpsburg Road at the south of the gap, and Hooker on the Martinsburg on the north. There was a seven-hundred-foot altitude to overcome; and the fighting lasted from early morn till late at night, the enemy taking refuge behind stone walls, and making a stubborn resistance. Gen. Reno was killed here late in the afternoon, of whom Gen. McClellan said, 'He was a skilful soldier, a brave and honest man.'

"Gen. Franklin's orders were to relieve the troops at Harper's Ferry; but, when the mountain pass had been opened, that portion had gone up, and the troops of Gens. McLaws and Anderson confronted him in Pleasant Valley, and barred the way.

"At early morn on the 15th the men are in line looking for the enemy. Gen. Lee is making a rapid concentration of his army on the banks of the Antietam Creek and near Sharpsburg, with the apparent intention of fighting a defensive battle. The cowardly surrender of Harper's Ferry has left his supplies in a satisfactory condition, and he considers himself in a position to throw down the gage of battle. The Army of the Potomac are right after him. It was late in the day, so no attack was made on the strong position of the enemy. A large part of the day was spent in reconnoitring the position of the foe, and at two P.M. Gen. McClellan gave the word 'Go!' 'Fighting Joe Hooker,' who commands the First Corps with its three splendid divisions under Meade,

Ricketts, and Doubleday, opened the ball by marching out from Keedysville, a little village two miles or less from the line of attack. The programme laid down is for Hooker to turn the enemy's left, and double it back on his centre; but he little more than got his position on the other side of the stream when darkness set in, and the men bivouacked down on the ground won from the enemy. He had carried his objective point, planted his artillery, and was ready for the morning's fray. During the night the veteran Gen. Mansfield, who had but a short time before assumed the command of the Twelfth Corps, moved over the creek in the darkness and rain, following the tracks of Hooker; and during the morning his men snatched a brief hour of troubled sleep.

"Any one who has read up the battle of Antietam has read a great deal about the Dunker Church. This church was in the edge of quite an extensive wood, as I viewed it from the left of it, or more properly from the centre of the line. The ground fought over, as far as my observation went, was ledgy and ridgy. The rebels were under cover of the woods and rising ground, and along this line was a sunken road with a heavy stone wall for shelter when they were quiet; while our side had to make their advance over open ground in the face of the enemy's scathing fire.

"Early in the morning of the 17th the rebs opened with picket-firing and bursting shells, but Hooker was up and ready before daylight. At sunrise the Federal infantry is on the move to envelop the Confederate left; they sweep across the open fields, driving the enemy before them; they strike the road near Dunker Church, and Jackson's and Hood's divisions at the same time; they falter, then turn, and flee from that deadly storm of lead and iron, and the advancing hosts of Lee. Hartsuff's brigade of Ricketts's division is moved up to the front, and pour in their volleyed thunder upon the exultant foe; and they in turn take to the woods, when Hooker makes a counter-charge, to be again hurled back with thinned and diminished lines.

"Hooker has come to the conclusion that the woods about Dunker Church is the key of the battle-field, and must be carried.

"There is a peculiarity about this key business: if there is an unlikely hole to get into, and a good smart chance of losing a few thousand men, military genius always imagines there is a key there lying out in the cold, which they are in duty bound to gather in, which they most always don't. Now, I always had a crude, unscientific idea, that, when the enemy had concentrated their minds and forces to hold on to that particular key, we could make a better success of key-finding on some weaker spot in their line. There were Sumner and Franklin and Burnside, — yes, and the greatly abused Porter, — had they been looking for a key as persistently as Hooker was, Lee would have looked for his key to the situation along towards the city of Richmond if he was able to. But as Hooker was the only one at that time that tried to unlock the position, we must follow him.

"At seven o'clock Gen. Mansfield with the Twelfth Corps had gone into the field, and made his fight directly opposite the church. Hooker was at the right of it. They raged on; lines wavered and broke; serried columns staggered and melted away.

"Blue and gray lay stretched in the cold grasp of death; and yet the carnage must go on, though mothers weep, and widows moan; though homes are desolated, what care we? we are making history with thundering noise, writing it in letters of blood. A small army is pressing to the rear: some limp with shattered limb, or hold fast to a mangled arm; some crawl away from out the murderous fire to die, — a ghastly array of the battle's fruits to be garnered by the surgeons, who with saw, knife, and probe are in their glory.

"At nine the Second Corps with the venerable Sumner comes on the field. The bluff, brave Sedgwick sails in with his division, and is roughly handled by the adversary. Twice is he seriously wounded, and leaves the field. Hooker has been wounded and retired, while Mansfield is killed. Our forces have gained ground all along the line, but are unable to get at the key which our generals declared must be wrested from the grasp of the enemy. But Hooker is disabled, and Sumner is in command of the right, and he demands that no more assaults shall be made, as it would imperil the whole army. He forbids Franklin from making any further attack, but to hold his ground. The enemy is exhausted and shattered, and are in a critical situation, if our side should open as they ought all along the line; but Gen. McClellan's judgment is overruled by Sumner, to whom he looks up, and in whose judgment he has confidence.

"It is near noonday, and the brazen lips of cannon are hurling out their rations of death and dismay, while the men hug the earth in fond embrace. The infantry fire on the line has become quiescent. But where is Burnside? He has not been heard from. McClellan ordered him at eight A.M. to carry the bridge on his front; three times orders were sent him to carry the bridge, which was not done; then, after three hours' delay, Inspector Gen.-Col. Sackett was sent with orders for Burnside to take the bridge immediately, if he had to do it at the point of the bayonet; and Col. Sackett was instructed to remain with Burnside, and 'see that the order was executed promptly.'

"At one o'clock the bridge was carried by a brilliant charge of the Fifty-first Pennsylvania and the Fifty-first New-York Regiments.

"After his troops were across the creek, he halted until three o'clock, when he was twice ordered to push on before he moved. Then he fought his way through to the outskirts of Sharpsburg, where he met fresh troops direct from Harper's Ferry, who forced him back, when night came on, and the fighting ceased all along the line."

CHAPTER XIII.

MOVEMENTS FROM ANTIETAM TO THE FRONT OF FREDERICKSBURG.

ON the 20th we were engaged in driving back Stuart's cavalry across the river at Williamsport. The regiment and brigade were under a very severe artillery fire for over three hours; but Stuart finally sullenly retired, throwing solid shot through and around us for an hour or more after his right was driven in. The regiment spent the most of the 21st on a range of heights about one mile back of the line we held on the 20th.

While moving back to encamp in a piece of woods to escape the sun, Sergt. John O. Hill of Company E was fatally shot through the heart by the accidental discharge of a gun that had fallen from a stack of arms. He was beloved by all his company and regiment. A fine soldier and a sincere friend, his death was most sincerely mourned. But such is the fate of soldiers.

We remained in the woods two days, when we moved to Downsville, some two miles, and encamped. Here we performed picket and guard duty, and enjoyed the beautiful autumnal weather, while Gen. McClellan prepared the army for another invasion of Virginia.

We were in a sad plight in regard to clothing. Very many of the men had no shirts or shoes; some even were without blouses, except what remained of what were once called by that name, which were in rags and tatters; and very few had stockings. And with his army in this condition, McClellan was blamed because he would not move from his line of communication until the men were properly clothed to meet the inclemency of the coming winter.

Oct. 18, 1862, we were ordered to Hancock, Md., to oppose a threatening move made by the enemy's cavalry. After marching twenty-eight miles, we reached Hancock on the evening of the 20th of October. The scenery on this line of march is wild and picturesque. For many miles the road runs along the North Mountains, the river on the farther side, and the canal on the side next the road. Hancock is very pleasantly situated on the river-side, and was quite a large village for that part of Maryland. It had a church and cemetery, and several stores where very poor or raw whiskey was sold, a fact which many of the men and officers were not long in finding out. But Col. Russell soon had a guard to stop the run of this brain-upsetter; Company F, under Capt. Bliss, being detailed as a provost.

The 21st of October marched back to Cherry Run to meet a move of Stuart's cavalry; encamped, and by this change lost our winter quarters. On the 27th marched back through Clear Springs, and bivouacked near Williamsport. The 29th we marched to Downsville. The regiment suffered extremely on these marches from lack of clothing, as our route was mostly among mountain heights, and the clear, frosty air was very benumbing. While encamped at Downsville, Frederick Cook of Company K died. He was a noble soldier.

On the 31st we began the movement for the invasion of Virginia, and reached Rohrersville after marching fourteen miles. We had a loyal reception from the Union people all along the line of march. Nov. 1, 1862, the regiment marched ten miles, and bivouacked near Berlin. At this place large quantities of clothing were issued, of which the troops were sadly in need.

This delay in providing the army with necessary supplies caused the soldiers a great amount of suffering; and for this the cabal at Washington were responsible, for they hampered the commanding general in every possible way. It was well known that Edwin M. Stanton was inimical to Gen. McClellan; and if it had not been for President Lincoln, who always had confidence in McClellan as a military chieftain, he would never again have commanded the army after his removal from the Peninsula.

We were now launched forth upon a campaign with a large and well-appointed army; the rank and file much improved in *morale*, and commanded by the only general who ever gained a substantial victory over Lee, except Meade at Gettysburg the year following. The weather was crisp and cold, and the thousands of the army covered the sides of the mountain with their camp-fires. As we fell in for roll-call, with roll of drums and blare of trumpets, on that early winter evening, the sight was really grand and beautiful.

We waited here in camp one day, while Couch was covering the gaps in the Blue Ridge, as the army debouched into the valley east of the Blue Ridge. On the 3d marched ten miles, crossing the Potomac into Virginia, and encamped near Wheatland. On the 4th marched fifteen miles, and encamped near a small, straggling village, called Union Village.

This part of Virginia is a very finely wooded section; oak, walnut, and chestnut being very plentiful. The boys gathered nuts to eat, and large quantities of leaves which made us excellent beds, and on which the soldiers slept as peacefully as the children in their far-off Northern homes.

On the 5th took up the line of march, and encamped near Upperville; and on the 6th marched fifteen miles, and encamped at White Plains. The orders were very strict in regard to foraging; but, as there were sheep and pigs in the vicinity, fresh lamb and pork would find its way into camp in spite of all the boys could do.

On the 9th marched five miles, and encamped on Hog Mountain, near New Baltimore, Va. It was here that the army was called upon to part with its commanding officer, much to the regret of the soldiers, who from raw recruits had been drilled, organized, and formed into one of the grandest armies of modern times, whose great intelligence and discipline, as it fell from his hands, saved it from annihilation many times while under the leadership of the incompetent generals who followed. They were the favorites of political cliques or that meddler in the civil war, Edwin M. Stanton, the would-be autocrat, the remover of such men as Sherman, McClellan, Rosecrans, and Don Carlos Buell, who saved Grant at Shiloh (see Grant's Memoirs). At the time when McClellan was in the midst of a movement which promised the annihilation of Lee's army, he was ordered to Trenton. N.J., to await further orders, while the army was handed over to the weak and vacillating Burnside, who had no capacity for such a command, and even fought the great battle of Fredericksburg without any fixed plan. Surely, "whom the gods would destroy, they first make mad;" and it did seem as though they had hold of Stanton and the clique at Washington. That the army was often saved from defeat, was not due to the generalship of the leading officers, but to the excellent discipline of the men, and their sturdy determination to win.

And now, as the regiment is about to enter a new epoch in its history, let us take a glance in retrospection, and see a summary of its work. It performed an immense amount of work in building corduroy roads and fortifications in a very unhealthy region on the Peninsula. It marched in its different campaigns over five hundred and seventeen miles, without counting the miles and miles of marching it did on picket-duty and special details. Its losses were as follows: killed in battle, one lieutenant and three privates; wounded, one sergeant and twenty-five privates; died of sickness, forty-eight; while others who were mortally wounded are not recorded as among the dead. It captured twenty-five prisoners in its cavalry engagement in the Seven Days' Fight, and also, as per Adjutant-General's report, one sergeant and six privates at various other times. One major, two captains, and nine enlisted men, were killed or mortally wounded by the regiment, and left in its hands.

Notwithstanding the demoralization of the General Government, the regiment was always ready to render quick obedience to the demands of its commanders; for this was a thinking body of men, who had, by reason of a firm belief in the justice of their cause, resolved to be ever ready to suffer hardships, and, if duty so required, give even life itself in sustaining the honor of the flag, and in the preservation of the Union.

EDGAR ROBINSON,
Captain Co. "L."

CHAPTER XIV.

REMOVAL OF McCLELLAN. — ARMY COMMANDED BY BURNSIDE. — BATTLE OF FREDERICKSBURG.

ON the 7th of November, Gen. George B. McClellan was relieved from the command of the army. He was a very superior officer, and the idol of the old Army of the Potomac. He took leave of the troops on the 10th of November, 1862, sacrificed to a political clique at Washington, the imbecility of the War Department, and that self-sufficient strategist Halleck, who was appointed to the command of the United States armies after his "great victory" at Corinth, Miss., where one division of his army had dug a whole day before they were informed that Beauregard was forty miles away, and a part of the Union forces were in the city. Halleck was a strategist after the politician's own heart, Stanton's idol, and a California lawyer, who understood intrigue fully; in fact, a vast deal better than he did Jomini, whose work on strategy he translated from the French.

Then was opened one long chapter of disasters and gloom, no less than forty thousand men being sacrificed by the inefficiency of the commanding officers and want of knowledge at Washington. Gen. Burnside, the new commander, was a faithful officer, but of no great military capacity. He was thoroughly honest and fearless, but many a subaltern could have handled the army better than he did. After waiting a week in the vicinity of the upper Rappahannock, he commenced his fatal march to Fredericksburg, giving up at once the great strategic advantage gained over our old antagonist Lee, whose army had been separated, and our immense force driven like a wedge through his centre.

So on the 16th we left Hog Mountain, and marched to Weaversville sixteen miles. On the 17th marched fourteen miles, crossing the Orange and Alexandria Railroad at Bristoe Station, and reached Stafford Court-House, where we remained till Dec. 5, when we proceeded to Belle-Plain Landing.

I may say here that Couch's old division had been merged into the Sixth Corps after the battle of Antietam under Franklin; and, when Franklin was appointed commander of Burnside's left grand division, Gen. Smith commanded the corps, and Gen. Newton the division; while the Seventh, Tenth, and Thirty-seventh Massachusetts Volunteers, with the Second Rhode Island and the Thirty-sixth New York, were a brigade in that division, commanded by Gen. Charles Devens, a gallant and superior officer, a native of the old Bay State, a man who possessed a fine education and good military capacity, and who has since held high positions and various trusts of great importance in the councils of the nation and State.

After we had remained in camp four days, we moved up by White-Oak Church, some twelve miles from the landing. In the mean time the weather had grown cold and frosty. On Dec. 11 we broke camp at daylight, and started on the march towards the Rappahannock River, about a mile below Fredericksburg. As we moved out on the bluffs overlooking the river, a grand and fearful sight greeted our eyes. Burnside had given the order to bombard the city, and the roar of over two hundred cannon thundered in our ears as we debouched upon the plain at Franklin's Crossing. Here we lay, while the companies of the United-States regular engineers were building the bridge upon which we were to cross. The report of the adjutant-general of the State furnished by Lieut.-Col. Harlow says that we waited till about five o'clock, when we crossed the river under a very severe fire of sharpshooters, which killed and wounded some four or five men of the brigade. The regular engineers had laid two bridges, some twenty rods apart. The regiment crossed the upper bridge, covered by two batteries of field-artillery. Our brigade, composed of five regiments, was the first to cross. The Seventh supported the Second Rhode Island and the Thirty-seventh Massachusetts on the upper bridge. Gen. Newton sat on his horse by the side of the batteries, which were throwing shell, spherical case, and canister. There was a large house on the banks of the river, which afforded the rebel sharpshooters a fine cover; and the bluffs, which were lined with large bowlders, gave them a fine shelter also. After the regiment had crossed the bridge, we were immediately advanced as skirmishers, and we drove the rebs up to the sunken road that led to the city. The enemy lost quite a number of men killed: for, as we reached the bank, they ran up the slope, and were a fine target for canister and spherical-case shot. We found some five or six lying on the bluff as we deployed our line as skirmishers, and advanced into an apple-orchard out beyond the house and barn on Barnard's estate. Col. Russell gave orders for the front rank to stand to arms the first half of the night, while the rear rank took the latter half; that is, from twelve o'clock till morning. Nothing of importance took place the first half; and the only incident that happened was the demolition of Barnard's barn, and the slaughter, after they had been milked, of a cow or two; the soldiers forming themselves into a commissary department, and issuing a ration of fresh beef. The morning opened foggy and chilly. Soon Franklin's grand division began to cross the river. About ten o'clock the fog blew away, and the sun came out hot for a winter's day. We lay in line of battle, but were not on active duty. The rebels gave us some shelling, and there was terrific cannonading on our right up towards the city of Fredericksburg.

Dec. 13 we lay in line unmolested until about one o'clock, when a battery opened on our right, and gave us a severe shelling for an hour or more, killing one of Company I's men. The shell burst all around and over us; but, as we had a small rise of ground in front, we escaped with but few casualties. But such a fire is more trying than when infantry are plying their deadly warfare at close quarters. About two o'clock we were ordered to the extreme left to support the troops of that flank, as it was apparent that Jackson contemplated a decisive movement. As we were proceeding down towards the left, the division was subjected to a galling artillery fire; and Gen. Bayard, a brave and capable cavalry officer, was killed by a solid shot thrown at Newton's moving division. After we had been in position about two hours and a half, all at once the rebel artillery of Hill and Jackson opened in terrific style, and for about two hours the shell screeched and burst amongst us, and just over our heads; but after a while we were placed in the rear of the sunken road which runs to Hamilton's Crossing. We were ordered to unsling knapsacks, preparatory to receiving the expected attack as we moved to cover. When the fire had slackened, about half-past six P.M., we went to get them, and found that the rebel shot and shell had made sad havoc with them. It was very fortunate that the regiment and brigade had been advanced to the line last held, for we should have suffered severely if we had remained where we were first stationed. It was a severe and well-directed fire, ordered by Jackson to demoralize our line, as he had determined to attack us, and, as his biographer says, to drive us into the river. I think it was fortunate for the rebels that Jackson altered his mind; for, his force being inferior to the Union one, he would have failed, and, no doubt, would have received a disastrous repulse, as our artillery ploughed over every foot of ground in front of our position. We lay here until about eight o'clock, when we passed to the right about half a mile, where we remained the rest of the night without being disturbed.

The next day drew rations, and remained on the bank of the river until the morning of the 15th, when we moved to the front line of battle. In the mean time the right grand division had received a crushing defeat, while the left had fared no better; some twelve thousand men had been lost by the want of generalship in our commander. While he had dashed division after division against an impregnable position above us at Fredericksburg, Franklin on the left had been hampered and delayed by orders not easily understood, and altogether wrong so far as military tactics were concerned. Longstreet has well said in his "Century" articles, "If Franklin had massed his forty thousand men, and hurled them upon Jackson, no doubt our right would have been forced out of position, and then Burnside's success would have depended upon the skilful handling of his army." But no orders came for the massing of troops, but to attack with a division, and to keep its line of retreat open. Meade made a most gallant fight on the left with Burns's division as a support; but his force was too small, and Franklin's orders were so confusing that he did not know what to do. We had taken our position in front line at daylight, or just before, and remained there all day, waiting for darkness to cover the retreat of the army. Our brigade was the last to cross the river. The Seventh moved over on the morning of the 16th, being the rear of a defeated and disheartened army of men, who felt for Gen. Burnside's misfortune, but did not think much of his ability as a general.

The casualties of the regiment across the river were one killed and two wounded. We marched back towards White-Oak Church, about two miles, encamped, and prepared for winter quarters. At this camp we parted with our gallant colonel, David A. Russell, who had been promoted to the command of a brigade. He took leave of the regiment in his usual quiet and subdued way, and carried with him the love and respect of his men.

CHAPTER XV.

COL. RUSSELL'S RECORD.

HAVING addressed a letter to Major-Gen. Schofield, commander of the Eastern, or Atlantic division, asking for a short biographical sketch of Col. Russell, my request was referred to the commandant at West Point, who very kindly sent me the record of our colonel while at the academy, which I present to my readers with great pleasure.

HEADQUARTERS UNITED-STATES MILITARY ACADEMY,
WEST POINT, N.Y., June 23, 1887.

Corp. N. V. HUTCHINSON, North Abington, Mass.

Dear Sir, — Referring to yours of the 9th inst. addressed to Gen. Schofield, and referred by him to the superintendent, I am directed to say that the records of the academy give the following history of Gen. David A. Russell: —

Appointed from Salem, Washington County, N.Y. Admitted July 1, 1841, aged nineteen years, six months. Born in the State of New York. Father, David Russell of Salem, N.Y.

Fourth class, first year, general merit, No. 32, class of 76 members.
Third class, second year, general merit, No. 40, class of 67 members.
Second class, third year, general merit, No. 38, class of 55 members.
First class, fourth year, general merit, No. 38, class of 41 members.

Cadet Russell was a corporal in his third class year, a sergeant in his second class year, and a lieutenant in his last class year. Graduated July 1, 1845. Promoted brevet second lieutenant, First Infantry, July 1, 1845. For further history, see Cullum's "Biographical Register," vol. ii. pp. 136, 137, and 138.

Very respectfully
Your obedient servant,

W. C. BROWN,
First Lieutenant First Cavalry, Adjutant.

I have copied this letter entire as a mark of courtesy for the exceeding kindness of the commandant of West Point, and also to call attention to Gen. Cullum's History of West-Point Cadets, which is a very valuable and interesting work, containing a full account of Col. Russell's services to the government in various positions in the army.

I have also received from Gen. Couch a full account of Col. Russell's military record, containing many extracts from Cullum's West-Point Biography, which I am sure will be read by the men of the Seventh with interest and affectionate remembrance.

David A. Russell was engaged in the war with Mexico. Participated in the combats of Pasco Las Vegas, Cerro Gordo, and Las Anemancos, and was brevetted first lieutenant, Aug. 15, 1847, for gallant and meritorious conduct in these engagements. Served in different stations in the West, and was engaged in various conflicts with the Indians. Appointed captain Fourth Infantry, June 22, 1854. Was located in California, and while there was in command of a post, and had as his first lieutenant, Philip Sheridan, late lieutenant-general, commanding the army. In the war of the Rebellion, served in the defence of Washington, and appointed colonel Seventh Massachusetts Volunteers, Jan. 31, 1862. Engaged in the Peninsula and Maryland campaigns, where his services gained for him the promotion to brevet lieutenant-colonel, July 1, 1862. Major of the Eighth Infantry, Aug. 9, 1862. Was promoted to brigadier-general of volunteers, Nov. 29, 1862, and in command of a brigade of the Sixth Corps. Took an active part in the Rappahannock campaign, and was engaged in the battle of Fredericksburg, Dec. 13, 1862. Engaged in the storming of Mayre's Heights, May 3, 1863. At battle of Salem Church, May 3 and 4. Was in the Pennsylvania campaign, and fought in the battle of Gettysburg, July 2 and 3, and pursued the enemy to Warrenton, Va. Appointed brevet-colonel United-States Army, July 1, 1863, for gallant and meritorious conduct at Gettysburg. Engaged in the Rapidan campaign, October and December, 1863. Captured the rebel works at Rappahannock Station, taking two thousand prisoners and several cannon. This he achieved with his own brigade, supported by the Seventh Massachusetts, Nov. 7, 1863. Participated in the Mine Run operations, Nov. 26 to Dec. 3, 1863, and was in command of a division of the Sixth Corps in the Richmond campaign. Engaged in the battles of the Wilderness, May 5 and 6, 1864, and was brevetted brigadier-general for his gallant conduct, May 6. In the battles about Spottsylvania, May 9 and 21, he took an active part, having organized the attack on the evening of the 10th; Gen. Upton, commander of one of his brigades, leading the charge. They captured the rebel works, and broke their lines; but their almost certain victory was lost by the non-support of Mott's division, Second Corps (see Grant's Memoirs). Was at North Anna, May 23 and 24; Tolopotomy, May 30, 1864, where Gen. Wright, being ordered by Meade to send his best division general to cross the river, and seize the crossing leading to Hanover Junction, Va., selected Russell; and what better choice could he have made for so important an operation? Engaged in the battles and actions of Cold Harbor, June 1-13, 1864; siege and battles about Petersburg, June 23 to July 10, 1864. In the Washington campaign, and in the action before Fort Stevens, D.C., July 12, 1864. This fort was one that the Seventh had helped to build in the fall of 1861, and was first named Massachusetts, but afterwards changed to Stevens in memory of a regular officer who died. Took part in the skirmish at Snicker's Gap, July 18, 1864, while in pursuit of Gen. Early's rebel raiders to Winchester, Va. Engaged in the Shenandoah campaign, commanding a division of the Sixth Corps, August and September, 1864. Fought in the battle of the Opequan, where he was killed Sept. 19, 1864, aged forty-two. Was brevetted brigadier-general United States Army for gallant and meritorious services in this engagement.

Gen. Couch has always said that David A. Russell was the best colonel of infantry in the war, and I think no competent military man will gainsay him in his judgment of the abilities of that wonderfully efficient officer.

I present below a copy of a letter to Gov. Andrew from Gen. Devens in regard to Massachusetts troops in the field under his command: —

HEADQUARTERS SECOND BRIGADE, THIRD DIVISION, SIXTH CORPS,
NEAR FALMOUTH, VA., Dec. 20, 1862.

To His Excellency JOHN A. ANDREW, *Governor Commonwealth of Massachusetts.*

Sir, — Your letter of Nov. 7, enclosing circular issued by your order, and dated Nov. 5, was received by me early this month; but I trust the stirring events which have occurred in this army will be my excuse with your Excellency for any seeming delay in my reply. The Fifteenth Massachusetts Regiment was commanded by me in the battle of Ball's Bluff, October, 1861; in several skirmishes in the valley of Virginia during the month of March, 1862, and during most of the siege of Yorktown, I having been transferred from the regiment just before the close of operations there. Since that time it has participated in all the important battles of Virginia and Maryland, and on all occasions it has behaved with the most distinguished gallantry and determination. Called upon both at Ball's Bluff and at Antietam, where it was commanded by Lieut.-Col. (now Colonel) Kimball, to endure the terrific loss of more than half of its men engaged, it exhibited a courage and fidelity more than worthy of veteran troops, for it was worthy of the *holy* cause which had drawn its men from their peaceful homes.

Having taken command of this brigade during the latter portion of the operations against Yorktown, the Seventh and Tenth Massachusetts came under my command as a portion of the brigade. At the battle of Williamsburg, May 5, the Seventh Massachusetts was under fire for the first time, and engaged with the enemy on the left of our line, losing several men. The Tenth Massachusetts was in reserve, and not actively engaged. In moving up the Peninsula, the first passage of the Chickahominy was made by the left wing of the army under Brigadier (now Major) Gen. Keyes; and the Seventh Massachusetts was the first to cross, with a loss of several men. The same night the Seventh and Tenth Massachusetts, with one or two other regiments from other brigades, formed an improvised brigade under my command, and held the Richmond side of the Chickahominy during the night, and until the afternoon of the next day, when the crossing of the left wing was effected.

At the battle of Fair Oaks, May 31, the Seventh and Tenth Massachusetts were both actively engaged. But the Seventh was in a far less exposed position than the Tenth, and suffered much less severely. After the line to the left of it had been broken, the Tenth Massachusetts was forced back in some confusion, — the colonel having been carried from the field, wounded, and other field-officers being absent, — but it was again re-formed, under my own immediate supervision, by Capt. Ozra Miller, the senior captain, and twice again led forward, displaying the greatest gallantry, and materially checking the progress of the enemy on this portion of the field. Having been disabled at the battle of Fair Oaks, I did not command the brigade during the subsequent six weeks, but have on undoubted authority that the Seventh and Tenth both participated with the greatest credit in the battles of the seven days' retreat of the army to Harrison's Landing, more especially in that of Malvern, in which action, as at Fair Oaks, the Tenth was more exposed, and suffered more severely, than the Seventh.

At the battle of Malvern the Tenth was commanded by Major (formerly Captain) Miller, who fell mortally wounded at its head. In any allusion that your Excellency may make to the heroic dead of Massachusetts, I know of no one more worthy to be mentioned by name than Major Ozra Miller of the Tenth Massachusetts. Accepting the command of his regiment at Fair Oaks, under the circumstances already mentioned, he proved himself fully equal to the task during the most trying scenes of that day. Dying at the head of his regiment only a month later at Malvern, he had lived long enough to inspire both those below and above him in rank with unqualified respect for his stern courage, his lofty patriotism, and his unswerving fidelity to duty.

The regiments composing this brigade, being among the last to embark from Yorktown, after the retreat down the Peninsula, did not arrive in time to take part in the battles in front of Washington at the end of August, although they marched directly from the boats at Alexandria towards Fairfax Court-House, without waiting even to disembark the horses of the mounted officers. On the day of the battle of Antietam the brigade marched twenty miles, reaching the field at nightfall, and were next day put in the front line; but, the battle not being renewed, only skirmishers and sharpshooters of our line were engaged.

On the fifth day of October, the Thirty-seventh Massachusetts, then fresh from home, was added to the regiments of this brigade. But since then the brigade, with the exception of some slight affairs on the Potomac, was not in action until the passage of the Rappahannock on Thursday, the 11th inst., when the brigade, including all its regiments, formed the advance of the left wing of the army, and, crossing the river at sunset, drove back the outposts of the enemy, and held the bridge until the next morning, when the main body crossed.

On Friday, the 12th inst., and on Saturday, the 13th, it was under very heavy artillery fire. On Monday it was in the front line of battle; and on Monday night, hearing that we were about to evacuate, I had so much confidence in this brigade, and the Massachusetts troops which formed a large portion of it, that I asked that it might be the last brigade to recross, and it was accordingly designated with the brigade of Col. Torbert of New Jersey for this purpose.

Throughout all these operations, the courage, earnestness, and fidelity to duty, of the Seventh, Tenth, and Thirty-seventh Massachusetts could not be excelled.

I have stated very hurriedly and briefly what the Massachusetts regiments under my command have done, because their deeds are their best eulogy. The commanding officers of the regiments will undoubtedly furnish, in answer to the circular of Nov. 5, in detail, the military history — so desirable to be preserved — of their respective corps; and I shall take great pleasure in calling their attention to its importance.

In conclusion, I cannot but express the sincere gratification and pride that every citizen must feel in the noble troops which the State of Massachusetts has furnished in this tremendous struggle against a rebellion whose wantonness and wickedness finds no parallel in history. Fully aware of their deep responsibility in girding on the sword for the defence of the country; cheerfully submitting to the hardships incidental to their situation; always obedient to the just and necessary, although often irksome, restraints of military life; in the hour of trial "no dangers fright them, and no labors tire," —

I have the honor to be

Your Excellency's obedient servant,

CHAS. DEVENS, JR.,
Brigadier-General United-States Volunteers.

CHAPTER XVI.

ARMY UNDER BURNSIDE. — COL. JOHNS. — ARMY UNDER HOOKER.

ON the 18th of December, 1862, we moved to a well-wooded position near White-Oak Church. Having selected a line for the regiment to encamp on, the officers of the different companies staked off their company streets, and we proceeded to erect our winter quarters, which were constructed with logs and shelter-tents. These tents were well made, and proved to be very serviceable. We generally built the sides with logs, some two feet high, and fastened the tents on top. The foot was the place for the chimney and fireplace, which was built up with split sticks and stones, plastered inside and out with Virginia mud. The head faced on company street. We raised the floor by using cross-logs some six inches through, and covered them with poles upon which we reclined to sleep and eat. We had sufficient wood to keep a fire in the fireplace, and, taken altogether, we were very comfortable. There was a small stream of water running through the centre of the camp, which was very useful for washing purposes.

We remained in this camp until the 20th of January, when we broke camp with the rest of the army, and started on Burnside's march up the river in an attempt to surprise the enemy, in which we wholly failed. A very severe winter storm overtook the army, and the inclemency of the weather caused the roads to become so soft and miry that it would often take twenty horses to move a twelve-pounder cannon over any unusual rise. We marched eight miles through Falmouth, and bivouacked in a dense woods. On the 21st

THOMAS D. JOHNS,
Colonel.

we marched three miles, and went into camp about a mile from Banks's Ford on the Rappahannock River. Here we tried to rest, a wet, tired, and discouraged body of men, "stuck in the mud," and unable to move forward; for the rebels had discovered our object, and were thoroughly prepared to receive us if we attempted to force a crossing. Their pickets on the river's bank used to exhibit strips of bark upon which were printed, "Burnside's stuck in the mud." On the 22d there was issued to us a generous ration of commissary whiskey; and this so stiffened up the backbone of the army, that it began the movement back to its old quarters on the 23d.

Gen. Burnside was soon afterwards relieved. He was a brave and loyal officer, well liked and respected, but he was not competent to handle large bodies of troops. He would have made a fine staff-officer or secretary of war, but was always making mistakes when in command of an army in active operations. The army did not grieve when he left it, as we all felt that he would sooner or later lead us to useless slaughter. It has been said that he gave McClellan a stinted support at the battle of Antietam. If this is true, surely the fates took ample revenge upon him; for of all the disasters the old Army of the Potomac suffered, the one under Burnside was the most useless, the army not inflicting any injury on the enemy, nor gaining one foot of ground, to compensate for its immense sacrifice of human life, while its *morale* was impaired to a serious extent.

And now the narrative is approaching another epoch in the regiment's history. After parting with Col. Russell, we had been under the command of that able and fearless soldier, Lieut.-Col. F. P. Harlow, whose firm and unfaltering fidelity to duty, and reasonable discipline, had kept the old Seventh's efficiency up to a high plane. He was in command of us until the 22d of February, 1863, when he was relieved by Col. Thomas D. Johns, a West-Point graduate, and resumed his former position of lieutenant-colonel of the regiment.

It was a matter of sincere regret to a large portion of the regiment to have Col. Harlow displaced.

Col. Johns was born in Pennsylvania. Appointed from his native State to West Point, where he was a cadet from July, 1844, to July, 1848, when he graduated, and was promoted to the army as brevet second lieutenant, First Infantry. Served on the Texas frontier, 1848–49. Served in California, 1850–51. Resigned Dec. 3, 1851. Merchant in San Francisco, Cal., 1852–60. Captain in California militia. Superintendent of silver-mines in Nevada, 1860–62. Served during the Rebellion. Colonel Seventh Massachusetts Volunteers, Feb. 22, 1863–64. Rappahannock campaign, Army of the Potomac, April and May, 1863, being engaged in the storming of Mayre's Heights, May 3, 1863, where he was twice severely wounded. In the operations to cover Washington, D.C., October, 1863. Operations of centre of Virginia, October, 1863, to December, 1863. In combat at Rappahannock Station, Nov. 7, 1863. At Mine Run, Va., Nov. 28 and 29, 1863. Movement of Sixth Corps to Madison Court-House, Va., May 4, 1864. Skirmish on the Rapidan, May 5 and 6. Battle of the Wilderness; battles about Spottsylvania Court-House, May 9–20, 1864. Skirmishes at Little River and Hanover Court-House, May, 1864. Battles of Cold Harbor, June 7–10, 1864. March to James River, June 13–16, 1864. Mustered out of service, June 27, 1864. Brevet brigadier-general United States Volunteers, March 13, 1865, for gallant conduct at the battle of Fredericksburg, Va., and for gallant and meritorious conduct during the Rebellion.

Gen. Johns has since died. He was a brave and loyal man, but was not fitted for an infantry command. He would have made a fine staff-officer, being thoroughly conversant with military law and official routine duty. He had some very superior qualities, not the least of which was his coolness in action, which made up for much of his rustiness, and lack of tactical knowledge. But he suffered in comparison with such officers as Couch, Russell, Davis, and Harlow, who were the best of tacticians. Such men as Bliss, Gurney, Leonard, Bowen of Company A, and other well-instructed officers, were kept in the background by Gov. Andrew, who always seemed anxious to secure West-Point officers, no matter what their qualifications or caliber.

During the winter months we were often on picket-duty by the river's banks, and frequently exchanged tea and coffee for rebel tobacco and other knick-knacks which the Johnnies had to offer in return. They were very short of salt, and a small cargo of the precious saline would be often hailed with delight by them when one of our miniature boats had made a successful voyage across the stormy Rappahannock. I believe it was Gen. Couch who first gave the order not to fire upon the picket-line of the opposing force, considering it nothing but murder to kill a poor picket while on duty. For his noble mind realized that the occasional killing of a sentry could have no weight in the mighty issues of the war, while the army was in winter cantonments.

While encamped at Stafford's Heights, we were reviewed by President Lincoln, Gen. Hooker having taken command of the army, Jan. 25, 1863. He was one of the most brilliant generals the war afforded, well known to the army as "Fighting Joe," and would no doubt have been as successful as Meade, at Gettysburg, the July following, if he had been retained in command. The grand review took place on the 8th of April. It was a fine sight; and the army was in great spirits, hoping soon to try conclusions with Lee's forces for the possession of Richmond.

During the winter Gen. Hooker re-organized the cavalry forces, and thoroughly reconstructed the Quartermasters' Department; and at no time during the war was the Army of the Potomac better cared for than while under Gen. Hooker's command.

CHAPTER XVII.

STORMING OF MAYRE'S HEIGHTS.—BATTLE OF SALEM HEIGHTS.

ON the 29th of April we moved down to the bluffs on the river bank. Hooker having broken camp, and started on his great flank-march around Lee, which was one of the most brilliant movements of the war. Here we remained quietly, except to make an occasional tactical movement to deceive the enemy as to the number of our forces, until the 1st of May. On the 1st and 2d of May the rebels shelled us very spitefully from the Heights, where we were repulsed the December previous. At ten o'clock on the night of May 2 we crossed the river at the old Franklin crossing. Our brigade was commanded by Gen. Henry Brown of New York State,— a very fine officer, and as brave as a lion. — Gen. Devens having been assigned to a division in the Eleventh Corps a short time previously. The brigade, one of the most effective the Army of the Potomac ever had, consisted of the Seventh, Tenth, and Thirty-seventh Massachusetts, the Second Rhode Island, and the Thirty-sixth New York, all old and well-tried veterans, the survivors of many a hard-fought battle; Fair Oaks, Williamsburg, Malvern Hill, Antietam, Williamsport, and Fredericksburg being the desperate engagements in which they had participated, while the skirmishes were numerous, and many of them had risen almost to the importance of battles.

During the night Gen. Sedgwick received orders to brush away the small force supposed to be opposed to him, and make a night march to join Gen. Hooker at Chancellorsville.

We were advanced to the Bowling-Green Road, when we faced to the right, and marched towards Fredericksburg. Gen. Newton commanded the division. Gen. Shaler's brigade led the advance: our brigade was second in line, while Gen. Wheaton's brigade brought up the rear. We reached Fredericksburg early in the morning, and were, with the Thirty-sixth New York, detached from the brigade, and put in position to hold the city against any attack the enemy might make against the division on the Telegraph and Plank Roads. We remained here under shell-fire until about eleven o'clock A.M., when the orders came to unsling knapsacks and all encumbrances, and prepare to lead the assault on Mayre's Heights. The necessary preparations were soon made; and we moved out on the Telegraph Road looking towards the Heights, at the foot of which rose, repellent and grim, the famous stone wall upon whose almost impregnable line the Second Corps under the gallant Couch the winter before had dashed in vain. With the stern order, "Forward, Seventh!" we moved towards the Heights; Col. Johns being mounted, and the troops advancing at common time in column of fours.

After we had crossed the canal that runs through the city, Col. Johns dismounted; and we moved forward in the charge, our guns uncapped, the order being given to depend upon the bayonet alone. I may here remark, that, just as we got in motion, the rebel batteries all along the Heights opened with shell, and one of the projectiles struck the major of the Thirty-sixth New York, commanding our supporting regiment, and mortally wounded him, and also disabled some five or six of the men. On the column moved in mass by fours at common time, shell and canister cutting through it until we had got within a hundred feet of the stone wall, when Barksdale's brigade of Mississippians poured in a terrific volley from right and left, and checked us for about five minutes. The road, or gulch, was filled with the dead, wounded, and dying. Col. Johns was down, having been twice severely wounded. Lieut.-Col. Harlow was prostrated by a ball in the stomach. Lieut. Tillson of Company K was killed. Adjt. Dean, Capt. Oakman, Lieuts. Bisbee and Seaver of Company E. Capt. Bliss of Company F, and several other officers whose names I have been unable to obtain, were severely wounded. More than fifty men of the leading companies, F, E, and K, were killed or wounded. But still we lunge forward, the brave left companies nobly supporting the right wing. On we stagger, men falling around us like leaves in autumn. Soon out of the confusion rings the clarion shout of Lieut.-Col. Harlow, "Forward, forward, boys!" and led by that gallant officer, ably seconded by his brave comrades, the old Seventh struggled through and over the stone wall, bleeding at every step. Turning to the right, we rushed over the rebel redoubt, capturing two pieces of artillery which had occupied the same position the previous December, and had done such fearful execution upon the noble Second Corps as to draw forth the encomiums of Gen. Lee.[1]

In the space of twenty minutes, the Seventh Massachusetts had lost over a hundred men killed and wounded, and captured two pieces of artillery and more than a hundred prisoners. In this glorious assault the regiment had in column four hundred and fifteen men, and lost over one-fourth of the assaulting force. We had present and absent on detached duty, about five hundred men: this report is taken from the adjutant-general's report of Massachusetts. I have been concerned about the account of this noble charge, and have given the exact data, for many errors in relation to it have already found their way into print. Gen. Doubleday, in his *brochure* upon Chancellorsville and Gettysburg, says, in speaking of this assault, that Col. Welch of the Thirty-sixth New York rallied the column, which is utterly without foundation; for Col. Harlow of the Seventh Massachusetts rushed to the front as soon as Col. Johns was wounded, and

[1] The flag of the Seventh Massachusetts was the first to wave over the rebel stronghold, it having been planted in the redoubt by command of Col. Harlow, Color-Sergeant Bowen of Company A having the honor to fulfil Col. Harlow's instruction.

CHAS. B. HATHAWAY,
2nd. Lieutenant Co. "F."

took command of his regiment, and, as he was the ranking officer, commanded the column as Col. Johns did before he fell.

In the mean time the rebels sullenly retreated, having saved two pieces of artillery from the extreme left of their battery; and soon they were vigorously shelling us again, having fallen back into a strong line of works with redoubts. We had advanced into a ravine, which the rebels swept with a raking fire, and were ordered to lie down. Gen. Shaler's brigade on the right assaulted the redoubts, and captured the cannon which had checked our column. It was here that I saw one shell knock over eight men of the left company of the left regiment of Gen. Shaler's brigade. Presently we were in motion again, and moving to the left towards Lee Hill. Gen. Brooks's division was putting in good work by capturing cannon and prisoners. We advanced slowly, the enemy contesting every inch of ground. The plain was alive with rebel infantry, artillery, and baggage-wagons. We moved along till we gained the plank road, where we rested until Gen. Brooks's division had taken the advance.

About five o'clock we were advancing towards Salem Heights, when the rebels opened with a very severe fire from a strong position near Salem Church. The brigade of Gen. Russell pushed forward, and developed a strong force of the enemy in line of battle on the edge of the woods. From a few scattering shots it became a rattle, then a roar, and finally came the thunder of the artillery. Newton's division formed on the right of the road, and Brooks's on the left. Almost immediately they became involved in a terrible struggle with the enemy. The brigade on the right of Newton's division met with a severe repulse, and then the Seventh Massachusetts was again called upon to breast the leaden storm. We had filed in upon the right of the main road, just back of the road that leads to Banks's Ford, and were listening to the roar of the battle, when down came a courier to Col. Harlow. "Is this the Seventh Massachusetts?" — "Yes, sir," responded the colonel. "Forward, then, double-quick! Wheaton's brigade is all torn to pieces, and is being driven like sheep. You must save the day!" So on the double-quick we started for a small hill in front, and were soon in position, and ordered to lie down. Gen. Brown, the brigade commander, rode along the lines, saying, "Keep cool, boys; keep cool. Seventh Massachusetts, you must stop them." Presently a massive column of rebel infantry broke from the woods, and advanced on the run, brigade front, four lines deep, uttering the rebel yell, and piling the plain with our poor boys, who had been broken to pieces by the ambush. At length they arrived near our front; then the order came, "Up, boys!" from Col. Harlow; then the command, "Ready, aim, fire!" and a crashing volley met that on-coming line of gray, and shattered them. "Fire at will," shouted the colonel. Still on they came, with yell after yell, shouting their battle-cry. They fall by scores, but on they press. Their colors fall: brave men grasp them, and wave them defiantly aloft. On they rush, great gaps in their lines; for by this time canister is reaping its harvest of death, being hurled through that dense mass of men by batteries on the right and left. Not until they reach the immediate slope of the rise upon which the regiment is in line of battle, do they halt or falter. The old Seventh has well sustained its record for steadiness and tenacity. Alone it threw back more than two brigades of McLaws's division, the very best fighting men in Lee's army. Next the order to advance was given; and the enemy was forced back more than a mile, with the assistance of the Tenth Massachusetts and Second Rhode Island, who had formed on our right. But we did not succeed in routing them; for darkness intervened, and stopped the advance of the Union troops, enabling the rebels to re-form their lines during the night, and present a solid front in the morning. The regiment lay in line of battle all night on the ground from which the foe had been driven.

In this short and bloody battle, the Seventh Massachusetts

PRENTISS M. WHITING,

Captain Co. "A."

held in check more than two brigades of the rebels for over an hour, until the brigade in our front which suffered defeat had time to re-form, and the rest of our own brigade in our rear could arrive, and help to check the exultant rebels.

Here it was that the noble Whitney of Company I gave his life in defence of the Union, and Lieut. John C. Bosworth of Company A was wounded while fighting for the preservation of the honor of his country.

Following is a list of the killed and mortally wounded in the battles of Mayre's and Salem Heights, and which may well be called, —

THE ROLL OF HONOR.

OFFICERS.

Killed. — Capt. Prentiss M. Whitney, Company I; First Lieut. Albert Tillson, Company K.

Severely Wounded. — Col. Thomas D. Johns; Lieut.-Col. L. P. Harlow, commander of the regiment; Adjt. Edward N. Dean; Capt. Zebe F. Bliss, Company F; Capt. Mathewson, Capt. Bancroft, Capt. Hiram A. Oakman, Company E; First Lieut. Wright Bisbee, Company F; Lieut. John C. Bosworth, Lieut. Seaver, Company D; and several other officers, whose names I have been unable to secure.

COMPANY A.

Killed. — Sergt. James L. Brightman; Privates James O'Neill, William Uncles.

Mortally Wounded. — Corp. James Clough.

COMPANY B.

Killed. — Corp. Michael Ryan; Private William Hazeltine.

Mortally Wounded. — None.

COMPANY C.

Killed. — None reported.

Mortally Wounded. — Privates James Kelly, William M. Dunham.

Company D.

Killed. — None reported.
Mortally Wounded. — Corp. Charles L. Wilbur; Private James Conlin

Company E.

Killed. — Private David Brown.
Mortally Wounded. — Privates George MacElroy, William Bole.

Company F.

Killed. — Sergts. Charles F. Dean, Gideon E. Morton; Corp. William H. Hammond; Privates John Brown, Seth Gibson, Loyal W. Pratt.
Mortally Wounded. — Privates Wesley Bridges, James Groves.

Company G.

Killed. — None reported.
Mortally Wounded. — None reported.

Company H.

Killed. — Privates Owen O. Mally, Eben Willard.
Mortally Wounded. — Private John Blanchard.

Company I.

Killed. — None reported.
Mortally Wounded. — Corp. Bartlett; Privates A. Keith, James B. Tisdale.

Company K.

Killed. — Privates Charles W. Reed, Marcus M. Levett.
Mortally Wounded. — Privates John B. Newcomb, John B. MacMakins, William W. Josselyn, Henry W. Beebe.

These are the silent heroes of Mayre's and Salem Heights; our comrades who fell on the field of honor, and gave their hopes, their aspirations, and their lives, for the purpose of sustaining the law and institutions of their country. In peace they were our friends, in danger our brothers, and in death they became our heroes. We mourn the loss of these noble men, many of whom, if they had returned to the peaceful pursuits of life, might have adorned any station where character, manhood, and virtue were demanded. In any position they would have been found faithful, even as they were on the field of battle. Their best monument is in the prosperity of our Union, and the benedictions of a grateful people.

Over one hundred other brave and noble men of our regiment were wounded in this desperate strife, many of whom died from the effects of their wounds in the subsequent years of the war. Many were maimed and disfigured, and health impaired; but as the rolls were so defective, it has been impossible to obtain their names in full; and also all were daring of record. The leaving out of any name would be a slight, and so we have recorded only the dead and mortally wounded of the privates and non-commissioned officers.

CHAPTER XVIII.

OPERATIONS OF GEN. SEDGWICK. — MOVEMENT OF GEN. HOOKER. — GETTYSBURG CAMPAIGN.

THE next morning Gen. Sedgwick gave orders to re-form the lines, so as to hold the road leading to Banks's Ford on the Rappahannock River. It was apparent from the forces met, that Lee could hold Hooker, and still confront Sedgwick with the greater part of his army. Rumors were rife that Hooker had been defeated. The wounded were sent to Fredericksburg; and Sedgwick made preparations to save the Sixth Corps from capture and annihilation, striving with only eighteen thousand men, wholly tired out, to hold in check Lee, who, with a force of thirty thousand men, fell upon the remnant of the Sixth Corps, and drove it towards the river; while Hooker, thoroughly whipped, remained cooped up in his fortifications with seventy-five thousand fighting men, furnishing an example for Butler to imitate a year later at Bermuda Hundreds. Hooker, in attempting to account for his defeat, tried to throw the blame on Sedgwick, who had performed the only redeeming act in this tragedy of errors. Lee, on the morning of the 4th, prepared for action on Sedgwick's front. Early moved up the telegraph-road towards Fredericksburg, and was soon firmly established upon Sedgwick's left flank. He had recaptured the Heights, and was ready by four o'clock P.M. to strike effectual blows in aid of Lee. He captured some of our ambulances loaded with the wounded who were moving into Fredericksburg from the battle-field of the night before. Lee formed his lines deliberately, and by so doing paid a greater tribute to Sedgwick's ability than he did to that of Hooker, whom he always immediately struck wherever he could find him. Soon after four o'clock huge columns of attack formed against Sedgwick's centre and left. But, as they were launched against that living wall of men who upheld the honor of the Sixth Corps, they were driven back in disastrous repulse. Charge after charge was made upon Howe and Brooks, and a part of Newton's line, but without avail. Darkness fell upon the defeated force of Lee, who had been repulsed by eighteen thousand men of the Sixth Corps; while Hooker, with eighty thousand men, had been unable to hold his own against some forty-five thousand infantry of Lee. Surely, further comment is unnecessary.

As the author lay wounded upon Stafford Heights, he could see the whole battle-field; and as the sand-bag battery of siege-guns exploded their huge shells over the charging columns of Lee, it was a grand and terrible panorama. First would come the solid column of gray, rushing on with its famous yell; and then the roar of the Union cannon, and a white flash of flame and smoke. And as the breeze blew across the battle-field, the smoke lifted, disclosing the columns of gray reeling in defeat and repulse. It has always seemed strange to the writer that Hooker did not, after he had been defeated around Chancellorsville, re-enforce the Sixth Corps with thirty thousand men, which he could have done as well as not, and have held the Heights and advanced position of Sedgwick, which would have compelled Lee to retreat beyond Spottsylvania Court-House, or across Hooker's front with Jackson's forces towards Orange Court-House; but such an idea seems to have never entered his mind. After letting the fruits of the best strategic move in the war slip through his fingers, he drew himself back into a tangled forest, where he could not deploy his men, by this move letting his enemy obtain the advantage of striking and massing against him at any point on his line at leisure. His cavalry was utterly useless. Instead of utilizing it as a screen and covering force, he sent it off on a wild-goose chase, to operate upon Lee's communications. If he had had ten thousand of his cavalry with him, he would have cleared the Wilderness, and Lee must have retreated behind the Annas. So much for criticism. But as I recall the thousands of the Sixth Corps who lay wounded, or silent in death, even at this late day I find no excuse for Hooker except in the belief of his lack of efficiency in handling large masses of troops in close contest with the enemy. The poor Eleventh Corps has been Hooker's scape-goat long enough. Let us put the blame where it belongs, which, summed up, is, weakness in generalship at the vital point of great combinations, and the lack of generalship to seize opportunities as they arise. Night closed the fight at Salem Church; and as soon as it became dusk, the Sixth Corps took up its line of retreat by Banks's Ford, Gen. Benham having by his foresight constructed two or three fine bridges at that point to facilitate the crossing of the Sixth Corps on its retrograde movement. Thus ended Hooker's grand campaign across the Rappahannock. That which had been inaugurated with every prospect of success, and a glorious victory to the Union arms, ended in disaster, gloom, and a crushing defeat, but with this advantage over Burnside's campaign, that, while we were defeated, and had received heavy blows, losing some seventeen thousand men, we had given Lee's army many a damaging blow in return, as his loss of twelve thousand men attested. After resting three days on the banks of the river, we took up our line of march back to our old camp, at White-Oak Church.

The regiment remained in camp until June 6, when they once more took up the line of march to the Rappahannock River, crossing at Franklin's old crossing, where they were thrown to the front on picket. Col. Johns having been wounded, Lieut.-Col. Harlow was in command of the regiment; and after his brilliant services at Mayre's and Salem

ZEBA F. BLISS,
Captain Co. "E."

Heights, the boys felt the utmost confidence in his courage, fidelity, and military capacity, he having shown himself a very cool and splendid officer in action. Of the officers wounded in the recent battles, Capt. Zebe F. Bliss showed great ability, cool and efficient under fire, firm and steadfast to duty; Capt. Hiram A. Oakman won golden opinions of Company E for his bravery and zeal; whilst Company I was called upon to mourn that gallant and brilliant officer, Prentiss M. Whitney, beloved by all. He met his fate with a stern resignation, begotten of a high and lofty patriotism, having had a presentiment of coming death, of which he had spoken to his comrades-in-arms. But by such men was the old Army of the Potomac led and directed, the ripened fruit of Liberty's educational systems, the vintage of our Northern civilization. June 11 we were relieved, and fell back to the banks of the river; June 13 recrossed, and bivouacked half a mile from the river. A campaign was now inaugurated by Gen. Lee, which was to finally terminate in his complete defeat among the hills of the State of Pennsylvania. In the histories published of that able general, it is said, that, after consultation with the War Department at Richmond, he determined to invade the North as a counterpoint to Grant's move on Vicksburg. But, alas for rebel dreams! it resulted in the most decisive defeat he ever received; and from the slopes of Cemetery Ridge, no doubt visions of Appomattox broke in upon his bitter reveries. The rebel army at this time was, no doubt, the strongest military organization on this continent. Under firm discipline, the veterans of many fields of battle, officered by graduates of West Point and the Southern military academies, it was a foe worthy the steel of any army that ever was organized; and surely the historian must give the old Army of the Potomac adequate praise that it should have met and defeated its old antagonist, after the disasters of Fredericksburg and Chancellorsville. But, as time elapses, it is apparent to the military student that Gen. Lee overrated the effect of the defeats the Federal Army had sustained, he not realizing the great moral reserve force of the Northern volunteer, which sustained him in defeat and disaster the same as in victory.

FRANKLIN P. HARLOW.
Lieutenant Colonel.

CHAPTER XIX.

LETTER FROM GEN. NEWTON. — WALTER S. GOSS. — MOVEMENT ON GETTYSBURG.

HAVING received a letter from one of the committee in relation to the previous services of the regiment, I shall take the liberty to insert it before trying to record the hardships, the fatigues and dangers, of the Gettysburg campaign, in which remarkable operations every regiment of the brigade and corps bore a conspicuous part. It was published in " The Boston Journal " of that year and date, and relates, as may be seen, to the operations in what is termed the Chancellorsville campaign.

HEADQUARTERS THIRD DIVISION, SIXTH ARMY CORPS.
OFFICE OF ADJUTANT-GENERAL, MAY 15, 1863.
TO HIS EXCELLENCY JOHN A. ANDREW, GOVERNOR MASSACHUSETTS.

Sir, — Permit me to call your attention to the excellent conduct of the Massachusetts regiments under my command during the late operations of the Sixth Corps. The Seventh Massachusetts stormed the Heights of Fredericksburg in column, without firing a shot, and suffered severely. To Lieut.-Col. F. P. Harlow, who commanded the regiment after the wounding of Col. Johns, I mainly attribute this fortunate result. Col. Harlow proved himself a hero. As this was a charge not exceeded in brilliancy and daring by any operation of the war, the Seventh ought to receive adequate praise. The Tenth and Thirty-seventh, although under fire in Fredericksburg on the morning of May 3, rendered their principal services in the afternoon and the following day at Salem Heights. Their coolness under fire, and admirable discipline, merit the warmest acknowledgments. The Tenth was under the command of Major Parker during the most important period of their operations, Col. H. L. Eustis having command of the brigade.

The conduct of all these regiments at such critical juncture has been an ample return for all care bestowed by your Excellency and the State upon their organization and discipline.

I have the honor to be your obedient servant,

JOHN NEWTON, *Major-General.*

Having also received another contribution from W. S. Goss of Company A. I take great pleasure in having it inserted as a very essential contribution to the history of the Chancellorsville campaign.

"The Army of the Potomac lay fronting the enemy, who were intrenched on the hills at the rear of Fredericksburg, while the muddy waters of the Rappahannock rolled between. This army, under the lead of bad generalship, had won several gallant defeats. The most of us had been through the not very enviable discipline of the Peninsula campaign; had sounded the depths of its mud, its swamps, and its fruitless victories; had struggled with Pope at the second Bull Run disaster, and successfully resisted the invading horde at Antietam. Again that devoted army, full of the fighting spirit, had it a general to lead it, was surging against the bristling, thundering heights of Fredericksburg, only to be swept back, broken and bleeding, as the effect of its ill-advised, wasted energies. Then came the renowned Burnside 'mud march' that upset the gravity of the army, and at which mud-bedraggled officers and men poked fun because of its ludicrous situations. Never before had that army, even in the face of defeat, fallen back in a more demoralized condition. The brave and valiant Burnside was looked upon with distrust as a commander, and there is no doubt he retired from his command with a feeling of relief that bordered on the frayed edge of disgust. The retirement of Burnside brought 'Fighting Joe Hooker' to the front as commander; and the army now expected lively business, and 'lovely fighting all along the line.' Gen. Hooker's first business appeared to be with the Commissary Department.

"He was a firm believer in the doctrine of good food and plenty of it. It is doubtful whether there was ever an army so well fed as was Hooker's during those weeks previous to his ill-fated move on the enemy's left flank. The thickly wooded hills where first lurked the hidden army were soon laid bare by the sturdy blows of these Northern pioneers. Even the limbs and brush, which at first were discarded, soon disappeared through the necessities of this denizen horde who had pre-empted the land of the F. F. V's. With the early days of spring the chips began to fly from the standing stumps, and they disappeared like a 'presto, change' performance. While we were beginning to wonder where our wood for cooking purposes was to come from, the solution came in the form of an order for each soldier to draw ten days' rations of salt pork and hard-tacks. These were the regulation campaign rations, interspersed at intervals by fresh beef from the drove of scrawny-looking cattle which followed the army afar off afoot. These beeves obtained a certain hardened toughness by their army discipline, and the masticators thereof had a realizing sense of its toughness. They called it mule-meat. In the field each man was his own cook; so the animal was divided from neck to rump into small slices, which were all passed off as steak. But there was a remote suspicion abroad in the ranks that rump and sirloin did not fall so low in rank as to honor their bill of fare by their presence. These fancy cuts of steak were usually cooked by being affixed at the bayonet's point, or on a forked stick, and broiled over a fire. They were well seasoned with smoke or ashes, as best suited the tastes or mishaps of the man at the other end of the implement. But the patriotic North was getting nervous over the protracted supineness of the army; and the valiant and intrepid editorial staff of the Union journals were shedding gallons of ink in the heroic interrogatory, 'Why doesn't the army move?'

"Campaigning on paper may be a pleasurable occupation; but when it has to be written in mud, it is of the *vice versa* pattern, in view of which we privates were willing to supine some more, and the commander appeared to second the motion, notwithstanding editorial inquisitiveness, and the pressure of red-tape strategists at Washington.

"But as the days of April were fading out of the calendar of 1863, we packed our little ten days' rations of salt pork, coffee, and sugar in our haversacks, chinking in the extra space with the typical parallelogrammatic 'hard-tacks,' which still left a surplus to be stowed away in our knapsacks. The inner man looked after, then came the ammunition; one hundred rounds in cartridge-box and pockets are the rations provided for the enemy, provided we can get them there.

"Our old soldier-homes, which had been fitted up with an eye to comfort, were dismantled, for 'Pack up and fall in' was the order, 'Forward, march!' the command. With head of column faced enemyward, we again entered upon a season's campaign, prepared to strike another blow for national unity; to write one more livid page of our nation's history.

"The 30th of April found us again on the banks of the Rappahannock, near Franklin Crossing, where once before we had so bravely passed over, but had come back again like unfledged heroes. Here we staid for three days. There were three corps below Falmouth; but they were gradually drawn away, up river, by Gen. Hooker, to participate in this grand movement, the climax of which was not illustrated with a great display of grandeur.

"On the evening of May 1 we were drawn up in line, and listened with rapt attention to a general order setting forth the 'splendid achievements of the Fifth Corps,' and supposed by its tenor that the rebellion had received a paralytic shock by some subtle stroke of strategy while we were not there to see. As the other corps left us, we were ordered to stretch out and cover the ground of two corps. So to keep up the simulation, and to lighten our loads, we charged on the ten days' rations, and mustered them out of the service as rapidly as possible. But of little avail were our efforts in that direction, for three days' rations more were added to condone the wastage.

"Before crossing over the river, the regiment that was honored by my presence was paid off for four months' service. The paymaster, who had been over a week paying the rest of the brigade, paid off this regiment in less than two hours. The closing of accounts was celebrated by the Johnnies popping shells over at us during this monetary crisis; and the non-combatants who carried the sinews of war that rejoiced the soldier's and sutler's heart, were anxious to clear us from their books, that they might seek a peaceful solitude in the distant rear.

"On May 2, as the setting sun was bidding its last goodnight to many of our numbers, we were in line on the river's brink ready to cross over. Away in the distance we hear a faint rebel yell; down their line it travels, increasing in volume until it comes from our immediate front with a distinctness that is bewildering to us, because ignorant of its import. While the yell was at its height, an officer rode along the line, shouting, 'Cheer, men! cheer, every mother's son of you!' So we set up a hurrah with all the power of healthy lungs, and discounted the rebels at their own game. But they had good cause to cry aloud with joy; for the news that came down their lines was of the dire defeat that had overtaken Howard's corps, shattering it, and mobilizing it into a disorganized rabble. But that news was not to be made known to us through any bombastic general order.

"As the shades of evening settled down upon the murky waters of the river, we crossed over the pontoon bridge, and commenced a series of spasmodic hitches towards Fredericksburg, by going a few steps, and then sitting down to think it over, the reason of which was unknown to us until near morning, when we found that we were simply following up skirmishers who were feeling their way through the darkness into the town, the first intimation of which was the discovery of the wounded who had fallen out by the way.

"We had a jolly Irishman in our company, who, during the night, was suddenly stricken with what was termed in the army as moon-blindness. While fording a run, he became dazed, and exclaimed, 'Byes, if yez wants me to help yez fight, yez will have to lade me!' So he was piloted through until daylight, and helped on the fight that day; was wounded; and, when I saw him afterwards in the army hospital, the surgeons had him blistered just abaft each ear, — 'For the eyes of me,' he said: but what sympathetic cords connect the bumps of combativeness with the sense of vision, I have never been able to gather up science enough to solve, except that the aforesaid bumps may be promoters of fistic encounters.

"As the rising sun ushered in that beautiful and quiet newborn sabbath morn, gilding the murderous hill-top with a glory that spoke to the soul of man, not of fratricide carnage, but of a peaceful calm, we were entering the town through a cut that hid us from the view of the enemy; but our telltale bayonets glistening in the sunshine attracted their attention. With malicious intent, and an emphasis that was startling, they plunged their solid shot in unhealthy proximity to our heads. A numbness began to creep over me, and I saved myself from falling by clinging to a comrade while I called for water. A lieutenant brought me a canteen, and inquired the whereof of my faintness. I told him, 'I was scared, I guess.' — 'Oh! I guess not,' said he; and I have tried to 'guess not' ever since, as it was the only time I ever felt faint under fire; although 'scared' does not begin to express the feelings of a fellow when he plunges into a fight while all the time he is striving to look brave and unconcerned; yet oft his nonchalance partakes of the ludicrous.

"From among many instances that I have seen, I will note the following: At the first battle of Fredericksburg we were lying under a terrific fire of bursting shells, when the brigade general cried out, 'For God's sake, colonel, move your men forward out of that murderous range!' We moved forward amid the boom of bursting shells; and as I glanced along the line, I noticed that every man's head (but mine) was bowed to earth. A tall, thin corporal, who was in advance of the line, I noticed particularly, because of the crookedness of his outline, his long nose near to earth, apparently on the principle of 'root hog or die.' I afterwards heard him laughing at the reverent attitude of the rest of the line, while he boasted of the perpendicularity of himself.

"In the town we take position behind a church on a corner-street. Our crowd is not feeling remarkably hilarious, for they know that there is a solemn work ahead of them, and that many of those who watched the rising sun will never more witness its setting.

"On the open space where the streets intersect are Gens. Sedgwick and Newton with their staff-officers. The enemy are sending shells down the street, and a piece of artillery in front of the staff-officers returns the compliment. A fine-looking aged matron, whose brick mansion is in range of rebel fire, comes out and accosts Sedgwick with, 'General, I wish you would remove that gun; you are drawing fire right on my house.' To which the sturdy general replied, 'Well, madam, if you are afraid, you had better go down cellar.' The forenoon of the day is wearing away, and still we lay nibbling hard-tack, waiting for orders to move. At length Gen. Sedgwick came and looked us over with a solemn expression which seemed to say, 'There will be a thinning out in your ranks very soon; at least, that is what I read in his countenance.' Without uttering a word, he turned on his heel, and walked away. Then the order came to pile up knapsacks; and soon we were in line as the head of one of the storming columns which were to assail Mayre's Heights, the famous 'stone walls' being our objective point.

"At eleven o'clock we lead off, the Thirty-sixth New York

following close in our rear. The last cautionary word is passed along the line by officers. 'Don't fire a gun. whatever the provocation. but give them the cold steel.' Onward and up the street we go at a slow, steady tramp, with arms 'right shoulder shift,' while our artillery at the rear were smashing shells through the houses ahead. to drive out rebel sharpshooters. An ominous silence prevails all along the enemy's line; they are biding their time. as we go marching 'into the jaws of death. into the mouth of hell.' We are nearing their earth-works, and are beginning to know how a man feels when he looks into the mouths of cannon. Right ahead is the first line of works in the form of rifle-pits. The occupants appear to be asleep. as they do not greet us with a single complimentary shot.

"They were expecting that the column would deploy into the field on their front. so a prisoner told me after; but the street was cut through the abrupt hill for an easy grade, so that for a space we were lost to their view, and, to their utter astonishment and discomfiture, the head of our column popped out to the rear of them. Then there was a scrambling among the Johnnies, several throwing down their arms; and they all scuttled for cover behind their more formidable breast-works, while we howled at them, 'Hurry up, Johnnies! go it, graybacks;' and other like endearing epithets until they were lost to view. There is a solemn silence for a moment, then the storm of battle burst upon us with all its withering fury. Our long column, that like a thin wedge was penetrating the enemy's centre, has become entangled in the vortex of an enfilading fire. There is the music of missiles filling the air; the swoop and screams of shells; the sharp, piping *ping* of canister; the zip, zip, zip, of minies, — all singing the choral of death. From the front, from the right and from the left of us, came the swift messengers on their errands of hate.

"In a moment five files at the head of the column are mown down by one swift stroke. and the whole length of the line is shattered and gory. Two comrades in the file with me are stricken down, and the man behind covering me is sent to the earth by a ball crashing through his brain; he brushes me as he goes down; I turn and glance at his prostrate form, then pass on again. The head of the line is staggering under its heavy load, while the rear is pushing to the front. I notice a lieutenant up ahead urging on his men, when a missile strikes him down. He scrambles to his feet, waves his sword, shouting, 'Forward, boys!' and is again felled to the earth, never more to rise. A long limbed youth grasps his gun by the tail-band, steps from the ranks, waving it aloft, and heroically shouts above the battle's din, 'Come on, boys, they can't lick us!' Just then he is stricken in the leg by a bullet, and fell, his courage quickly flowing from an ugly wound. A shell made a dip at our colors and exploded as it struck its azure field, and it was no longer a starry banner, but a hole with a rag around it! It now rests in Doric Hall, beneath the gilded dome, a memento of the vicissitudes of Southern storms.

"We are showing an inclination to push ahead, seeing which, the colonel came to us saying, 'That's right, boys.' I was getting in a hurry to have the job through with, so we suggested to the colonel that he give us the order 'double quick.' He swung his sword over his head, shouted 'Forward!' and very soon was stricken down by a rebel bullet, severely wounded in the leg, and was taken to the rear by some of our boys. Concluding I was needed at the front, I left the colonel to his fate, and joined forces with the color-sergeant of the Thirty-sixth New York, who had a fit of heroism, and came up shouting, 'Come on, boys, let us take the Heights!' I had got all over wanting the Heights, but I was willing to help him get them if he had any particular use for them, so I told him I would go color-guard with him. 'Well, come quickly,' said he, and away we started, but had not advanced more than two or three rods, when down went the brave sergeant, colors and all, dead. Then I discovered that we were making that charge alone, and to the left of the main line of advance.

"Looking over in the field on our left, I saw the Sixth Maine making one of their famous charges in line of battle. Their men were dropping fast, but they drew fire and relieved some of the pressure upon the main column of attack, which came up under the command of Lieut-Col. Harlow. With a rush we sweep through the rebel lines, and they break to the rear with a rush, in squads and singly. The Seventh Massachusetts takes two brass cannon from the famous Washington Artillery, with prisoners, which are sent to the rear. This fearful charge, which seemed to me to have occupied over an hour of time, was in fact but of a few minutes duration. The Heights were won, and our tattered banner was planted on the parapet of one of the forts. After a short rest the brigade was formed in line, and advanced in pursuit of the enemy, towards Salem Heights, where in the afternoon he was met in force, having been heavily reinforced from Lee's main army, where a very severe fight took place. Early in this fight I received a wound in the leg by a bullet, which necessitated my retirement, with numerous rests, in the direction of Fredericksburg, faint and sore, where my sinking spirits and fast oozing strength was stimulated by copious 'swigs' of brandy from a canteen furnished by a member of the 'Christian Commission.' I remember that valuable adjunct of the army with grateful reverence, notwithstanding their persistence in deluging me with a plethora of religious tracts while I for weeks lay prone upon an army hospital cot. In my rearward flight I threw away my haversack with all its stores of provisions, around which had clustered the hopes and fears of previous days, and found my knapsack, to which I clung with the tenacity of a householder. All the wounded that were able to get there, lay in Fredericksburg that night, and when morning dawned a glance in that direction revealed the fact that the enemy were making preparations to retake the Heights, from the direction of the Telegraph road. They soon reoccupied their old positions in rear of the city. Hooker, who had shown a lack of that tenacity so much needed in a leader, had allowed Lee to throw his forces upon Sedgwick, nearly surrounding him, and had left him to cut his way out as best he could, which he did, but at a fearful sacrifice of men.

"In Fredericksburg the surgeons were hastily loading the ambulances with those who were unable to walk, whilst all who could hobble along were left to the tender mercies and solicitudes of themselves. I set out on my journey with a heavy heart and a heavier leg. I commenced my pilgrimage with a long staff clutched in both hands, and carried in front of me as a lever to pull myself along. My knapsack trailed at the rear, dragging on the ground, a strap being hooked to my belt. There was a bridge across the river at Fredericksburg, and over this bridge of boats I started to cross. A train of ambulances came thundering over, and their jolt and jar were beyond my powers of endurance, so I crawled into a pontoon boat and dangled my legs in the water, which proved a great relief to me from the excruciating pain caused by their ceaseless jar on the bridge. There I sat until the procession had passed over, when I again started from the debatable ground, which I was anxious the river should separate me from. It was with feelings of relief that I struck what appeared to me as solid Union territory beyond all debate, and sat myself down on the friendly knapsack, when a major of artillery came along, and told me not to stop there. I expostulated with him, telling him that I was unable to go another step, which I shortly proved to be a mistake, for he informed me that they were expecting an attack on the bridge, and all they had to defend it was one regiment of infantry and his battery ; adding : 'You do not want to get hit again, so you had better get over the hill.' I got there in time. Over the hill I found a large company of wounded, and here I had a good rest. Soon a mounted orderly rode into our midst and said : 'It is the general's order that you go to Falmouth Station, where you will be taken away by cars.' The news was encouraging, but the tramp discouraging. I asked him how far it was, and was informed that it was less than a mile. There was misery in every inch of that mile, and I did not share it alone. It took nearly four hours to cover that distance, and I covered it more by sitting than I did by walking.

"At Falmouth Station we were finally put in box cars with liberal carpets of straw, and taken a few miles to Potomac Creek. On arriving at the landing, several of the men had completely broken down, and were carried to the hospital tents on stretchers. A kind-hearted settler offered his services with his team to transport those unable to walk. Three of us were laid on the straw in the bottom of his hard spring vehicle, and the carting commenced. We struck a road built of logs, and, oh ! misery of miseries ! such rolling, such pitching, such tossing to and fro over and under each other. And ungrateful wretches that we were, we cursed the driver, begging him to let us get out and crawl. He stopped his team, and with sympathetic tears dimming his eyes, told us he was doing the best he could, and that it was but a little farther anyway. So not to hurt his feelings, though he did not seem to spare ours, we suppressed our grief and remained as quiet as circumstances would permit. I know not how long that ride was, but a life-time of woe seemed to be concentrated therein, and as long as life lasts will the vital remembrance of its tortures arise in my mind as it reverts to Hooker's movements around Chancellorsville, and his generous donation of ten days' rations to the army under his command."

The regimental narrative gives the following record of the marches of the regiment in the movement on Gettysburg.

June 11, was relieved and fell back to the bank of the river, where the regiment furnished its proper quota of men to help fortify a line of defence drawn from near Hazel Run to near the Bernard house, touching the river on either flank. June 13, during the night, we recrossed and bivouacked one-half mile from the river. The intention of the enemy having been fathomed, the movements of the regiment and army, as now related, is a record of the most severe marching the regiment was ever called upon to endure in all its service. Lee had begun his grand invasion, and Hooker had commenced his masterly moves to checkmate him. June 14, marched ten miles to Stafford Court House; June 15, marched fifteen miles to Dumfries; June 16, marched fifteen miles to Fairfax Court House; June 24, marched five miles to Centerville. The regiment was very much exhausted on this march; it was rain, and mud, and sunshine, with a sultry and depressing heat. The roads were simply quag-mires of mud, and choked to almost impassability by the huge trains of siege guns of the reserve artillery and wagon trains.

But Lee is away to the North, marching with untiring energy on to the consummation of his dreams in the fertile plains of Pennsylvania, with its fields of grain and stock of cattle and horses, a rich field for the Rebel hordes, who hardly ever tasted the sweet wheaten bread of our Northern States. June 26, marched twenty-two miles to Drainesville; June 27, marched thirteen miles, crossing the Potomac at Edwards' Ferry, and bivouacked two miles from the river near Poolsville, Md. June 28, marched twenty-five miles to near New Market, Md.; June 29, marched twenty-three miles and bivouacked in the woods. These last few days had been so trying that it was absolutely necessary to rest the men. Tramping twenty miles a day is great marching in cool weather over our difficult roads, but in the midst of a hot and sultry summer it is remarkable how the Northern boys stood the severe tax upon their vitality, with nothing but disaster to cheer them on. Frowned upon by the authorities at Washington, they knew better than their harsh critics the valor and endurance hid under their misfortunes, caused mostly by the same government which so coldly frowned upon their commanders and men. June 30, marched twenty miles to Manchester; July 1, marched all night and until about 4 o'clock P. M. of July 2, making thirty-seven miles, when we arrived on the battle-field of Gettysburg, where we rested and filled canteens with water from Rock creek.

But while on this long and arduous march, Gen. Hooker had been relieved, and Gen. George G. Meade had been given the command of the army. A conscientious and capable officer, who had fulfilled every trust heretofore laid upon him. When called upon to take command of the Army of the Potomac he was in command of the Fifth Corps, had given no promise of superior generalship, but had attended strictly to his duties while in the field. Gen. Hooker, whom he relieved, was a very able officer for certain duties, but had not the broad and massive qualities of mind so necessary to successfully command a large army, as had his successor.

By great good fortune, the selection of Gen. Meade was the most fortunate move the powers at Washington had made in all its satanic meddling with the Army of the Potomac. And under God's kindly providence, Halleck's and Stanton's selection proved beneficial to the army, though not by any superior judgment on their part, but by the intrinsic worth of the man whom they

HENRY E. KAY,
Sergeant Co. "A."

had chosen to experiment with while in the face of the enemy.

Lee had launched his columns with great precision into the fertile valleys of Pennsylvania; had met but little opposition from the inefficient militia of the State under the gallant Couch, who commanded the Department of the Susquehanna. Meade, as soon as he took command, moved promptly to the rescue, and gave orders for concentration on the Pipe Creek line.

But providence ordered that this battle should be fought by the great armies on lines forced upon them by circumstances. Reynolds pressing forward with the First Corps, in support of the cavalry under Buford, struck the advance guard of Hill's forces, who were advancing upon Gettysburg as their point of concentration. Gen. Lee having learned of the change of commanders, and being afraid that his line of communication would be broken, had hoped to take up a position where the Army of the Potomac would have to attack him, but ere he could concentrate his army he met the noble Reynolds rushing on to avenge the invasion of his native State. And on the banks of Willoughby Run was opened the battle that was to decide the fate of the Union.

The first part of the battle was favorable to the Confederates Gen. Reynolds was killed; the First Corps suffered very severely, and the Eleventh which had come up to support them, had been very severely defeated later in the day, with the First, when overpowered by the onward rush of Ewell's Corps on the Cashville Pike. Reynolds was killed early in the fight, and the command of the corps was assumed by Gen. Abner Doubleday, when they performed herculean efforts and then only retreated slowly and in good order to Cemetery Hill. And now the great battle is on: the Second Corps is coming up; Howard and Hancock are a host in themselves; and by 9 o'clock P. M., the Union lines were firmly established to await the mighty crash of the victorious foe the next day. But succor is at hand. The Twelfth, Fifth and Sixth Corps are rushing on to the rescue, and the Rebel hosts are to be hurled back, broken and dismayed, by the brave old Army of the Potomac,— the loyal and true!

The battle of Gettysburg was no doubt the high-water mark of the rebellious efforts to disrupt the Union; in fact, the decisive battle of the war. Lee, with his eighty thousand veteran infantry and cavalry as the sum total of his forces across the Potomac, suffered his most disastrous defeat in this battle at the hands of the Federal Army, since he had been so roughly handled by McClellan at South Mountain and Antietam. Though the Seventh Massachusetts was not called upon to offer up a large list of brave men to the moloch of war, still they had marched and suffered as few were called upon to suffer. Through heat and dust, rain and mud, they had marched over one hundred and sixty miles. And then, when nature seemingly could do no more, the regiment with the brave men of the Sixth Corps made a march of almost unparalleled swiftness to help its hard pressed comrades upon the blood-stained heights of Gettysburg. How those long, hot marches still call up a thrill from the old soldier, as he recalls to mind the hunger and thirst, the heat, the want of rest, the blistered feet, the stiff joints, as morning after morning the early bugle roused him from his slumbers, to still press on and find the fleet-footed enemy.

The march to the battle-field of Gettysburg was of a most exhausting nature. The Sixth Corps had been thrown out to the north and east to protect and cover the strategic points leading to Baltimore, and was more than thirty miles from the main body of the army. After marching all day in the broiling sun, the tired soldiers of the Sixth Corps had filed into a level field to rest and encamp for the night.

Gen. Sedgwick had pitched headquarter tents and had prepared to spend the night at this place. As Newton's division filed in, the general said, "Put your division right in here, general; we rest here to-night." But hark! do you not hear the clatter of hoofs on the Baltimore Pike? And soon a courier, his horse covered with sweat, foam and dust, his original color unrecognizable, gallops up and gives an order to the gallant Sedgwick, who hastily opens and reads it. Soon the bugle sounds out on the evening air the "Assembly," and orders are given to "Fall in." The long and almost incomparable march has begun—and a night-march! Who of my readers have not known its irksomeness, its exhausting effect, the sudden halt, then the quick step to the "close column," then the rest for a moment, then the rising up half asleep, and stiff in every muscle? But on the column goes, with darkness to hide the pall of dust which choked the men, filling eyes and ears, mouth and nostrils, with its blinding and irritating effects. And as the weary men press on, what tidings have reached them! The First Corps is in, and all cut to pieces; Reynolds is killed; the Eleventh Corps is smashed; and so far, our Army of the Potomac has been whipped. Then the stern orders, "Close up! Close up!" On they rush; it is past twelve o'clock, midnight; word is sent back for our help. Boys, do your best. We must reach the field; the brave old army needs you. And so they stagger on; "having missed the way in the first part of the night, they were called to make an unnecessary march of eight miles, which many historians will fail to relate as they speak of the battle in general terms." Through the suffocating heat and dust—streams of water adding to the misery of blistered feet—the perspiration starting from every pore and dropping from their faces. And still the stern orders, "Close up! Close up!" The gray dawn is breaking, and on they rush a little faster. They have reached a point on the march when every few moments the sullen boom of cannon reaches the ears, not to dishearten, but nerving to stronger efforts. A short rest is taken; the order is given to make coffee, but before the water is hardly warm in the many dishes the bugle rings out its clarion notes of the "Assembly," and the half-boiled coffee is hastily poured into the soldiers' canteens, to be their only nourishment for the day. The morning comes and goes; the sun is pouring down its scorching rays as it climbs the eastern horizon. But there is no let-up to the march. It is on! on! on! Noon has passed. The column still is in motion, its leader still pressing on for the battle-field, as his soldier heart knows how great the responsibility resting upon him. This corps is the largest and strongest in the army, and he fully knows how much may depend upon its timely arrival. High noon is past; the sun is slowly sinking down the western sky, when the roar of battle shakes the earth.

Longstreet is opening the ball; his long lines are moving like an avalanche to strike the Third Corps in its exposed position, because Gen. Meade had not men enough to hold the line which Sickles had obtained. But the Third Corps was not to be driven from its position until Longstreet had received such punishment that in the terrific charge of Pickett's division on the third day of battle his corps was so surfeited with blood and carnage it gave but poor support to the gallant Pickett. As the sun had begun to throw its long rays to the east, the corps and regiment reached Rock Creek, to the right rear of our army. The welcome sound was heard to "rest," and men were sent to fill their canteens in Rock Creek. But word soon comes, "We are hard pressed upon the left; send your best division to support the noble Fifth Corps and what is left of the Third and Second." For the "Devil's Den" had been a den where the reaper, Death, had put in his sharpened sickle with intense lust and vengeance. As the tired divisions of the Sixth Corps were resting in column by brigade, there came word from our beloved commander, Sedgwick, "Tell General Eustis to bring his brigade to the front at once." Almost as by magic they spring to their feet with a cheer upon their lips. These tired, hungry, foot-sore men spring forward at the word of command, and swing into line on the double-quick. Readers and friends, can pen say more? After marching over forty miles through clouds of dust, through streams of water, and over rocky road beds, in a dark and sultry July night, stifling and depressing, they spring forward at the word with all their ancient vigor and zeal, ready to dare and die. As General Longstreet, in his *Century* article upon the battle of Gettysburg, says, "Preparing for another attack upon the Union lines, I rode forward to the front of our position; but seeing the enemy rapidly forming new lines of battle with fresh troops, I thought it prudent to desist from attack until our lines had been re-formed and were more compact, having suffered very severely in the assaults delivered upon the Union lines." Yes, there they stood, the brigades of the Second division of the Sixth Corps, of which the Seventh Massachusetts formed a part, firm, resolute, with not fifty stragglers in the whole number, ready to die for the maintenance of our institutions and for the repulse of the hosts of treason.

If Longstreet had organized his forces, and the Sixth Corps had been away to the rear, and yet upon the march, with the Third Corps shattered, Round Top torn from our grasp, and our whole line in retreat and broken, we leave the intelligent reader to judge of the results. No more rapid and indomitable march is recorded in any war. It ranks with Stonewall Jackson's rapid movements. It shows the discipline, the nerve, the soldierly qualities of its men, and it shows in the soldier-patriot, Gen. John Sedgwick, the qualities of great comprehensive and correct military judgment.

Comrades, my feeble tribute is written, blundering and halting, but thick with facts, richly laden with love of country and heroic sacrifices, which are ever green and fresh to those who loved and dared to die for their country's defence and life. We were not called upon to die amidst the flash of rifles, the hiss of shell, or plunging shot; but we were called upon to render all the service that lay within our power. And as time rolls on, the old Sixth Corps at Gettysburg will be remembered, not as Grouchy at Waterloo, but as Desaix at Marengo, under Napoleon the First. Round Top was saved by the foresight of Warren, the martyr, and the timely arrival of the Fifth and Sixth Corps; and as time moves on, Eustis and his brigade can claim their share in the chaplets of glory so gallantly won by all the Army Corps and brigades on that fateful field to Southern valor and aspirations, the rock-bound heights of Gettysburg, consecrated for all time by the blood of forty thousand men, a monument to the evils of class legislation and the oppression of the human race, washed from the escutcheon of our country's honor by the blood of its sons shed in defence of the Union of States formed by our forefathers, which is the best monument to the fidelity to duty of officers and men.

July 3, the regiment was constantly moving from right to left, under a terrific shell fire most of the time, acting as a support to different portions of the line as the enemy's movements became dangerous and determined. It was in these movements back and forth that the Thirty-seventh became involved in a vortex of fire, and lost thirty men in ten minutes. It bore itself very bravely, but would not have suffered so much if it had passed this point in open order as did the Seventh Massachusetts. General Russell always told his men to keep open order when under shell fire at a distance from the foe, he considering life of more consequence than exact military order. July 4, just before daylight, took position in front line of battle, where we remained until about noon, when we fell back two hundred yards and threw up rifle-pits.

On the morning of the 5th, it was discovered that Lee had retreated, pushing his way to the rear through the passes of the Blue Ridge, his long trains loaded with his wounded, although he left nearly fifteen thousand upon the field of battle and in its vicinity. The Sixth Corps was immediately ordered in pursuit, and as the Corps pushed out on the Emmittsburg Road, the sights were sickening in the extreme. Everywhere lay the debris of battle, thousands of men and horses swollen beyond recognition in the hot July sun, and the stench was almost unendurable. On every hand lay the wounded under temporary cover, while every farm house was filled to overflowing with the dead and wounded of Lee's army. The Corps this day made but six miles, as they had to proceed slowly to escape ambush while entering the foot hills of the Blue Ridge. On the 6th, started at 4 P. M., marched all night, making nine miles. General Meade had in the meantime given orders to pursue the foe by the Fairfield Road, as the numerous mountain passes to the West afforded Lee very strong positions where he could hold the army of pursuit in check with a very small force, and leave his trains free to press on for the Potomac with the booty gathered from the fertile plains of Pennsylvania. July 7, marched twenty miles and bivouacked on the summit of South Mountain. This night-march equalled the horrors of the one on Gettysburg, there falling every hour copious showers which drenched the men to their very skin. The roads were in a very deplorable state, and the mud was equal almost to Burnside's mud, the December previous. July 8, marched eight miles to Middletown, where the regiment drew rations and rested through the night. July 9, marched six miles to Boonesboro, and rested during the afternoon and night. The cavalry was vigorously pushing the enemy, under the gailant Pleasanton, Custer and Kilpatrick. July 10, marched five miles and formed line of battle in the enemy's front. July 11, remained in same position. July 12, followed the enemy to Funkstown, and formed line of battle. The Seventh was thrown to the front on skirmish line and had a very severe brush with the enemy, having four men wounded; remained on skirmish line and threw up rifle-pits. July 13, engaged in same work.

In the meantime Lee had crossed the Potomac, making his escape into Virginia. The question is, Why did Meade thus let Lee slip through his fingers? It would take an able military man to properly answer that question. We may venture one assertion. The Army of the Potomac had lost almost thirty-five per cent. of its number in its engagements thus far, and it was a serious question with Meade whether his army was strong enough to cope with Lee's in his strongly fortified position. July 15, marched fifteen miles to Boonesboro. Gen. Meade had now taken the line of advance that the great strategist McClellan had, the year before later in the season. July 16, marched fifteen miles to near Berlin, where the regiment rested two days. The weather was simply terrible, and many of the men were sunstruck upon those fearful long and hot marches. July 19, crossed the Potomac at Berlin, and marched ten miles to Wheatland. July 20, marched ten miles to near Union. July 22, marched five miles and bivouacked.

We were now on the same line of advance that McClellan gave to one of his most trusted lieutenants. The authorities at Washington had, in their experiment of removing McClellan from the Peninsula, thrown the burden of defence of the Capital upon the Union army, and relieved the rebel army from a like responsibility. They had sacrificed in the experiments of Pope, Burnside and Hooker not far from forty-five thousand men, and were substantially upon the

JAMES HOLLHOUSE,
Private Co. "B."

same ground as in the first year of the war. The South was getting exhausted in a measure, not from the military ability of Stanton or Halleck, but from natural causes.

July 23, marched eighteen miles and bivouacked in the woods. July 24, marched to near Ashby's Gap, and halted for dinner, then marched back to Orleans. July 25, marched fifteen miles and encamped two miles from Warrenton, where we remained in camp resting until September 15th, when we marched five miles to Sulphur Springs. The regiment had marched since it broke camp upon the Rappahannock, June 14th, three hundred and sixty-nine miles; and although it had not lost many men in battle, but by sunstroke and disability it had lost more than sixty. The marching is almost unparalleled in history. It stands as a monument to the great vitality of the Anglo-Saxon race.

The army was concentrated near Warrenton, well in hand to strike Lee another blow as soon as he gave Meade an opening, but ere it came, the army was depleted by the withdrawal of the Eleventh and Twelfth Corps, sent to reinforce Gen. Rosecrans' Army of the Cumberland, after its repulse at Chickamauga, who had appealed to the authorities at Washington in vain for reinforcements before he made his great stategic move across the mountains to Chattanooga, the Key of the Confederacy.

Gen. Rosecrans, after McClellan, no doubt was the greatest strategist the war brought to the front. He had for his great subordinate, the "Rock of Chickamauga," Major-Gen. George H. Thomas, the only general of the war who smashed an army of the Confederacy in the open field. Gen. Grant has very severely criticised Gen. Thomas' actions around Nashville, but his glorious victory no doubt allayed all fears for his lieutenant, as he was hanging on to Richmond by a very uncertain grip in the summer and fall of 1864. Gen. Thomas, in my opinion, had no superior as a general, either in our army or in the Confederate. He was a remarkable man.

CHAPTER XX.

FROM STONE HOUSE MOUNTAIN TO MORNING OF MAY 3, 1864.—BATTLE OF RAPPAHANNOCK STATION. — PRESENTATION TO LIEUT.-COL. HARLOW. — MINE RUN CAMPAIGN. — MOVEMENT TO MADISON COURT HOUSE.—LIFE IN CAMP.

SEPTEMBER 16, marched to near Stone House Mountain, sixteen miles, and took position in line of battle. October 1, about 11 o'clock P. M., started from camp and marched all night and the next day, to near Boulton's Station, twenty-four miles. Oct. 3, marched fourteen miles to Bristow's Station, where we remained in camp until the 13th, when we marched to Catlett's Station, and returned to Bristow's, sixteen miles. This movement was made to meet Lee's great flank march, by which he hoped to get between Meade's army and Washington, and force the Union army to attack him in his chosen position; but he was foiled at every step by the consummate generalship of Meade. While upon this march, Gen. Warren gave the corps of Hill a decided check at Bristow's Station, capturing cannon and prisoners. Oct. 14, marched fourteen miles to Centerville. Oct. 15, marched three miles and formed line of battle near the old Chantilly battle-field. Oct. 19, marched three miles to Gainesville. Oct. 20, marched twelve miles to near Warrenton. Oct. 22, marched three miles and went into camp on the same ground we left Sept. 15, where we remained until Nov. 7, when the regiment again advanced twelve miles to Rappahannock Station, where the enemy held a very strongly fortified position.

The Seventh was again detached from the Second Brigade, and sent forward in line of battle to strengthen the First Brigade. Here the regiment was exposed to a very severe shelling from the redoubts held by the enemy. Gen. Sedgwick, who had command of this wing of the army, had tried by a concentrated artillery fire to drive the rebels from their positions and force them across the river under his guns, but the works proved too strong for our artillery, and sent back a very severe reply of shot and shell.

As the day drew to a close, after a thorough reconnaissance, Gen. David A. Russell, who had command of the line of battle, reported to Gen. Sedgwick that it was feasible to carry the works by assault, and asked permission to do so, which was given by Gen. Sedgwick. Gen. Russell chose as his forces for the assault his own brigade and the Second of the first division, commanded by Gen. Horatio G. Wright, who was to gain a name in the future amongst the renowned chieftains of earth. The brigades composing the assaulting force were commanded by Colonels Ellsmaker and Upton. As the shades of evening drew on, these gallant men rushed forward to the assault with a stern and decisive step, and soon were up and over the rebel works, capturing some fifteen hundred prisoners and four cannon. The total Union loss was 371 in killed, wounded and missing. Gen. Russell led the charge in person, and was in a critical position for some time. The Seventh was detached to strengthen his line of reserves, by his own request to its division commander.

Nov. 8, crossed the Rappahannock, and occupied the works abandoned by the enemy. Eight companies of the regiment were sent to the front on picket, where they remained until the afternoon of the 9th, when the regiment re-joined its brigade at Kelley's Ford, distant five miles. Nov. 12, returned to Rappahannock Station, crossed the river on the enemy's pontoons, marched seven miles, and encamped one mile from Brandy Station, Va., where we remained in camp until Nov. 26, 1863.

In the operations beginning with the assault at Mayre's Heights and ending at Rappahannock Station, the regiment was under the command of that zealous and faithful officer, Franklin P. Harlow. Having received a short autobiographical sketch of his life, I insert it as a tribute to his fidelity to duty and as a rich treasury of reminiscence for his comrades in arms.

"Lieut.-Col. Franklin P. Harlow, commander of the Seventh Massachusetts Volunteers in many of its important battles and campaigns, was born in the town of Springfield, State of Vermont, Dec. 8, 1827. In early manhood moved to the State of Massachusetts, where he served ten years in the Massachusetts militia previous to the war of the rebellion. He resigned as captain of Company E, Fourth Regiment, Massachusetts Volunteer Militia. In 1859 he was commissioned captain of Company K. April 21, 1861, was ordered to Taunton and assigned to Company K, of the Seventh Massachusetts Volunteers, Col. Couch commander; was promoted Major Aug. 1 following; was promoted Lieutenant-Colonel Oct. 25, 1862, in which capacity he served until the muster-out of the regiment at Taunton, 1864. He bore a very honorable part in the Peninsula campaign, being the trusted and zealous helper of Col. Russell, who had perfect confidence in his military capacity and judgment. He had command of the detachment that crossed the Chickahominy May 20, 1862; was in the engagement of Fair Oaks, Golden's Farm, Malvern Hill, Antietam, Fredericksburg, first and second, leading the charge after Col. Johns had fallen at Mayre's Heights, Gettysburg, in the Rappahannock campaigns, including Rappahannock Station and Mine Run, in the Wilderness campaign, from the Rapidan to Cold Harbor, was detailed to command the Thirty-seventh Regiment of Massachusetts Volunteers after the battles at Spottsylvania Court House. After Edwards took command of Eustis' brigade, and Lieutenant-Col. Montague of the Thirty-seventh had been very severely wounded in that hard and desperate struggle at the "Angle," he rejoined his regiment at Cold Harbor. He returned home with the regiment, and was mustered out of service June 27, 1864. Col. Russell said of him, 'He is the best volunteer officer I ever met with, and one of the best tacticians in the army.'

"The civil record of his life is as follows: Member of the House of Representatives in 1871 and 1872. His ordinary occupation is superintendent of the finishing department of boots and shoes in one of our largest firms in the State of Massachusetts, which position requires great tact and address, and a thorough knowledge of men and mechanical means. While lying at Brandy Station, Va., the officers of the Seventh Regiment presented Col. Harlow with a magnificent sword and belt. An account of the presentation was published in the papers at home, furnished by others, as our worthy Colonel is a very modest man. I hereby insert the account as a very pleasant part of our history. It reads as follows:

A SURPRISE PRESENTATION.

On Saturday evening last, Lieut.-Col. Franklin P. Harlow, of the Seventh Massachusetts Regiment, was the happy recipient of a splendid sword, sash and belt, the gift being a slight testimonial of filial regard of the veteran officers of the regiment, all of whom were present at the surprise presentation. The late special orders of the army forbid the acceptance of donations of presents to superior officers, but in this instance the money was all subscribed before the order suppressing such testimonials was issued. Col. Harlow came out in the Seventh Massachusetts Regiment as a Captain, and after remaining in this position a few months he received the appointment of Major, and a short time since again rose to the rank of Lieutenant-Colonel. No officer in this army has a stronger hold upon the sympathies of both subordinates and privates, and, without any desire to flatter, few officers are more deserving of this honor and respect, if undoubted bravery, pure patriotism, calm judgment and Christian fortitude are traits worthy of appreciation. The past record of this soldier claims some such public acknowledgment as his comrades in arms have seen fit to bestow upon him. In a neat speech Lieut. Nichols of Company I presented the souvenirs to the astonished colonel, who was suddenly called to the hospital tent of the regiment, as he supposed, to see one of his men, but where he was amazed to find every one of his officers in secret conclave assembled. The surprise was too much for the gallant officer, who, with considerable emotion and great modesty, feelingly replied to the donors. After a pleasant interchange of thought and a few witty speeches, a sumptuous repast was served in Capt. Bancroft's quarters. The whole affair was an enjoyable one, and, although impromptu, it passed off to the entire satisfaction of all present. The following is the presentation speech of Lieutenant Nichols of Company I: "Col. Harlow.—The officers of the Seventh Regiment have bid me bring you these as an expression of the high estimation in which they hold your character. They bid me tell you that since you have been associated with them as an officer, your conduct has been such as to command their admiration and win their love, for many months we have been laboring for country and against rebellion. The same great cause has inspired us all; we have all shared in common the exposures, the fatigues, and the dangers of a soldier's life. We have stood side by side in the same line of battle; we have sat together around the same camp-fire. It is fitting we present you some testimonial of our respect for you as an officer, of our gratitude to you as a leader, and of our friendship for you as a man. Whatever reputation for efficiency or bravery our regiment has obtained, either here or at home, is largely due to your efforts and example. You have instructed us in camp, your fortitude has encouraged us amid hardship, and your heroism has inspired us upon the battle-field. Take, then, these tokens; and to you, and to your children after you, let them speak of the esteem and friendship in which you are held by the officers of the Seventh Regiment, Massachusetts Volunteers.

CAMP SEVENTH MASSACHUSETTS VOLUNTEERS,
NEAR BRANDY STATION, VA.,
DEC. 19, 1863."

But to return to the narrative of active operations. Nov. 26, Thanksgiving day, broke camp, and took up the line of march for the Rapidan. Nov. 28, marched eight miles to Robertson's Tavern, and bivouacked in line of battle. Nov. 29, joined Second Corps, marched eight miles, and formed in line to the extreme left and front of our line of battle. Nov. 30, advanced to the front, formed line of battle, and engaged in a very sharp skirmish with the enemy without serious casualty on our part. During the night changed position nearer the Plank Road leading to Fredericksburg. At 9 o'clock P. M., Dec. 1, fell back and marched all night, recrossing the Rapidan at Culpepper Mine Ford. Dec. 2, at seven o'clock, A. M., marched ten miles and bivouacked for the night. Dec. 3, marched four miles to Brandy Station, and pitched tents on same ground that we left Thanksgiving day. No movement was made up to Dec. 31, which closed the narrative for the year 1863, in the Adjutant General's report for the State of Massachusetts.

The campaign just closed was one of the most arduous the regiment had been engaged in for the year. The weather was terrible cold, and the men suffered greatly. Gen. Meade hoped by a swift movement to interpose between the different corps of the rebel army and whip them in detail, but the operations were so hampered by thick forests and poor roads, and by the mistakes of one of his corps commanders, that the rebel Gen. Lee had ample time to concentrate his army in the impregnable natural fortress of Mine Run, and when Meade had got his army into position to strike an effective blow, Lee was ready and even anxious for him to attack. After a thorough reconnaissance of the enemy's works by Warren on the left, he reported to Meade that he had found a vulnerable point in Lee's lines, but it was so near the close of day that it was impossible to attack with success, and it was deferred until morning. But when morning broke the rebel army had thoroughly covered their front with rifle-pits, and cannon was planted to cross-fire over all their front. Warren, under the circumstances, advised against attack, and when Meade had by personal observation examined the enemy's lines, he concurred in Gen. Warren's judgment. Sedgwick the meanwhile had prepared to attack, and was impatiently waiting for the sound of Warren's guns, when he received an order from Meade to defer the attack until he could confer with Warren, in whose judgment Meade concurred as already stated. During the Mine Run campaign the regiment was under the command of Col. Johns, he having recovered from his wounds received at Mayre's Heights the May previous.

In the Adjutant-General's report of 1863-64 is found the following:

The last annual report of the Seventh Regiment, Massachusetts Volunteers, brings the narrative up to Dec. 31, 1863, Camp Sedgwick, near Brandy Station, Va., between the Rappahannock and Rapidan rivers, where it remained performing the usual routine of camp and picket duty until Feb. 27, 1864, when a winter's march from Camp Sedgwick, Va., to assist in the operations of Gen. Kilpatrick in his attempt to enter Richmond and liberate the Union prisoners confined in the "hell-holes" of Libby Prison, and on Belle Island in the James river, was ordered by General Meade. The narrative, as found in the report, says: On that day we moved with the Sixth Corps to cover and support the cavalry movement under Brig.-Gen. Custer, in the direction of Madison and Charlottesville Court House. The regiment marched fifteen miles on that day, through Culpepper towards Madison Court House, and bivouacked for the night near Jamestown City, Va. On the 28th, marched to south bank of Rapidan river, and took position in line of battle, where we remained until the night of March 1, in the midst of a severe rain and snow storm. The cavalry having returned, we recrossed the river, and bivouacked one mile from the north bank, the snow still continuing. The object of the movement having been accomplished, March 2, marched twenty miles over the same line of march as we came, to our old camp near Brandy Station, and resumed camp duties. The winter was unusually severe for Virginia, and caused much suffering upon the picket lines.

Nothing unusual occurred until the night of May 3, 1864, when we received orders to break camp at 3 o'clock next morning, and hold ourselves in readiness to move. During the winter months we had very hard work to get sufficient fuel to keep warm, having to go as far as Hazel Run to the right of the army's lines. The regiment had constructed comfortable tents or houses, and the men kept very comfortable, considering the lack of fuel. The picket duty of the men had become very arduous on account of the small number of men reported present for duty in regiment, there being about 225 reported as fit for duty on muster-rolls. At this time several executions took place in New York and Pennsylvania regiments for desertion. We spent the time in camp playing checkers and drawing lots to see who should go and get the wood and water. We were reviewed several times by Generals Grant and Meade. When Generals Russell and Sedgwick rode along the lines of the Sixth Corps, the former spoke of the Seventh as his regiment, for Russell was always proud of his old command. The boys were as proud of him as he was of them. When the boys were out on the march towards Madison Court House,

Gen. Custer rode by at the head of the cavalry command, and was very warmly received by the infantry. He looked every inch the dashing cavalry man that he was, and the boys felt that he would give a good account of himself when the opportunity should occur. And no doubt my many readers will remember how gallantly he escorted the rebel Gen. Rosser out of the valley after Rosser had declared himself the saviour of the valley. No doubt he felt that his escort rather hurried him, but under the circumstances it was the best Custer could do for him; for the invincible Sheridan generally required of his subordinates quick fulfillment of his wishes.

Before the spring campaign opened, the old Army of the Potomac had undergone a thorough reorganization, though many military men think that the consolidation of the different corps impaired their morale and efficiency. The following is the roster as found in the reports in the Adjutant-General's office at Washington:

General commanding the armies, Lieut.-Gen. Ulysses S. Grant, headquarters with the Army of the Potomac, with Major-General Geo. G. Meade, commanding the army; Major-General A. A. Humphreys, Chief of Staff; Brigadier-General Henry J. Hunt, Chief of Artillery; Major James C. Duane, Chief Engineer.

Major-General Winfield S. Hancock, commanding the Second Corps, had under his command four Divisions, commanded by the following generals: First Division, Brigadier-General F. C. Barlow; Second Division, Brigadier-General John Gibbon; Third Division, "old Third Corps," Major-General D. B. Birney; Fourth Division, "old Third Corps," Brigadier-General G. Mott, commanding.

Major-General G. K. Warren, who had been promoted to the command of the old Fifth Corps after the Mine Run campaign, had under him the following very able leaders: First Division, Brigadier-General Charles Griffin; Second

FRANK BARKER,
Private Co. "A."

Division, Brigadier-General J. C. Robinson; Third Division, Brigadier-General S. W. Crawford; Fourth Division, Brigadier-General J. S. Wadsworth, commanding.

The Sixth Corps was under the command of the illustrious soldier and patriot, Major-General John Sedgwick, who had for his division commanders, Brigadier Horatio G. Wright, commanding First Division; Second Division was commanded by Brigadier-General G. W. Getty; Third Division by Brigadier James B. Ricketts.

The Cavalry Corps, composed of three Divisions, was commanded by the renowned Major-General Philip H. Sheridan, who added new lustre to the armies of the Union by his almost incomparable generalship.

The division commanded by General George W. Getty, and to which Eustis' Brigade was attached, having been transferred from the old Third Division, commanded by Major-General John Newton, who had left the Army of the Potomac to serve in the army under Sherman, consisted of four brigades, commanded by the following named officers: First Brigade, Gen. Frank Wheaton; Second Brigade, Col. Lewis A. Grant; Third Brigade, Brig.-Gen. Thomas H. Neil; Fourth Brigade, Brig.-Gen. Henry L. Eustis, formerly colonel of the Tenth Massachusetts, a very fine soldier, and a most excellent engineer.

The Fourth Brigade consisted of only four regiments, commanded by the following officers: The Seventh Massachusetts, Col. Thomas D. Johns; Tenth Massachusetts, Col. Joseph B. Parsons; Thirty-seventh Massachusetts, Col. Oliver Edwards; Second Rhode Island, Col. Horatio G. Rogers.

CHAPTER XXI.

ROSTER OF REGIMENT, MAY 3, 1864.—MOVEMENT ACROSS THE RAPIDAN.— BATTLE OF THE WILDERNESS.—MOVEMENTS AND BATTLES OF SPOTTSYLVANIA COURT HOUSE.

THE Seventh Massachusetts in the campaign of 1863 and up to the morning of May 3, 1864, had marched in direct marches seven hundred and five miles, besides the untold number of miles marched while on picket duty; and had lost in killed and wounded, and discharged from sickness and disabilities, two hundred and fifty men, so that the muster rolls, upon the morning of May 3, 1864, had but three hundred and eighteen men present for duty.

On the morning of May 3, 1864, the roster of the regiment was as follows:—Colonel, Thomas D. Johns; Lieutenant-Colonel, Franklin P. Harlow; Major, Joseph B. Leonard; Staff: Edward N. Dean, Adjutant; Daniel Edison, Jr., Quartermaster; Surgeon, William H. Lincoln.

Commanders of Companies were:—Co. A, Capt. C. C. Weston; Co. B, Capt. T. R. Mathewson; Co. C, Capt. William H. Gurney; Co. D, Capt. William M. Hale; Co. E, 1st. Lieut. Charles E. Cady; Co. F, Capt. Zeba F. Bliss; Co. G, Capt. Ward L. Foster; Co. H, Capt. John R. Whitcomb; Co. I, Capt. D. C. Bancroft; Co. K, 1st Lieut. Leonard Hathaway, Capt. Daniel Packard of the company being on staff duty with Major-Gen. Russell, formerly colonel of the Seventh Regiment. There were many first and second lieutenants whose records are worthy of all praise, and will be mentioned as the history progresses.

CHRISTOPHER C. WESTON,
Captain Co. "A."

The Seventh Massachusetts, under the great military leaders, Grant and Meade, was about to engage in one of the most bloody campaigns the world ever saw. General Grant, fresh from his fields of labor in the West, where he had gained victory after victory over his foes, where others had failed, came to the East well crowned with honors gained in his country's service. And while perhaps he underrated the great chieftain against whom he was pitted, and scarcely understood the heroic mould of the army he was called upon to command, yet, as he warmed up to his work, he grew to recognize the great power and fidelity to duty which permeated the grand old Army of the Potomac, upon whose shoulders rested the fate of free institutions. And while perhaps he did not show the consummate ability of Lee, he did show equal and greater moral training, and by his constant hammering broke the grand old Army of Northern Virginia to pieces, and plucked a piece from the brow of the greatest general of all rebeldom. Therefore all honor to Grant; many may laugh at his immobility to death, still the fact remains, he conquered the rebels and gained us peace and a nationality among the nations of the earth! He knew the worth of his volunteer soldiers and trusted them implicitly, and through this common-sense trait in his own character, and a mind of unparalleled tenacity, he drove the "cold steel" into the vitals of the rebellion and united the land of his fathers. General George Gordon Meade, his subordinate, was a most meretorious officer, bold and tenacious, conscientious and kind. With Christian fortitude he achieved for himself a name and fame among the illustrious names of the war. And Grant and Meade will go down in history one and indivisable, at the right and left hand of Mars, who overthrew the great slave-holders' rebellion from Constitutional authority.

Early on the morning of May 3, 1864, the orders were given to be ready to break camp at a moment's notice, or at 3 A. M. the next morning, and hold ourselves ready to move. Eight days' ration had been issued with sixty rounds of ball cartridge, and early the next morning the tents were stripped from our little log houses, never more to return to them, which awakened many thoughts of our far away northern homes, for the term of service of the Seventh Massachusetts was soon to end; and knowing that the coming grapple with the enemy must be fierce and deadly, it gave to many faces a sad and thoughtful cast.

But soon the order came to fall in, and we were launched upon the hardest and most bloody campaign the army had ever experienced.

General Lee occupied about the same position that he did the fall previous, his lines running to the Rapidan on his left, while his return rested upon Mine Run. His position was impregnable to a front attack, and so Generals Grant and Meade planned a flank movement by his right, hoping to cross the river in safety, and pass through the Wilderness, and seize the roads leading south towards Richmond. The first part of the plan was successful, but the last part failed in a very important particular. General Lee decidedly objected to having his right flank turned, and with desperate haste hurried his legions into the Wilderness to strike Grant's army a staggering blow in flank, before he could march his army through it.

On the morning of May 4, the Seventh Massachusetts broke camp, and with the rest of the brigade formed column of march, heading for the Rapidan, with the division of General Getty of the Sixth Corps. The day proved very warm, and as we made a rapid march, the road was encumbered with the paraphernalia of camp life which the troops preceding us had thrown away as they warmed up to their work. Blankets, extra caps and coats were soon dispensed with. The regiment marched fourteen miles and crossed the Rapidan a few minutes after 1 o'clock P. M., the brigade then advanced some four miles and bivouacked for the night. Meanwhile the Second Corps had crossed at Eley's Ford and encamped near Chancellorsville under the command of General Hancock.

The Fifth Corps had preceded the Sixth Corps in crossing the Rapidan, and, preceded by Wilson's cavalry division, had bivouacked at the intersection of the Germania Plank Road with the Orange Court House and Fredericksburg Turnpike. The head of the Sixth Corps was some four miles from Germania Ford, at which place the rear of the corps had encamped for the night. The orders given to the different corps commanders for May 5 contemplated moving the Second Corps under Hancock to Shady Grove Church, and then extend his right toward the Fifth Corps, under Major-General Warren, at Parker's Store. But ere this move could be carried out in its entirety, the rebels had appeared on the Orange Court House Pike in such force, that General Warren halted his corps and sent word to General Meade of the interruption of his line of march. Meade replied to Warren's aid, "Lee has left a division here to fool us while he prepares a position behind the Annas." But the force confronting Warren soon developed into a very strong force, and Warren formed line of battle and awaited orders.

Now let us turn to Lee, and see what he has been doing. In the meantime, while the Army of the Potomac has been crossing the Rapidan, in the movement past Lee's right flank, General Lee had correctly divined the intent of the Union commanders, and had informed his corps and division commanders when they assembled upon Clark's Mountain with him May 3, that he anticipated that Grant would move around his right flank, and gave orders to his corps commanders to hold themselves in readiness to march upon Grant's army and strike it a blow in flank before it cleared the Wilderness, that field of battle offering substantial advantages to the Confederates, as the Army of the Potomac could not use its immense park of artillery to any advantage in the wooded tangles of this dark and gruesome ground, and where the Southern knowledge of bushwhacking would more than counterbalance the preponderence of numbers of the Union army. It was a field well chosen, but it did not prove as decisive as Lee had hoped. The "clock of destiny" had begun to strike the death knell of the Confederacy, and Grant kept striking the clock until the death stroke had been delivered at Appomattox Court House, almost a year from the opening blow struck in the Wilderness.

May 5, the Second Division under General Getty of the Sixth Corps, marched to the left and took position upon the left of the Fifth Corps, but the demonstrations becoming so powerful upon the Orange Court House Road, the cavalry reporting under Colonel Hammond that the enemy had appeared in great force out beyond Parker's Store, and that he was slowly being driven back to the junction of the Brock and Turnpike Roads. General Hancock had received orders by 11 o'clock A. M., to hold his forces at Todd's Tavern, and be in readiness to move up the Brock Road to the help of General Getty, who, with the Second Division of the Sixth Corps, had been detached from that corps and had been hurried to the junction of the Brock Road and Orange Court House Pike, as soon as it was apparent that Hill's Corps was advancing in force upon the Pike. The division arrived at the junction shortly after 11 o'clock A. M. One brigade under General Neil had been detached from the division, and ordered to support Major-General Wright of the First Division, on the right of the Fifth Corps under Major-General Warren. The other three brigades, consisting of Wheaton's, Grant's and Eustis', formed line of battle across the Pike, and threw out skirmishers shortly after 1 o'clock P. M. The line was formed with the Second Brigade, General Grant's, on the left of the Plank Road, General Wheaton's, the First, and General Eustis', the Fourth Brigade, upon the right of the Pike, Wheaton's Brigade in the front line, and General Eustis' Brigade in two lines of battle in support, the Thirty-seventh Massachusetts on the right, and Tenth in front line, the Seventh Massachusetts and Second Rhode Island in second as support.

General Getty had, after arriving at his destination in the morning, advanced his skirmishers until he had met the enemy's, and had developed such force that he thought it prudent to desist from attack until a part of the Second Corps should arrive upon the ground, and while waiting, the men intrenched slightly in front of Wheaton's and Grant's Brigades.

General Hancock's troops did not arrive as promptly as expected, and the attack was not made until near 4 o'clock, and then it was too late to obtain a decisive victory. The Brock Road was very narrow, and Hancock had encumbered it with his artillery, and therefore he had a very severe march to get to the assistance of Getty. Some one must have thought very decidedly that Lee would retreat, or they never would have left the Orange Court House Pike guarded by only 500 cavalry, and have blocked the only road with artillery from which it was possible to reinforce the right wing of the army; and the army only escaped disaster from the non-arrival of Longstreet's Corps upon the 5th.

The narrative says, shortly after 4 o'clock the advance to attack was sounded, and the enemy was successfully engaged until dark, when we occupied the grounds from which the army had been driven, and slept on our arms for the night. This was one of the severest engagements the regiment had been engaged in.

Colonel Parsons, of the Tenth, in his narrative says, "The

lines were immediately formed, with the Tenth Mass. and Second Rhode Island in the front line, and on Wheaton's right, and the Seventh and Thirty-seventh Massachusetts composed the rear line ; and it would seem to me as if this was the correct formation. Other formations have been given, but I think this the correct one." Mark what follows : "I was now ordered by General Eustis, commanding brigade, to throw out skirmishers and cover his front, after which we were ordered forward to attack the enemy. The woods at this point, were so thick that we moved forward by the 'right of companies to the front' for about a half mile, when the skirmishers became engaged, and we promptly formed line, and soon became hotly engaged with the enemy. At this juncture the regiment on our right gave way, and we received a destructive fire on the right flank, in addition to the fire in front. Men fell like leaves in autumn, yet the regiment stood firm, never wavering till the ammunition being expended, was promptly relieved by Lieut.-Colonel Barlow and the Seventh Massachusetts. Would I could sound a note to his (Harlow's) praise, than whom none is more worthy."

The Tenth Massachusetts suffered a loss of 115, while the Seventh suffered a loss of 85 in kill and wounded, in this deadly embrace in the tangled woods on the Turnpike.

In the meantime Hancock had arrived, and with his aid, Hill's Corps was driven back more than a mile. The three companies of skirmishers thrown out to the right front of the brigade, had a very severe skirmish, and drove back the rebel skirmishers almost to the opening at Chewnings, where they attained a very strong position, and sent in word to the division commander who sent Owens' Brigade to their support, from which position he attacked the rebels, but was severely repulsed, losing some 200 men.

Meanwhile, on the right of the army, the battle had been carried on with fearful carnage. Assault after assault

ALFRED A. SEAVERNS,
Private Co. "E."

had been delivered upon the rebel lines, with no appreciable results, by Sedgwick and Warren. Meanwhile, Gen. Burnside had joined the army, and early in the day had been put into position to attack the rebel center, on the left of General Warren. He advanced to the attack but gained no advantage over the enemy. Towards 6 o'clock in the evening, Generals Gordon and Early organized an attack upon the right flank of the Sixth Corps, getting in on the right and capturing some six hundred men, with Generals Seymour and Shayler commanding brigades in the Third Division of the Sixth Corps. This division was annexed to the Sixth Corps after the reorganization of the army. It had joined the army after Gettysburg, and had not had the necessary pounding and experience to withstand the onslaught of Lee's veterans of so many fields of bloody battles. But subsequently they retrieved themselves nobly, it being a question of seasoning; General James B. Ricketts being one of the finest officers in the army. The First and Second Divisions were never broken, and were the nucleus around which clustered the glory of the old Sixth Corps, as do the stars in Orion's belt on a winter's night.

During the night, preparations were made to renew the battle promptly on the morrow; Hancock was reinforced by Wardsworth's Division of the Fifth Corps, and General Stevenson's of the Ninth. The next morning promptly at 5 o'clock, the attack commenced from the Union lines. May 6, General Hancock had under his command seven divisions, or about two thirds of the army. Soon after the advance was sounded, the enemy was met, consisting of Heath's and Wilcox's Divisions of Hill's Corps. After a fight of an hour or more they were broken and forced back in great confusion, almost amongst the cannon at Widow Tapp's and Chewning's, at which point General Lee had established his headquarters. But ere Hancock could secure the results of his brilliant fighting, Field and Kershaw of Longstreet's Corps were met, and under the inspiration of the leadership of Lee and Longstreet, they checked and then drove back the troops of Hancock on the left of the Pike, until they were nearly parallel with the Pike. It was in this retrograde movement that General Wadsworth, commanding a division of the Fifth Corps, was killed; he was a noble and conscientious man.

Before Hancock could re-form his lines the enemy had come upon him in such force, he felt compelled to withdraw and re-form on the Brock Road. The division in the front of Getty's broke early in the morning, which brought it into the forefront of battle again, and it yielded up a large quota of its soldiers in death and wounds, to help stay the oncoming tide of rebel success. The Seventh Massachusetts suffered a loss of thirty-five on this eventful day, while the Thirty-seventh was called upon to make one of those heroic sacrifices which the soldiers of the old Bay State were called upon to make so often, in that sea of blood from 1861 to 1865.

After the repulse in the morning, we were re-formed on the Brock and Germania Plank Roads, where we rested until Lee delivered his attack in the afternoon. When the company which had been out on the skirmish line returned to the regiment as they lay in line waiting the enemy's attack, they asked, "Where are the boys, colonel?" "Here is all there is left of us," he replied, with quivering lips. There were about one hundred and twenty-five men with the colors, and as we brought in about thirty men the loss was very apparent.

The rebels let us rest in peace until about 4 o'clock, when they delivered their famous charge upon Hancock's lines, and after a temporary success they were driven off with great loss. Shortly after 8 o'clock we took up our march for the right of the army, to rejoin our old corps, very glad to get home after being jammed to the extent of our ability, to help Hancock's Corps reap the laurels to which they lay strong claims.

The gallant division of Getty had lost over twenty-five hundred men in this bitter and desperate battle, and the gallant Getty was very severely wounded. The division was commanded by General Wheaton, and afterwards by General Thomas Neil, while General Getty was recovering from his wounds.

The Seventh Massachusetts lost in the ensanguine battle of the Wilderness, in killed, wounded and taken prisoners, one hundred and twenty-one men. The following is

THE ROLL OF HONOR.

COMPANY A.

Killed.—James H. Wordell.
Mortally wounded.—Corporal William Hill, Charles W. Terry.

COMPANY B.

Killed.—Richard H. Quinley, Edward P. West, William Warhust.
Mortally wounded.—None reported.

COMPANY C.

Killed.—Corporal John L. Hamilton, John Hart, George A. Warren.
Mortally wounded.—John Fox.

COMPANY D.

Killed.—None reported.
Mortally wounded.—Corporal Benjamin Williams, Corporal James B. Allen, George W. Boston, Thomas Davis, Jeremiah Durgan, James Goodwin, George T. Lee, Horatio Hudson, William Ricker, Joseph E. Sandford.

COMPANY E.

None reported.

COMPANY F.

Killed.—James McCormick.
Mortally wounded.—Sergeant Joseph Elliott.

COMPANY G.

Killed.—None reported.
Mortally wounded.—Jacob Roach, Daniel Donovan, Corporal James McCullough.

COMPANY H.

None reported.

COMPANY I.

Killed.—None reported.
Mortally wounded.—William H. Hill, First Sergeant John D. Peacock.

COMPANY K.

Killed.—None reported.
Wounded.—James C. Bates.

These are the heroes of the Wilderness, who fell in its tangled thickets, and of whose sepulchre no man knows to this day. They sleep where they fell, with thousands of others, only to awaken when the Lord shall come in the glory of His might, and when wars shall be no more, and all tears shall be wiped away, and peace, universal peace, shall reign supreme; when nations shall learn war no more forever, when the widow and orphan, the brother and son, the father and mother, shall be united never more to part, and all nations shall know of His righteousness and love.

On the morning of May 7, went into position upon the extreme right of the corps, and commenced throwing up rifle pits, to resist a threatened attack upon the right flank of the army. As we were making this move, the regiment passed General Sedgwick standing by a battery, looking with evident pride and pain at our decimated ranks. At 5 o'clock in the afternoon he thoroughly inspected his lines, in anticipation of an attack from the enemy, but no attack was made upon us, and shortly after dark we were moved out on the road towards Chancellorsville, and then marched on the road towards Spottsylvania Court House.

From the results of the battle just fought, the military student will conclude that Grant underrated the fighting powers of Lee's army, and with greater numbers he could have defeated Lee at the outset of the campaign. Therefore it must be said that he commenced his campaign after inadequate preparation. The same question could be asked of him as of McClellan at Antietam. Why did not Grant attack upon the Eighth? Simply because he could not drive Lee away from his flank, and the only thing for him to do was either to retreat or move by the flank. He wisely chose the latter, (perhaps more in deference to Halleck's, Stanton's, and the President's wish) for an overland campaign. If Butler had been with us, we would have had Spottsylvania Court House, and no doubt Lee would have suffered a disastrous defeat.

The regiment marched all night in the dark, making some ten or twelve miles. May 8, marched eight miles on the road to Spottsylvania Court House, where we met the enemy in force; the Fifth Corps had preceded us, and had met with a severe repulse at the hands of the rebels, but after some severe fighting they established their lines. Soon after noon the Sixth Corps began to come upon the ground, when General Sedgwick took command of the troops and began forming lines of attack with the Fifth and Sixth Corps. The Second Corps was still to the rear at Todd's Furnace, where the Brock Road and Shady Grove Road connect with the Catharpian Road. The rebels were meanwhile pushing forward with all their might to obtain the position around the court house and fortify the same, so as to block Grant's advance. There was an open field at Alsop's, which was favorable for deploying troops, and where artillery could be planted to command approaches to the Union lines, and which position had been seized by Warren in the morning. General Robinson of the Fifth Corps had been severely wounded in the morning's fight. The rebel lines were held by two divisions of General Anderson's Corps of the rebel army, he having been promoted to the command of Longstreet's Corps after his wounding in the Wilderness.

PHILANDER W. FECTO,
1st. Sergeant Co. "G."

CHAPTER XXII.

FROM SPOTTSYLVANIA COURT HOUSE TO COLD HARBOR.—DEATH OF GEN. SEDGWICK.—FIGHT OF THE "ANGLE."—MOVEMENT ACROSS THE ANNAS.—LETTER OF COL. JOHNS.

GENERAL SEDGWICK by 6 o'clock had formed his lines and was ready to assault the rebel lines. There was quite a severe artillery duel in the meantime, and shortly before 6.30 Brown's New Jersey brigade made an attack, but was repulsed with severe loss. General Crawford's division of the Fifth Corps had formed in the meantime with Eustis' brigade as a support in rear line. This charge was in a measure successful, but should have been made two hours earlier to have been of any great help in carrying the rebel position, as the most of the troops were withdrawn in the night to their original positions held before the charge.

The narrative says: Formed in line of battle with the Sixth Corps, and at dark charged on the enemy, who was in a strong position on elevated ground. Their line was broken, and the Seventh Massachusetts captured the color-standard, color-guard, and thirty-two men of a Georgia regiment, losing but two men killed, four wounded, and two taken prisoners. The latter were recaptured while on their way to Richmond, by Sheridan's cavalry, and subsequently returned to the regiment. It was in this charge that Sergeant William H. Hill of Company I, and Corporal William Hill of Company A, were mortally wounded, dying the same day. The next morning commenced throwing up rifle pits.

It was upon this day, May 9, 1864, that the army and Sixth Corps were called upon to yield up to this grand carnival of death, the immortal Sedgwick, who yielded up his life on this eventful day, a holocaust to his country's liberty. Noble, generous and brave, he ruled his troops by the quiet impressions that a great character of his ability always holds over his men. He never was given to the glitter and pageantry of war, but seemed to be endued with the good strong common-sense characteristic of Grant, using a soldier's fare and comforts when campaigning. The Sixth Corps lost in Sedgwick one who had gained their affections, by the tender care of his men in camp and on the march, and by his great skill in handling them in action. The news was brought to the regiment by Marcus Ames of Co. K, and a soldier from Co. E, who had gone for water to the right rear of the Corps. We could not believe it, the blow was paralyzing; and many a tear dropped on well-worn blouses and uniforms, as the sad news was pressed home to every heart, that Sedgwick was no more. This unfortunate fatality occurred at the angle of the lines which ran in the direction of Alsop's. General Sedgwick was on the outer lines, giving the directions for putting cannon into position to command the approaches to this part of the line. The sharpshooters had been busy all the morning, and wounded and killed several in the immediate vicinity. As he stood there in his calm serenity, Gen. Sedgwick said, "Pooh, man, they can't hit an elephant at that distance," when a sickening thud, and a sudden reel, and the soul of the gallant Sedgwick had left its frail tenement of clay for eternity, there to walk the streets of paradise with the congenial spirits of those who had gone before him. He fell into the arms of his faithful Adjutant-General, John McMahon. In his death the Sixth Corps lost a great commander; the country, a noble patriot; the army, a soldier and able general.

DEATH OF GEN. SEDGWICK.   185

As soon as Sedgwick's death was known at army headquarters, Major-General Horatio G. Wright, commander of the First Division, Sixth Corps, was appointed to the command of the corps; he was a very able general, and filled in a large measure the place left vacant by the death of Sedgwick, he being the general chosen by Sedgwick to succeed him if he should be killed or disabled. Major-General Russell took command of the First Division formerly commanded by General Wright.

On the 10th, threw up rifle pits and supported Brown's Rhode Island Battery, he opening a very heavy fire in aid of the assaults delivered upon the enemy's lines on the left of the division. General Thomas H. Neil was in command of the Second Division of the Sixth Corps, in the movements around Spottsylvania. May 11, was ordered to the front on skirmish line, where we remained two days on constant duty. In the meantime preparations for the grand assault on the morning of the 12th were being made. Hancock's Second Corps was withdrawn from the extreme right of the army, where it had operated across the river Po, in the attempt to seize Lee's wagon train, "but it was severely handled, and gained no advantages over the enemy to compensate for its loss of life," and was massed in rear of Landstren's house. Early in the gray morning of the 12th, the columns of attack were moved forward, and soon with a rush and cheer were over the rebel works, where they captured General Edward Johnston's division almost entire with some eighteen or twenty cannon, but after they had advanced about one quarter of a mile, they met with the severest opposition and were slowly pushed back to the lines from which they had advanced. But the Sixth Corps under Wright was at hand, and moving up to the west face of the "Angle," commenced a very heavy attack with Upton's and Eustis' brigades. The fighting was severe and bloody, there being a continuous battle of twenty hours' duration. General Eustis' brigade, now commanded by Colonel Edwards of the Thirty-seventh Massachusetts, General Eustis being detached temporarily to the command of the Fourth Brigade, First Division, suffered very severely in killed and wounded.

The Seventh Massachusetts had been left upon the picket line in front of the old line held by the brigade previous to the battle of the "Angle." The skirmishing was very severe all along the lines. We were holding a very important point of the line with a Pennsylvania regiment who were not under the best of discipline, for the larger portion of a company left the lines and gathered around a fire to make coffee, but were soon dispersed by rebel shell and the field officer of the day, Lieutenant-Colonel Franklin P. Harlow of the Seventh Massachusetts, who ordered them back to the skirmish line or be shot in their tracks, for leaving their posts in face of the enemy. The regiment fired some forty rounds on the skirmish line this day.

On the evening of May 13, rejoined the brigade and rested until 2 A. M. of the 14th, when we marched five miles and formed line of battle on the left of the Fifth Corps. These movements were made in the midst of rain, mud, and extreme darkness. The men were beginning to feel the strain of this constant fighting by day and marching by night. It was at this time that Lieutenant-Colonel Harlow was detached from the regiment and sent to command the Thirty-seventh, Lieutenant-Colonel Montague being wounded very severely at the "Angle." May 17, marched all night towards the "Angle," and went into position as support to the Second Corps in the second attack upon the "Angle;" charged with our division on the enemy's works, but we were met with a fearful fire of shell and shot, and the general commanding seeing the uselessness of further sacrifice, gave the order to fall back, which we did under a fearful fire of shot and shell.

MUNROE F. WILLIAMS,
1st. Lieutenant Co. "E."

After we had moved to the right rear, the rebels, still keeping up a severe shelling, dropped a shell into a cluster of officers who were chatting together as they thought under good cover. Colonel Johns, Lieutenant Hathaway of Company K, Adjutant Dean, and one or two others were in the bunch. They were soon under better cover, with only the adjutant slightly wounded. The casualties this day were six wounded. We rested in line of battle until dark, when we took up our march back to our old position on the left of the Fifth Corps, crossing the Ni River, threw out pickets and bivouacked for the night. At this time the weather was extremely sultry and depressing, and the army was much exhausted. We had gone in on the 18th, lost some twelve hundred men, had accomplished nothing, but expended a good deal of our strength, and had begun to think that this constant hammering was very severe work for the army, with no advantage gained to compensate for the terrible slaughter experienced in these useless and aimless attacks without adequate preparation.

Grant rested here some four days and received reinforcements from Washington, bringing up his army to very nearly seventy-five thousand effective infantry, when, seeing the futility of his efforts to break through Lee's lines around Spottsylvania Court House, he commenced his movement towards the North Anna River. He had lost some eighteen thousand men around the court house, which with fifteen thousand lost in the Wilderness, made the sum total of thirty-three thousand men killed and wounded in this series of desperate battles. Surely the overland campaign was bloody enough to suit most any strategist of Stanton's or Halleck's stature.

The following letter, printed in the Boston *Journal*, June, 1864, may be of interest to the readers of this history, and is copied entire, with corrections in the fatalities as time has shown the need of correction:

SEVENTH MASSACHUSETTS REGIMENT.

The term of service of this gallant regiment will expire on the 15th of June, when they will leave the army to be mustered out of service. They have lost one hundred and eighty men since they crossed the Rapidan, in killed and wounded, and also a few men taken prisoners. On the 7th of June, Col. Johns had a very narrow escape from death, a spherical case-shot exploding within a few feet of him and showering balls all around, but none of them striking him, although his horse was killed. In a previous engagement in the Wilderness, when the regiment was engaged with Hill's Corps upon the Orange Court House Pike in advance of the Brock Road, where the fighting was very close and deadly, Color-sergeant Hetherston was very severely wounded; Color-corporal Hill, who seized the colors, was mortally wounded; Color-corporal Thomas Sherman, who next took them, fell severely wounded as the regiment advanced; Sergeant Sweet, who next took them, was severely wounded, when Corporal Knowles, who succeeded the others, escaped their fate and carried the colors until the close of the action without serious casualty. The Seventh Massachusetts in the contest of May 8, at Spottsylvania Court House, in the charge just at night on that day, had a most spirited contest for the colors of the Sixth Georgia regiment, but only succeeded in capturing the color-standard, the color-sergeant of that regiment having previously stripped the colors from the staff and threw them away, and in the dusk of evening it was impossible to find them, but we succeeded in capturing the color-bearer and two of the color-guard. After the attack was over and the roll had been called, it was found that the Seventh had captured thirty-two officers and privates besides the color-guard, while the Georgians had captured only four of the Seventh's men, who were afterwards recaptured by Sheridan's cavalry while they were marching upon the road to Richmond, in his great cavalry raid around Lee's army, and have rejoined the regiment. It was in this charge that Corporal William W. Bouldry of Co. G, exhibited fine traits of valor, dashing ahead and calling on the boys to follow, capturing single-handed, a rebel lieutenant and private, the first prisoners taken, and pushed them to the rear at double-quick. This, too, after he had had a musket pointed at his heart and had been summoned to surrender.

JOHN HOWARTH,
Sergeant Co. "F."

There were many men who distinguished themselves in this charge: Lieut. Wade of Co. I, Bowen of Co. A, Giles of Co. K, Nye of Co. B, Capts. Wm. Hale and Bancroft, and Lieut. Fisher; and of the non-commissioned officers there were Sergeants Fecto and Wilbur of Co. G, Byron, Howarth and Aldrich of Co. F, John Cook, Sergeant, and Corporal Needham of Co. E, Hazeltine and Paine of Co. C, Davis and Cahoon, Sergeants, of Co. B; while McEwen, Key and Bennett of Co. A, Hall, Sweet, Snell and Bliss of Co. I, Sergeants, and Corporals Hayward and Pidge, with Calvin Porter, Sergeants Bain, Alden and Brown of Co. K, stood firmly by the old flag, and dared to die in its defence. But where all were heroes it is invidious to select.

The three hundred men who crossed the Rapidan under Grant were veterans of many fields of battle. They had stood within the sound of the cannon at Bull Run; they had slept in the trenches at Yorktown; they were the first to cross the Chickahominy, and previous to that had received their first baptism of fire at Williamsburg, under the gallant Couch and Russell; they were in the sanguinary battle of Fair Oaks and Golden's Farm; they had covered the withdrawal of the Fourth Corps to the banks of the James; they had stood with Hancock on the heights of Malvern; had slept upon the battle-field of Antietam, and had been with Burnside at Fredericksburg, where human blood flowed like water; they had been with Hooker in his disastrous campaign of Chancellorsville, where men had yielded up their lives like the leaves of autumn which fall from the trees; they had been at Gettysburg, Rappahannock Station, Mine Run, and in the Wilderness, under Grant and Meade. These were the veterans who followed the colors of the Seventh Massachusetts in the bloody campaigns of Grant and Meade. Is it necessary to say more, after men had had such experience and schooling in the arts of war?

May 21, started at 9 P. M., on the road all night, marching fifteen miles towards North Anna River. Early in the morning halted for breakfast and rested in column until near 2 o'clock P. M. The boys spent the time in sleep and in bathing in a tributary of the North Anna. This part of Virginia had thus far escaped the ravages of war, and was a peaceful valley, with fine plantations. In this movement General Hancock's Second Corps led the army and crossed the rivers Po and Mattapony, and was ordered to take position at Milford Station, on the right bank of the Mattapony. General Warren was directed to march on the 21st to Marrapona Church, crossing the Mattapony at Smith Mill, the Po at Stannard's Mill, and then move south by Mud Tavern and Thornburg. Burnside was to follow Warren and Wright, who were ordered to concentrate their corps in the vicinity of the Gayle House, but were withdrawn on the 21st, and followed Hancock's route.

General Lee, in the meantime, had learned of the movements, and moved his army immediately into position to check the advance of Meade and Grant upon the roads leading to Richmond. General Hampton's cavalry was on the road between the Mattapony and Telegraph Road. General Breckinridge was at Hanover Junction, where he had come to reinforce Lee's army, after defeating General Siegel in the valley.

On the 22d, passed Guiney's Station, Virginia. In the interim, the army had come up to the banks of the North Anna River, the Fifth Corps under Warren at Jericho Ford, and the Second Corps to Chesterfield Ford and bridge. The banks of the river were steep, and the engineers began laying the bridges and preparing the approaches as soon as they reached the river. General Warren was ordered to cross his corps at once, and to form line of battle to protect the bridges. Crawford was on the left, Griffin in the centre, and Cutler on the right. Before Warren's lines were fully formed he was attacked by the enemy, and a very severe engagement ensued. The head of the Sixth Corps had reached Mount Carmel Church when the attack upon the Fifth Corps was commenced, and they immediately moved to the support of the Fifth Corps. General Edwards' brigade of the Second Division leading the corps early on the morning of the 24th, crossed the river and advanced to the right of the Fifth Corps, and threw up rifle-pits. On the 25th, marched one mile, crossing the Virginia Central Railroad at Noel's Station, and were put out on the picket line. The men of the Seventh at this time were without food, except some very tough beef which had followed the army afar off. The men being out of hard-tack, coffee and salt, the army was now crawling upon its belly, as Napoleon says, our base of communication being moved to the Pamunky. On the 26th, the regiment was thrown to the extreme front, near Little River, where the enemy was in a formidable position.

To fully understand the obstacles the army was meeting, it will be necessary to give the position of the rebel army at this time. Its centre rested upon the North Anna, near Ox Ford, extending along the bank of the river south about one mile, while its wings were withdrawn so that it gave Lee's army the appearance of a huge wedge; and as General Meade could not break the centre of Lee's army, he had no alternative except to cross above and below his centre, which necessitated the crossing of the river some four miles apart twice in reinforcing either wing. The left wing of Lee's army crossed and covered the Virginia Central Railroad, near Lowry's, and extended towards the Little River, resting upon an extensive swamp, while his right wing crossed the railroad near Miller's, and the return covered Hanover Junction. This position of Lee was an exceedingly strong one, and offered but poor opportunities for a direct attack with any prospect of success. Grant, therefore, determined to withdraw his army and continue his movement to the south.

The narrative says: The Seventh Regiment, with others, covered the withdrawal of the Sixth Corps, re-crossing the Virginia Central Railroad and North Anna River, marching all night, and crossing the Fredericksburg and Richmond Railroad at Chesterfield Station; distance marched, eighteen miles. General Russell of the Sixth Corps had had the advance, and with the cavalry divisions had crossed the river under Sheridan. On the morning of the 27th, Sheridan reported that he held Hanover Town, and that the crossing was made without much opposition. The other two divisions of the Sixth Corps, under Neil and Ricketts, were following Russell's division very closely. On the 28th, marched five miles, crossing the Pamunky River, where we rested for the night. On the 29th, marched to Hanover Court House, four miles, and threw up rifle-pits. On the 31st, threw out pickets, and covered the withdrawal of our division from this position. June 1st, marched fifteen miles to Cold Harbor, which we reached at 2 P. M. The enemy was found in position. Sheridan on this day and the day before had a very severe action at Cold Harbor, but had been ordered by Meade to hold it at all hazards. He had dismounted his men, and had constructed rifle-pits, from which the rebels could not dislodge him. At night Sheridan held the ground, and to his assistance the Sixth Corps was marching with rapid strides to succor and sustain, before Lee could concentrate to crush him. After the Sixth Corps came upon the ground, General Wright immediately formed his corps into columns of attack.

But before we give a description of this battle, we will try to give a description of the movement of the army for two days previous to the battle of Cold Harbor. On May 28, the Sixth Corps had crossed the Pamunky, and was in position across the Hanover Court House or river road, at

Crump's Creek. The Second Corps took position immediately on our left. The Fifth Corps crossed the Pamunky and was posted on the road leading to Richmond, its left near the Totopotomoy, near Hawes' Shop. The Ninth Corps crossed about midnight, leaving General Wilson with a division of cavalry on the north bank covering the trains. Gen. Warren received and repulsed a very spirited attack in the morning and evening of this day. Gen. Hancock was ordered to attack early in the day, but found no opening. On the night of the 31st, General Wright was ordered to make a night march and relieve Sheridan at Cold Harbor.

But to fully understand the movement which culminated at Cold Harbor, we must take a glance at the Army of the James under Butler. When General Grant commenced operations in the Spring, he had concentrated about thirty thousand men at Fortress Monroe, to move up the James and secure a point as near Richmond as possible, and operate upon that stronghold from its southern approaches, a movement which has been very severely criticised.

The Army of the James consisted of the Tenth and Eighteenth Corps, commanded respectively by Major-Generals Quincy A. Gilmore and Wm. F. Smith (Baldy Smith), and its cavalry division by Brigadier-General A. V. Kautz.

The Tenth Corps was composed of three divisions, commanded by Brigadier-Generals Terry, Turner and Ames, and numbered seventeen thousand nine hundred and twenty-six men present for duty, with sixty-six cannon.

The Eighteenth Corps consisted of three divisions, commanded by Brigadier-Generals Brooks, Weitzel and Hinks, numbering fifteen thousand three hundred and thirty-seven men, making in all as the number of infantry, officers and men, under General Butler, thirty-three thousand two hundred and sixty-three, with eighty-two cannon.

The cavalry numbered ninety-seven officers and two thousand eight hundred and four enlisted men, with six cannon, and in addition thereto was a colored brigade under Colonel West, numbering one thousand eight hundred strong.

After a week or ten days of operations on the lines around Richmond, General Butler was forced back into his lines at Bermuda Hundreds, where he was safe from assault. He had followed the letter of his instructions, and therefore failed to seize Petersburg, the key to Richmond. The fault was with General Grant; but if General Butler's force had been at Fredericksburg, probably Lee never would have reached Richmond, as Grant would have grasped Spottsylvania with his force, and Lee would have been forced to retreat to the west of Richmond. After it was apparent General Butler could not be successful, and the Army of the Potomac had reached the lines around Richmond, General Grant directed Butler to send him all of his forces that he could spare and still retain his grasp on Bermuda Hundreds. General Butler immediately dispatched some sixteen thousand men, sixteen cannon, and a small squadron of cavalry, to the Army of the Potomac, the whole force being under command of Gen. W. F. Smith. His division commanders were Generals Brooks, Ames and Devens. The first commanded a division in the Eighteenth Corps, while Ames and Devens commanded divisions under Smith in his own corps, the Tenth. These reinforcements were more than welcome, after the great slaughter on the overland route to Richmond.

As the Second Division of the Sixth Corps was resting in line on the road leading to Old Cold Harbor, the division commanded by Gen. Devens of the Army of the James passed us as they filed into position on the right of the Sixth Corps. As Gen. Devens met his old companions-in-arms who had not seen him since the previous April, in 1863, the greeting he received must have warmed his heart, as cheer upon cheer rent the air as he passed the old brigade, which had been commanded by such men as Couch, Devens, Brown, Eustis and Edmunds. The boys were glad to see him, for General Devens always held a warm place in the affections of his men. This march through the night and the broiling sun of the day had been very exhausting, and the men were soon resting in all shapes beside the road in the shade of the trees. But soon the dogs of war were to open their mouths and reap their usual harvest of death on this bloody campaign.

Shortly after 2 o'clock, General Wright formed his corps in mass by brigade, the First Division under Gen. Russell moving on the left of the Richmond road, while the right of the corps under Ricketts moved upon the right. Getty's old division, Gen. Neill commanding, formed on Russell's left in single line as support. Gen. Smith in the meantime had formed on the right of the Sixth Corps, Gen. Devens' division connecting with the right of that corps, Brooks next, and Martendale on his right and rear front.

Promptly at 6 o'clock the lines advanced with a rush and cheer, and carried the rebel rifle-pits, capturing some six hundred prisoners and ten cannon. But then they were checked by the severe artillery fire from the rebel lines. Smith's corps kept pace on the right of the Sixth, capturing a number of prisoners and cannon. While this movement was being made, the left brigade of Russell's division was much endangered by a flank movement of the Confederates, when the Fourth Brigade, Second Division, under Edmunds, was moved on the double-quick to the extreme left of the line to protect that flank, under a very severe artillery fire.

A very ridiculous incident occurred on this movement while we were forming line of battle. The rebels pushed forward a battery of artillery, supported by a brigade of infantry. In front of our lines there was a Virginia snake-fence. The rear rank held every other man's gun in the front rank while they made a charge upon the fence as a basis for a rifle-pit. The rebels saw us coming and made a break for the cover of the woods, and gave us a very severe artillery fire. We threw up rifle-pits and rested for the night. The next morning, June 2, marched to the right of the corps, and went into position where General Ricketts had charged the night before.

In the meantime General Hancock had formed upon the left of the Sixth Corps, prolonging the line to the left with the cavalry until it rested upon the Chickahominy River. On the morning of the 3d received orders to attack at 4 o'clock A. M. Gen. Wheaton's brigade formed the first line, Gen. Edmunds of the 37th Regiment, commanding the Fourth Brigade, supporting him in rear line. This assault, like all others except that at the "Angle," failed with immense slaughter. It is said that President Lincoln was so depressed at this useless slaughter that he came very near ordering a cessation of hostilities, as he thought he could not face his Creator and continue the sacrifice of life.

The regimental narrative says: The Seventh was on constant duty by day and night, constantly exposed to the enemy's fire, and losing men daily, having been greatly reduced in numbers by the serious casualties of the campaign thus far. The duties of the regiment were unusually arduous, the necessities of the position requiring almost constant duty in the front line. The regiment lost at Cold Harbor, and on the march from Spottsylvania Court House, thirty-nine killed, wounded and taken prisoners.

On the night of the 12th the regiment moved out of the lines at Cold Harbor and marched towards the James River. On the 13th marched twenty-five miles, crossing the Chickahominy River, and encamped for the night.

I may here state, parenthetically, that Seth T. Dunbar, of Company G, was the last man killed in the regiment, being shot through the throat, and bleeding to death in ten minutes. We buried him where he fell. James F. Bradley, of Company K, was the last man wounded. June 14, marched four miles towards Charles City Court House, where we saw the waters of the James River.

B. FRANK GERRY,
Private Co. "A."

CHAPTER XXIII.

RELIEVED FROM DUTY AND ORDERED HOME. — LETTERS OF GENERALS NEILL, DEVENS AND DAVIS.—MUSTER-ROLL OF THOSE WHO DIED IN FIELD AND GENERAL HOSPITALS.— FORMAL MUSTER-OUT.

JUNE 15, 1864, bivouacked on the banks of the James River. The term of service of the Seventh Massachusetts having expired this day, it was relieved from duty and ordered to Massachusetts to be mustered out of service. It was not without many a heart-ache that it was called upon to turn from its path of glory, which it had followed with such honor to its country, state and county, and leave its many friends in the other regiments of the brigade.

During the battle of Cold Harbor the regiment had been under the command, for a part of the time, of Captain Zeba F. Bliss, who always proved himself capable of fulfilling all demands made upon him. He was a most excellent officer. Colonel Harlow returned to the regiment from the Thirty-seventh, which he had commanded since the battle of Spottsylvania Court House, May 13. Col. Johns had been to the rear sick, and Capt. Bliss had command of the regiment in his stead in the absence of Lieut.-Colonel Harlow and the Major, Joseph B. Leonard. The regiment slept sweetly and peacefully on the banks of the James, the first time for thirty days, for they had marched and fought constantly during that time, and no part of the lines or army had been exempt from being under fire for that number of days.

In special orders from division and brigade commanders, the regiment was thanked for the gallant and efficient service they had performed. On the morning of the 16th embarked upon the steamer *Keyport*, and left Wilson's Landing, Virginia, on the James River, for Washington, D. C. Arrived in Washington about 11 o'clock on the 17th, and at 6 P. M. took a special train for New York. At Philadelphia we met with a flattering reception and hospitable entertainment by the citizens at the Soldiers' Home. At New York we were comfortably quartered at the Park barracks, and on the evening of the 19th took a special train on the New Haven Railroad for Taunton, Massachusetts. Arrived in Taunton about 5 o'clock A. M. on the 20th, unexpectedly, but as soon as the citizens knew of our presence they turned out en masse, and after a most cordial reception by the mayor, who had wished us God-speed three long years before, they provided us a most bountiful collation upon the Green. After the men had partaken of the repast furnished by the citizens, they were furloughed until the 4th of July, when they paraded and assisted the citizens of Taunton in the celebration of the anniversary of our National Independence.

Having received several letters paying tribute to the gallant and meritorious services of the regiment, I take great pleasure in inserting them as a part of our history:

LETTER TO HON. JOHN D. LONG.

ADJUTANT GENERAL'S OFFICE.
WASHINGTON, July 29, 1886.

HON. JOHN D. LONG, *House of Representatives, Washington, D. C.*

Sir.—Acknowledging the receipt, by reference from the War Department, of your letter of the 23d instant, requesting copies of an order of commendation and some final orders relating to the Seventh Massachusetts Volunteers, when the regiment left the army, I have the honor to invite your attention to orders from Headquarters Second Division, Sixth Corps, dated June 14, 1864, a copy of which is enclosed herewith.

I am sir, very respectfully,
Your obedient servant.
R. E. DRUM, *Adjutant-General*.

In pursuance to a request of mine to Governor Long, he very kindly forwarded to me the following order, obtained from the War Department, and the author would here personally extend to Governor Long the very respectful thanks of the historian of the committee for the promptness with which he responded to the call upon his very valuable time and patience, while in the House of Representatives at Washington, in procuring official dates for the completion of the Seventh's history:

[COPY.]

HEADQUARTERS SECOND DIVISION, SIXTH CORPS.
June 14th, 1864.

ORDERS.

The term of service of the Seventh Massachusetts Regiment having expired, the General commanding the Division desires to express his satisfaction with their conduct during the time they have been under his command. Of the previous history of the Regiment it is not needful that he should speak. He knows that the Seventh Massachusetts has always borne itself with great honor, and he feels that its name and that of its gallant leaders are too well known to require any praise from him.

But he desires more especially to thank them for what they have done while under his command; above all for their courage and steadiness in the battles of Spottsylvania, where through the whole day of May 12 they, in conjunction with Brown's Rhode Island battery, on skirmish line at the right of the "Angle," and in conjunction with the rest of the Fourth Brigade, bore the brunt of the conflict and repulsed the repeated attacks of the enemy.

In taking leave of the Seventh Massachusetts, the General commanding congratulates them on the credit with which they have carried their colors through the many and bloody actions they have been engaged in, and hopes that the remembrance of their deeds may excite their remaining comrades to maintain the honor of their old brigade.

Signed, T. H. NEILL,
Brigadier-General commanding Division.

Official: J. C. KELTON, *Assistant Adjutant-General.*

A. G. *Office, July* 29, 1886.

LETTER OF GEN. DEVENS.

BOSTON, MASS., June 27, 1887.

Dear Sir and Comrade.—I am very glad you will undertake to write the history of the Seventh Massachusetts Regiment, which is certainly one of the most gallant regiments which Massachusetts sent forth to battle. It was in the First Brigade, which I had the honor to command, and to which I was assigned when we were before Yorktown in April, 1862. I was with it in all the engagements of the Peninsula, except during the "seven days" battles, when I had been disabled on account of wounds received at Fair Oaks, and was absent from the brigade about six weeks. I rejoined it during the stay at Harrison's Landing, and participated with the brigade at Antietam, Fredericksburg, and in all its other battles until April, 1863, when I was assigned to a division elsewhere.

I cheerfully render my tribute of respect and regard to the Seventh Massachusetts. Often and often I have seen it under fire and in action, and have never seen it where it failed. Its men were of our best New England stock, and its officers were worthy of its name. They were patient and uncomplaining under hardships, they were obedient to the sternest duty, they were brave and devoted in battle, and they were loyal to the great cause of country. I revere the memory of their gallant dead who are gone before us, and I respect and honor the living who remain.

While I was commander of the brigade, Col. David A. Russell was the colonel of the Seventh. He was the model of a soldier, simple in manners, careful in discipline, wise and resolute in action. He died nobly a soldier's death, but his name will never be forgotten by the soldiers of the Seventh Massachusetts.

I wish it had been in my power to have commanded the brigade in which the gallant Seventh served better than I did, but the respect and kindness I have received from its soldiers since the war was over, and the brave and unyielding support I had from them while it endured, will never be forgotten.

Wishing you success in your enterprise, I remain always,

Your old friend and comrade,

CHARLES DEVENS.

Comrade N. V. HUTCHINSON.

LETTER OF BRIG.-GEN. DAVIS.

NEW YORK, May 6, 1887.

Corp. N. V. HUTCHINSON, *North Abington, Mass.*

My Dear Sir,—I have just returned from a five months' absence. Your favor of the 3d instant is at hand. You justly pay tribute to the gallant services of the old Seventh Massachusetts Volunteers in storming successfully, May 3, 1863, Mayre's Heights in Virginia. I have reason to be proud of the faithful, efficient, gallant and patriotic services of said regiment, not only on that day, but throughout the late civil war; first, because it came from my native state, and secondly, because once I had the honor to command it.

Its war record is a rich legacy to leave to the posterity of its members. I join with you all in commemorating the events of your campaigns, and in shedding the silent tear in the privacy of our own souls for the many brave comrades-in-arms who fell upon the bloody battle-fields of Virginia, whose only requiem is the sighing of winds and the song of birds.

Health, prosperity, and a long life, with my cordial good wishes to you all, to whom I send greeting.

Yours very truly,

NELSON H. DAVIS,

Brigadier-General U. S. A., (*Retired.*)

ROSTER OF THOSE WHO DIED IN FIELD AND GENERAL HOSPITALS.

By Companies.

COMPANY A.—Lawrence Harding, Major Monks, Daniel H. Peckham, Thomas A. Reed, Lincoln Ryerson.

COMPANY B.—Hiram S. Beers, Bartley Galligan, Thomas A. Wallace, Stephen Hays, John G. Wright.

COMPANY C.—George L. Dunham, Sergeant; Michael Carey, James Scanlon.

COMPANY D.—Henry Beach, Corporal; Charles Burt, Orville S. Chase, William Craig, James T. Dean, John Dewsnap, Benjamin Farrell, James L. Gay, Royal Hathaway, James Henry, Andrew Leonard, James Mitchell, Charles A. Payton, Henry B. Smith.

COMPANY E.—Samuel Ewell, William O. V. Rockwood, George Bent, John O. Hill, accidently shot Sept. 28, 1862, Sylvester Wheeler, John Scott, Andrew Fais.

COMPANY F.—Webster Wordell, Corporal; John Buckley, Charles H. Corbett, Leonard A. Francis, Edward W. Hall, Luther Smith, Philo B. Wilbur, William J. Whitcomb.

COMPANY G.—James A. Humphreys, Jason F. Eldridge, Samuel H. Gilmore, Edward Hudson, Otis D. LeBarron, Henry Woodward.

COMPANY H.—William A. M. Cobb, Charles A. Morse.

COMPANY I.—Abraham B. Savery, 1st Sergeant; Baylies B. Richards, Sergeant; Henry P. Davenport, William Remlinger, Artemus W. Stanley, George H. Willis.

COMPANY K.—Benjamin F. Hutchinson, Corporal; Frederick Cook, Augustus F. Ehns, George F. Graves, James G. Harvey.

These are the larger part of the men who died in field and general hospitals. There were some of the wounded who died from their wounds after the regiment was mustered out, but this is as correct as can be given after twenty-seven years have elapsed since first the regiment was mustered into service.

I have prepared this roster that the friends of those who died in hospitals can see they are remembered as well as those who suffered fatalities upon the battle-field, and are held in the same just and sacred remembrance as those who died upon the fields of battle. The whole number who died in field and general hospitals was sixty-one.

July 5 the regiment was formally mustered out of service to return to the pursuits of civil life, the same honest, earnest citizens of the Commonwealth as when they started three long years before from its honored precincts to put down armed rebellion, and with the great armies of the North returned to the ordinary pursuits of citizenship, with their morality and Christian character unimpaired.

Comrades and friends, the work is completed, and although very imperfect, it has cost abundant labor in time and money. Many obstacles have arisen to make it thus imperfect. More than a quarter of a century has elapsed, and the muster-roll of our dead is far greater than that of the living, and in their breasts are locked many incidents which only the resurrection to life can renew. Therefore judge leniently of its imperfections.

The flag of the Seventh rests in Doric Hall, State House, Boston, Massachusetts,—the emblem of liberty, and which its men followed through heat and rain, sickness and pain, wounds and death! Its sacred folds are dear to their hearts, and may its honor never be sullied by the generations to come.

ROSTER OF THE ARMY OF THE POTOMAC WHILE UNDER THE COMMAND OF MAJOR-GENERAL GEORGE B. McCLELLAN.

After the defeat of Brigadier-General Irwin McDowell, at Bull Run, the Army of the Potomac was organized into divisions, commanded respectively by Franklin, McCall and King, Sumner, Richardson, Blenker, Sedgwick, Heintzelman, F. J. Porter, Hooker, Hamilton, Keys, Smith and Casey, Banks, Williams and Shields.

ARMY CORPS.

On the 8th of March, 1862, President Lincoln ordered the formation of Army Corps. The following is his order as issued.

EXECUTIVE MANSION,
WASHINGTON, D. C., March 8th, 1862.

General War Order No. 2.

Ordered, 1st. That the Major-General commanding the Army of the Potomac proceed forthwith to organize that part of said Army destined to enter upon active operations (including the reserve, but excluding the troops to be left in the fortifications about Washington,) into four Army Corps to be commanded according to seniority of rank as follows:

First Corps to consist of four divisions, and to be commanded by Maj.-Gen. I McDowell. Second Corps to consist of three divisions and to be commanded by Brig.-Gen. E. V. Sumner. Third Corps to consist of three divisions and to be commanded by Brig.-Gen. S. P. Heintzelman. Fourth Corps to consist of three divisions and to be commanded by Brig. E. D. Keys.

2d. That the divisions now commanded by the officers above assigned to commands of army corps shall be embraced in and form a part of their respective corps.

3d. The forces left for the defence of Washington will be placed in command of Brig.-Gen. James Wadsworth, who shall be military governor of the District of Columbia.

4th. That this order shall be executed with such promptness and dispatch as not to delay the commencement of the operations already directed to be undertaken by the Army of the Potomac.

5th. A Fifth Army Corps, to be commanded by Maj.-Gen. Banks, will be formed from his own and General Shields', late General Landers,' division.

ABRAHAM LINCOLN.

In compliance with the order of the President, General McClellan issued the following order:

ARMY CORPS.

HEADQUARTERS ARMY OF THE POTOMAC,
FAIRFAX COURT HOUSE, VA., March 13th, 1862.

General Order No. 101:

In compliance with the President's War Order No. 2, of March 8th, 1862, the active portion of the Army of the Potomac is formed into Army Corps as follows: First Corps, Maj.-Gen. Irwin McDowell, to consist for the present of the divisions of Franklin, McCall and King. Second Corps, Brig.-Gen. Sumner, divisions, Richardson, Blenker and Sedgwick. Third Corps, Brig.-Gen. S. P. Heintzelman, divisions, F. J. Porter, Hooker and Hamilton. Fourth Corps, Brig.-Gen. E. D. Keys, divisions, Couch, Smith and Casey. Fifth Corps, Maj. N. P. Banks, divisions, Williams and Shields. The cavalry regiments attached to divisions will for the present remain so. Subsequent orders will prevail for the regiments as well as for the reserve artillery, regular artillery and regular cavalry. Arrangements will be made to unite the divisions of each army corps as promptly as possible. The commanders of divisions will at once report in person, or where that is impossible, by letter, to the commander of their corps.

By command of MAJOR GENERAL MCCLELLAN.

A. V. COLBURN, *Asst. Adj't. Gen'l.*

The infantry troops sent to the Peninsula under the command of Gen. McClellan consisted of the Second Corps under General Sumner; Third Corps, Heintzelman; Fourth Corps, E. D. Keys.

The Second Corps had as division commanders, Richardson and Sedgwick, consisting of the following brigades: Richardson's Division—First Brigade, Howard's; Second Brigade, Meagher's Irish Brigade; Third Brigade, French's. Sedgwick's Division—First, Gorman's Brigade; Second, Burns'; Third, Dana's. Blenker's Division detached and assigned to the Mountain Department.

The Third Corps, General Heintzelman, consisted of Porter's Division of three brigades—First Brigade, Martendale's; Second, Monell's; Third, Butterfield's. The Second Division, commanded by Hooker, consisted of the following brigades: First Brigade, Sickles'; Second, Nagle's; Third, Col. Starr's. The Third Division consisted of the First Brigade, Jameson's; Second, Birney's; Third, brigade officer unknown.

The Fourth Corps, infantry, General E. D. Keys commanding, consisted of First Division, Maj.-Gen. D. N. Couch, commanding—First Brigade, Graham's, consisted of the following regiments: 67th New York Vols., (1st L. I.), 65th New York Vols. (1st U. S. Chass.), 23d Penn. Vols., 31st Penn. Vols., 61st Penn. Vols. Gen. Peck's Brigade consisted of the 98th Penn. Vols., 102d Penn. Vols., 93d Penn. Vols., 62d New York Vols., 55th New York Vols. Gen. Devens' Brigade consisted of the following regiments: Couch's Old Brigade; Third Brigade: Second Rhode Island Volunteers, Col. Frank Wheaton; 7th Massachusetts Volunteers, Col. David A. Russell; 10th Massachusetts, Col. Henry L. Briggs; 36th New York, Col. Welch.

There was also sent to McClellan on the Peninsula, Franklin's Division of the First Corps, consisting of Kearney's Brigade, Stevens', Newton's; also McCall's Division of the same, consisting of Reynolds', Meade's and Ord's.

After the defeat of General Pope at Bull Run and the reorganization of the army under McClellan, it consisted of the First Corps, Second, Third, Fifth, Sixth, Ninth and Twelfth, commanded as follows: First Corps by Maj.-Gen. Joseph Hooker; Second Corps by Maj.-Gen. E. V. Sumner; Third Corps by Brig.-Gen. Jesse L. Reno; Sixth Corps by Maj.-Gen. William B. Franklin; Fifth Corps by Maj.-Gen. Fitz John Porter; Ninth Corps by Maj.-Gen. Ambrose E. Burnside; Twelfth Corps by Maj.-Gen. Williams. The division of Couch was shortly incorporated in the Sixth Corps commanded by Maj.-Gen. Franklin.

After the battle of Antietam the army was further reorganized by the appointment of General Couch to command the Second Corps, Gen. Sumner having to retire from the effects of age and sickness. After the removal of General McClellan, General Burnside who was appointed in his stead as commander of the army, reorganized his army and formed it into three Grand Divisions as follows: First Grand Division commanded by Gen. E. V. Sumner; Second Grand Division by Maj.-Gen. Joseph Hooker; Third Grand Division by Gen. William B. Franklin. The Corps were, First Grand Division, Second and Ninth, Wilcox's, Hooker's, The Old Fifth and Third: the Left Grand Division, The Sixth Corps and First; commanded as follows: The First, Maj.-Gen. John Reynolds; The Second, Maj.-Gen. Darius N. Couch; Third Corps, Maj.-Gen. Butterfield; Fifth Corps, Maj.-Gen. Stoneman; The Sixth, Maj.-Gen. William B. Smith; The Ninth, Maj.-Gen. Cadmus Wilcox. The Sixth Corps at the first battle of Fredericksburg, under General Burnside, consisted of the divisions of Brooks, Newton and Howe.

Newton's Division consisted of the brigades of Cochrane, Devens and Rowley. After the defeat of Burnside, and

Gen. Hooker had reorganized the army, it consisted of the First Corps, Third, Fifth, Sixth, Eleventh and Twelfth, commanded as follows: First Corps, Maj.-Gen. John Reynolds; Second, Gen. D. N. Couch; Third, Maj.-Gen. Daniel Sickles; Fifth, Maj.-Gen. George Gordon Meade; Sixth, the lamented Sedgwick had command; Eleventh, Maj.-Gen. O. O. Howard; Twelfth, Maj.-Gen. Williams.

There was no material change in the commands of the corps and divisions until after the battle of Gettysburg, when Meade reorganized the army, and Gen. Sickles retired from the command of the Third Corps, on account of wounds, and Gen. French took command. Gen. Couch had in the meantime resigned his command of the Second Corps, feeling that the men would be cruelly slaughtered under the command of Gen. Hooker, and Gen. Winfield Scott Hancock took command of the old Second Corps. Maj.-Gen. Newton retired from the command of the Sixth Corps, and took command of the First Corps, and General Terry took command of Couch's old division.

After Gettysburg the Second Corps was commanded by Maj.-Gen Warren, the Sixth by Sedgwick, the First by Newton, the Twelfth by Slocum, and so remained with few changes until the army passed under General Grant's command, when the roster of the army was changed as follows: The First Corps was broken up, as also was the old Third, and the different regiments were merged in the Second, Fifth and Sixth Corps, commanded respectively by Maj.-Gen. W. S. Hancock, Maj.-Gen. Goveneur K. Warren and Maj.-Gen. John Sedgwick. The cavalry was commanded by the renowned Maj.-Gen. Philip Sheridan.

The Sixth Corps had as division commanders: First Division, Major-General H. G. Wright; Second Division, Brigadier-General George W. Getty; Third Division, Brigadier-General James B. Ricketts, formerly commanded by Smith.

The changes of the Sixth Corps were :—The wounding of Getty in the Wilderness and the appointment of Wheaton to command; the wounding of Wheaton and the appointment of General Thomas Neill to command; the killing of Sedgwick, May 9th, and appointment of General Wright to command of corps; the transfer of General Eustis to command of Fourth Brigade, First Division; appointment of Colonel Edwards of the Thirty-seventh Massachusetts to command of brigade; the wounding of Lieut.-Col. Montague of the Thirty-seventh and transfer of Lieut.-Col. F. P. Harlow of the Seventh to command the same, until his term of service had expired and Col. Montague had returned to command the Thirty-seventh.

Which ends the term of service of the Seventh Massachusetts in the war of the Rebellion, and for reference to further work of the old Division you are referred to Sheridan's Valley Campaigns and Humphrey's Campaigns of the Army of the Potomac in the years 1864-5.

CHAPTER XXIV.

INCIDENTS OF FIELD AND GENERAL HOSPITALS. — VISIT OF PRESIDENT LINCOLN TO COLUMBIA COLLEGE HOSPITAL. — SIGHTS AT THE REAR OF LINE OF BATTLE.

AS soon as the Seventh Massachusetts Regiment had established camp at Kalorama, Surgeon Holman, and his assistant, Z. Boylston Adams, had their tents erected, and, as the climatic change began to operate upon the boys, the castor-oil began to run, and some of it went down many of the poor soldiers' throats, with added paregoric or sulphuric ether, which quenched the ardor of many a hospital visitant as its diffusive influences were felt in the soldiers' system.

There were no very severe cases of fever or other diseases in this camp, as it was situated upon a very convenient ridge of hills. The surgeon of the regiment, S. Atherton Holman, and his assistant, Z. Boylston Adams, with C. H. Eldridge, hospital steward, and his assistant, J. Gallagher, made a very efficient corps with which to entrust the sick and wounded. After the regiment removed to Camp Brightwood, on 7th street, and as the fall of the year came on, and the men were exposed to the effects of the chilly nights, standing guard around the camp and on picket duty on the Rock Creek road, leading to Tennellytown, the roll of the sick increased. Typhoid fever became very prevalent, from which disease Major Monks and Michael Cary, of Co. A, died; also, Samuel Elwell of Co. E, and Augustus Elms and James G. Harvey of Co. K. These were the first to succumb to that fatal and dreaded disease.

ALBERT S. PALMER,
Sergeant Co. "A."

General McClellan, in his report furnished the War Department, says: "For the operations of the medical department, I refer to the reports transmitted herewith of Surgeon Chas. S. Tripler and Surgeon Jonathan Letterman, who in turn performed the duties of medical director of the Army of the Potomac,—the former from August 12, 1861, until July 1, 1862, and the latter after that date. The difficulties to be overcome in organizing and making effectual the medical department were very great, arising principally from the inexperience of the regimental medical officers, many of whom were physicians taken suddenly from civil life, who according to Surgeon Tripler, 'had to be instructed in their duties from the very alphabet,' and from the ignorance of the line officers as to their relations with the medical officers, which gave rise to confusion and conflict of authority. Boards of examination were instituted, by which many incompetent officers were removed, and by the successive exertions of Surgeons Tripler and Letterman, the medical corps was brought to a very high degree of efficiency. With regard to the sanitary condition of the army while on the Potomac, Dr. Tripler says that the records show a constantly increasing immunity from disease. In October and November, 1861, with an army averaging one hundred and thirty thousand men, we had seven thousand nine hundred and thirty-two cases of fever of all sorts: of these, one thousand were reported as cases of typhoid fever. I know that errors of diagnosis were frequently made, therefore this must be considered as the limit of typhoid cases. If any army in the world can show such a record as this I do not know when or where it assembled. From September, 1861, to February, 1862, while the army was increasing in numbers, the sick decreased from 7 per cent. to 6.18 per cent. Of these, the men sick in the regimental and general hospitals numbered less than one-half. The remainder were slight cases under treatment at 'quarters.'" During this time, so far as rumor was concerned, the army was being decimated every month by many and various diseases.

The health of the Seventh Regiment remained in very good condition until the measles were introduced into the camp by some bummer from Washington. No doubt the arduous work of building the houses in which the regiment lived through the winter, with the very severe winter and early spring weather, prepared the systems of the men for the contagion to root and take hold of in the severest manner. There were in all sixty cases, of severe and slight attacks. Lieutenant Charles Hathaway of Co. F was quite sick, while Lieutenant Lothrop of Co. G had a more severe attack. A regimental hospital was established on 14th street, in a commodious brick building, to which place the infected were speedily ordered. The epidemic broke out in the middle of February, soon after the order of Abraham Lincoln that the armies of the Union should advance and attack the enemy. It did not discompose the enemy much, but those who were suffering from the measles were many of them fatally injured by their removal from the field hospitals to the general hospitals in Washington, by exposure to the inclemency of the weather, and by which exposure many of the cases were turned into the severest type of typhoid measles.

When the Seventh Massachusetts moved forward on the Manassas Gap raid, under General McClellan, it had twenty-five men in various stages of the disease. They were removed to Armory Square and Columbia College Hospital on Meridian Hill, Washington, D.C., and of the twenty-five, ten of them died in these hospitals from exposure in the transportation. Those who died were: In Company D, James Henry, James T. Dean, Henry Beach; Company E, William O. V. Rockwood, George Bent, Sylvester Wheeler, John Scoff, Andrew Fais; Company F, Philo B. Wilbur, William J. Whitcomb.

The weather was cold and stormy, raining and freezing into sleet. Some died in three or four days after the arrival at the hospitals. We arrived at the College at about 11 o'clock A. M., and were assigned rooms in the west wing of the building, in Mrs. Pomeroy's ward, who also had general supervision of nurses in the hospital. At that time, March 2, 1861, she was in the full power of strong and well developed womanhood. Calm and sagacious, she moved around among the suffering men with a quiet dignity we will never forget, and many were the silent benedictions craved for her well-being by the soldiers who felt her gentle touch and soothing presence. What Mother Bickerdilke was to the West, Mrs. Pomeroy and others were to the Army of the East.

The College hospitals and others were under the supervision of Dr. Abedee, and his assistants were Drs. Hervy and Dubois. While in this hospital the President made us a visit, accompanied by Lord Lyons, Secretary Seward, Chase, Stanton, and one or two others whose names I do not bring to mind at present. Previous to this visit, the crew of the *Congress*, one of our naval vessels, had reported and rendezvoused at the College. Shortly after 1 o'clock, May 15, 1861, Abraham Lincoln and his escort came to the hospital. After he had rested he came to the upper wards first. Those who could stand did so, while others who were too weak sat upon the edge of the army bedstead of substantial iron frame. As that tall, homely form came into the room, every man gave him a respectful salute. With a firm step and eager countenance he grasped the hand of every soldier in the room, with a kindly word for all, and a "How are you getting along?" He came and went a nature's nobleman. That rugged, honest countenance had only to be seen once, and that giant intellect always left its impress, never to fade so long as the mind can retain its action. Of all the cortege, only Lincoln's face comes up distinctly and plain after twenty-eight years have passed away. After he had visited every ward and soldier in the hospital, he went to see and shake hands with the crew of the sunken fleet at Fortress Monroe. Among them were several men whose skin was of sable hue, but Lincoln treated all alike. God bless his noble memory,—a spectacle to the world and a warning to the effete monarchies of the old world, that in a true republic all men are equal before the law, no matter what color or previous condition of life. This, I think, was the crowning incident of that visit, the virtual acknowledgment that the negro was his brother man. The incident was long remembered and talked about in the hospital.

The boys were slow to recover from the effects of the measles. Spring had come, the birds had carolled their songs, the buds had blossomed, the leaves were growing finely, and the College grounds seemed almost a paradise upon earth, when the monotony was broken by the arrival of fifty wounded from the battle-field of Williamsburg, some with ghastly wounds in legs, arms and body. All was bustle and confusion, and many of the boys thought that war was indeed a horrible thing. Mrs. Pomeroy was present almost everywhere; she seemed ubiquitous. The writer saw her hold a basin for the cleansing of a wound where a piece of shell had struck the thigh and shattered the bone very much. She held the water with not a tremor, while Dubois probed to find the pieces of bone and remove them.

Soon the hospital became crowded, and those who had so far recovered were ordered to Fort DeKalb Convalescent Camp, Va., which had been established upon the estate of the rebel general Robert E. Lee. This estate of Lee's was, for scenic beauty, hardly equalled either on this continent or in Europe. It lay upon the right bank of the Potomac, a few minutes' walk below the Aqueduct bridge that enters the city of Georgetown, a suburb of Washington. The Potomac at the point where Lee's estate adjoined spread out into a broad and beautiful expanse of water, more like an inland lake than a river. Below the estate nearly one-half mile, and one mile below the Aqueduct bridge, Long bridge spanned the river like a long thread, and over this bridge the first invasion of the "sacred soil" was made.

The house known as Arlington, Lee's abode, was an old-fashioned manor-house, with a very large portico, supported by immense columns of brick and wood. The main building was rather small, containing some six or seven rooms, and was mostly portico, like the Southern Rebellion,—all portico and no principle behind it. However, this estate was the most beautiful the eye could scan. Beneath its heights lay the placid waters of the Potomac, while across the river in almost a straight line could be seen Pennsylvania Avenue, bordered with trees. At its head rises the Capitol in magnificent array, its marble porticos shimmering in beauty as the sun sinks behind the western hills at eventide, while his morning glory gilds the dome surmounted by the Goddess of Liberty. On either side are the Treasury buildings, Post-office, Smithsonian Institute, and the White House, embowered with the southern magnolia trees and other foliage most pleasing to the eye, while Georgetown above and Alexandria below, in the early days of the war, enterprising commercial ports, exporting large quantities of coal and tobacco, were in plain sight from the estate.

Early on the morning of June 3, 1862, some one hundred and fifty men were ordered across the river to the camp formed to receive them. The weather in the meantime had grown sultry and depressing, and as the boys formed in line gentle showers commenced falling, but we were soon under cover in the ambulances sent to convey us across the river. After a pleasant drive of over an hour we arrived at the house of Gen. Lee. We were soon divided into squads and given different rooms to sleep in during the night. Early in the morning the boys were astir, fell in, and took up their way to the camp, where there had been pitched some fifty Sibley tents, with floors to sleep on. The camp was most pleasantly situated, both as regards location for water to drink and to bathe in. The bathing was excellent, a quick stream breaking forth from the bluff and wending its way down towards the Potomac above the Aqueduct bridge, making a fall of some eight feet over a limestone formation, falling in gentle spray into a pool worn to receive it by attrition of the gentle falling waters, while under the spray rose a ledge of solid stone some four feet or more wide, upon which you could sit and receive the waters upon the person. This pool was embowered in thick foliage, and only a few knew of its position, the most of the invalids bathing in the Potomac.

Under the genial rays of the warm Southern sun, and with plenty of fresh air, the men quickly improved. They were free from restraint, being allowed to go anywhere except across the river, which gave some of the boys too free access to the "tangle-foot" of which they would freely imbibe. So the month of June wore away, and July was ushered in with heat and thunder-showers almost every afternoon.

McClellan had toiled up the Peninsula, only to be driven back to rest under the shelter of the gunboats and a strong position on the James, but as the morning of the 4th of July dawned it was determined to celebrate the anniversary of the day of our independence from British rule in a commendable manner. At early sunrise all the forts around Washington boomed forth the national salute of thirty-two guns to usher in the eventful day. By ten o'clock in the morning the boys had got very dry in the hot sun and bleaching winds of the South, so a scheme was devised whereby the moisture of the day could be increased. There happened to be in our camp a half-breed Indian from the Adirondack regions of New York, who was a most excellent swimmer. The Potomac river narrowed very suddenly just above the Aqueduct bridge, which carried across its waters the Chesapeake and Ohio Canal, and in the centre there happened to be a rock very nearly submerged, upon which a swimmer could rest. So after taking up a general contribution, he was sent across the river into Georgetown to get some good old rye whiskey, the river being about three-eighths of a mile wide at this particular point. With what palpitating hearts the squad of watchers scanned the water as he dove boldly in, reached the ledge, rested, and struck out for the opposite shore. We saw him slowly dress, (as he had swam the river with his clothes strapped on his head,) and go up into Georgetown. Soon he returned, bringing with him a two-gallon jug. He quickly stripped and plunged in, and after a struggle reached the half-way resting place. After stopping here a moment he struck out for the shore, which he soon reached. That jug went back and forth upon its mission several times that day, and as the day drew to a close the stars and stripes which floated from the flag-staff in Fort DeKalb seemed to be studded with legions of stars, and folds and stripes without number.

The jubilee wound up with a grand display of fireworks, but the boys were in the best of spirits and temper, and there were no serious abrasions. The sober restrained their weaker brethren, and the officers of the Fourth New York Heavy Artillery seemed to be about as deep in the mud as were the sick boys under their charge. About 10 o'clock the celebration wound up with a grand fusilade of rockets, red-lights and serpents, and quiet and rest fell upon a seriously exhausted battalion of convalescents.

Early on the morning of the 8th of July salt rations were ordered to be cooked, and it was rumored that we were going to re-inforce "Little Mac.," who was very tired after the pounding Lee gave him in the "seven days' fight." On the morning of July 10th salted rations and hard-tack were issued, with the usual small moity of sugar and coffee, and orders came to form line. Some two hundred were ordered to rejoin their regiments, which were with the Army of the Potomac. We fell into line and were put under an officer sent from Washington, who had been sick and belonged to the New Jersey brigade, under General Philip Kearney. After roll-call we started for Long bridge, and filed aboard the steamboat *Daniel Webster*, the same which had conveyed the Seventh in April, 1861, to the Peninsula.

We had a most excellent voyage down the bay. Wesley Bridges of Co. F was on the boat, and we soon became bunk-mates. Bridges was a good and earnest man; he fell mortally wounded in the charge on Mayre's Heights. Shortly after dusk of evening we sighted the immense fleet of war and transport vessels at Fortress Monroe, one of the most beautiful sights that an observer could see,—lights of red, white and blue, with fore and mizzen lights, fore-peak lights, and the glare of light from the huge frigates and line-of-battle ships, made a varying and beautiful panorama. At this time the wooden walls of Old England ruled the seas. But just around the point lay a new invention of Ericsson's which was to revolutionize the building of navies, and since that epoch of the fight between the Monitor and Merrimac, iron has been the material of construction used in the navies of the world.

Shortly after 9 o'clock we dropped anchor in Hampton Roads, after being challenged and boarded by the picket-boat of the squadron. We lay at anchor all night, when we steamed up the James river to find the army, which was at

CHAS. E. ROBINSON,
Captain Co. "C"

Harrison's Landing. After a tramp of three miles out to the front lines, Bridges and myself found our regiment, but very much decimated by disease. The boys welcomed us back with many a grim joke of "Tenderfoot!" and "You'll soon grow lean on hard-tack and pork!" We had got into fine condition after our measles, and before we had another chance to fat up we needed all we carried to the Peninsula.

CHAPTER XXV.

INCIDENTS OF FIELD AND GENERAL HOSPITALS (Continued.)—THE WOUNDED AT FREDERICKSBURG.—LIFE IN ST. JOSEPH'S HOSPITAL, NEW YORK.—AN INCIDENT OF THE NEW YORK RIOT.

THE Army of the Potomac under Hooker met with a very severe repulse at Chancellorsville, losing some seventeen thousand men, all told, in killed, wounded and missing. In the charge of the Sixth Corps upon the heights of Fredericksburg it suffered severely, more especially Newton's division, and Brown's brigade of that division still more severely, according to its numbers. The Seventh Massachusetts, which had been chosen by Generals Sedgwick and Newton to lead the assault upon the key-point of the position, lost about 150 men, all told, some twenty-nine killed and over one hundred severely wounded.

The surgeons were in their glory. Amputating tables were plenty, and many a poor boy felt for the first time the keen blade of the surgeon's knife as it carved its way to the bone, preparatory to receiving the saw. There were many who came out of that battle maimed for life, which no money can ever restore, or assuage the anguish, as they first come to realize they have lost a leg or arm, hand or foot, and must go through the world maimed and disfigured.

The field hospital of the Sixth Corps was established over the hill to the left of the Orange Court House plank road, and soon its capacity was filled to overflowing, and those who were not so seriously wounded lay around it beside huge fires of rails taken from the adjoining fences. The shrieks of the poor fellows were very heart-rending as the surgeons probed the wounds, and to any one who was wounded and had lost quantities of blood it was very jarring to the nerves. It is but a little while and then the shriek is past, the excitement is gone, and nature begins to assert her sway; limbs and body grow stiff and sore, and you can only be moved with intense pain. Some thirty of the Seventh lay in this hospital severely wounded.

On the morning of the 4th of May, 1863, orders came to send the wounded to Fredericksburg, as the rebels were making very severe demonstrations in that direction, and General Sedgwick gave orders to clear the field of the wounded. Soon a long ambulance train was loaded to its utmost capacity, and commenced its tortuous journey toward the city, over one of the most execrable roads in existence, broken and sadly out of repair. It was the longest three miles that was ever rode in this world. Just as we reached the city of Fredericksburg the rebel general Early captured some four or five of the rear end of the train. We went down into the city on the keen jump as soon as the drivers knew the "rebs" were after them. We were unloaded in front of a large tobacco factory, which was used as a hospital while the city was in possession of the Union forces. We had not been there more than an hour when the surgeon in charge gave the orders to every one who could crawl to make an effort to get across the river. Some ten or twelve of the regiment commenced the laborious work of crawling and hitching towards the bridge, and thence across the river at the upper portion of the city. It took us almost two hours to crawl that distance. In the interim the "Johnnies" had got the heights, and were sending the spiteful missiles into the streets of the city, while overhead whistled and roared the shot and shell from the siege guns on Stafford Heights, supported by a field battery. It was near 11 o'clock before we got across the river. Many were helped in their efforts by men of the construction corps, who made chairs of guns and pieces of wood, and carried many a poor soldier across the river to the land of safety. We were removed to the rear of the first bluff, where the second division hospital had been established to receive the wounded of the day previous in the charge of the Sixth Corps on the heights.

There were many of the Seventh Massachusetts who received very severe wounds in the thigh, necessitating amputation. In the hospital with the writer there was Williamson of Co. K, and Sergeant Edward James of same company; Goss of Co. A was in another tent a short distance away; Severns of Co. E, and others, who were very severely wounded. By sundown we were well under cover. During the night it rained very hard and cleared the atmosphere, which had been very sultry. As many of the wounds had been neglected, the cooling of the atmosphere by rain was very refreshing, and as we lay very near the edge of the tent upon the ground several of us thrust our wounded legs out into the rain, and never did any shower-bath relieve and allay the fever of limb better than that natural shower on Stafford Heights in May, 1863.

Shortly after the sun had risen on the 5th of May we were ordered to go to Falmouth Station, from which place we were to be taken in cars to Aqua Creek, Va., thence to be transported to Washington. After about one and one-half hours' ride we reached the landing, and were quickly put aboard the hospital boat, to be forwarded to Washington, D. C. Our destination was Campbell Hospital. While on the boat one of the Sixth Maine boys died from exhaustion and loss of blood. As he breathed his last he said, "I am going fast, boys. I am not afraid to die. The only dread is in leaving friends and loved ones at home and my comrades here. I am fully willing to give my life if we can only restore the Union and liberate the slave." He grew weaker and weaker, and with a trembling sigh his spirit winged its way to the mansions prepared for all men in the world beyond the river.

We soon arrived in Washington, and were rapidly transported to our several hospitals. As soon as we arrived at Campbell the surgeon in charge issued about three ounces of government whiskey to all who could drink it,—and he was a fine surgeon besides! We had as bed-fellows, on either hand, Sergeant White of the Second Rhode Island, a private of Colonel Speer's regiment, on the right, with a rebel captain as next bed-fellow, and Sergeant James of Co. K, of the Seventh, right across the alley-way on the west side of the room. The rebel captain was a red-headed, sanguinary sort of a man, rather positive in his nature, and very outspoken in rebel sentiment, to which he gave expression at every opportunity. The boys in blue stood his noise as long as they could, when they called upon the surgeon to take him out. Our sufferings and his secession sentiments couldn't be made to harmonize, besides he had a very irritating effect upon the boys.

The soldier on my right, a Pennsylvanian by birth, of Dutch descent, had two holes through his body, one in the shoulder and the other apparently through the chest, besides being wounded in the leg. He had a most excellent appetite, and did not lose a meal while I was in the hospital. Sergeant White of the Second Rhode Island was very severely wounded in the groin. He seemed to be doing nicely until the third night after we had reached the hospital, when his wound began to superate very severely and slough off. The surgeons of the hospital held a consultation, and they decided that the injury was such that it would be impossible to perform an operation and take up the artery, and the only safety for him lay in *anti-septis* applications to the wound. On this day he had a long talk with me, and said, "Friend, I am not going to get out of this. I feel as if I should bleed to death; my wound keeps superating and it will soon eat off the artery." I tried to cheer him up in my poor way, and said to him, "After you get over the shock you will recover. You have got a very strong constitution and splendid physique." He was six feet six, I think, and well-proportioned every way. Well, we chatted away, as old soldiers always will when thrown together, talked of home and the prospects of whipping Lee and ending the war, and both of us fell into a refreshing sleep. I was in hopes his fears were unfounded, but shortly after midnight he woke me up by reaching out his hand and touching me. "Say, corporal, my wound is bleeding; call the steward." I called aloud for him, and he was soon beside the couch. The blood then had begun to drip through the mattress upon which he lay. The surgeon was soon at hand, and everything was done that could be. They applied a compound to stop the hemorrhage, but it would push it away, and the blood would still run. He turned to me and said, "It's no use; I am going to bleed to death." I asked him if he had any word to send to his friends. He said, "No, except to tell them that I am not afraid to die." As he slowly neared the valley that leads to the waters of death, he grasped my hand and bade me good-bye, and passed away without a struggle. The Second Rhode Island lost many men in that terrible war, but none braver or purer than Sergeant White.

After stopping in this hospital about a month they transported us to New York City, to St. Joseph's Hospital, Central Park. On the same train that bore Sergeant James and myself North was Colonel Johns of the Seventh Massachusetts. Shortly after we left Philadelphia we ran off the track, and for a short time there was many a groaning and a good deal of cursing as one after another were thrown in a heap at the bottom of the car. We were delayed some three hours, when we steamed across New Jersey to New York City, where we took the transport *Elm City* and were landed in Harlem, and from there we went to the hospital.

St. Joseph's hospital, before it was accepted by the government as a hospital for wounded and maimed soldiers, was a Roman Catholic convent. It was most pleasantly situated at the outlet of Central Park, on what is called the Bloomingdale road, upon which thoroughfare many of the elite of New York used to try the speed of their horses. This hospital was in charge of Surgeons Gooley, Shrady, (General Grant's physician in his last sickness) and a Dr. Smith. Dr. Gooley was a sour, overbearing, crabbed, disagreeable man, while Drs. Shrady and Smith were the perfection of gentleness, with warm and sympathetic natures. Dr. Gooley was a great surgeon, no doubt, but that was no excuse for treating the soldiers under his charge as if they were common cattle.

While in this hospital the great riot in New York occurred. Gooley was quite excited, as they had given out word in Yorkville that they were going to clean out Gooley's pests up to the hospital. Well, we had two howitzers and about seventy-five fighting men, and if they had come they would have had all the fighting they wanted with one hundred other good men who would have defended the hospital against a determined attack.

The writer had been home to Scituate, Massachusetts, on a two weeks' furlough, only to find his home broken up and scattered. The mother had died previous to the war, and as business had changed, the brothers and sisters had changed their abodes. The family was never re-united. We await that reunion which is eternal on the banks beyond the rolling tide.

As my furlough called for my presence in New York, I started to fulfil it. I went to Boston, took the cars to

Fall River, (the home of A and B companies of our regiment) and the Old Colony steamer for New York, where I arrived safe and sound. But the wharves were lined with surging crowds of men. The captain of the boat advised me not to attempt to go across the city, but being young and inexperienced I set out. I followed Eleventh or Twelfth avenue right beside the water, and kept Uncle Sam's gunboats in line, so that if they murdered me they might get a charge of grape and canister in return. I took the middle of the street and only heard one menacing remark directed towards myself, which was, "There goes a d—— blue coat!" As ———— I got opposite Vesey street, I crossed over towards City Hall, and got aboard a Third avenue car. I asked the driver if he was going through. He said, "I am going to try; but you'll get killed." "Well, killed it is; if your car goes I am going, too." "Well," says he, "don't you show your head above the window-sill; if you do, they will shoot you." "All right," says I; and we started.

I had nothing but two good crutches and boundless cheek to protect me. All went well until we reached Yorkville, where there was a lively skirmish going on. Sometimes the police would charge, and fire a volley, which would be returned in earnest by the rioters. We got up to Harlem high bridge (the railroad bridge), at half-past four o'clock. When I went into the ward and reported, Gooley said, "How in —— did you get through?" I told him I got aboard a car, laid down, moved when the car moved, and stopped when the car stopped. But I have often wondered if a gang of "plug-uglies" had boarded that car what would have become of me. I guess that report would have been *killed suddenly*, *while on furlough.*

After I got back, gangrene, more properly called hospital gangrene, broke out, which necessitated the removal and breaking up of the hospital. The men were sent to St. T. Knight's Hospital, New Haven, Conn. We were

ordered aboard the same boat which had transported us to St. Joseph's. It was a most beautiful day in the first part of September as we took the steamer from the pier in East River, steamed up past Fort Trumbull, and out on to the waters of the sound. We arrived in New Haven harbor some time in early afternoon, and were transferred to the hospital. It was not equal to St. Joseph's, but was roomy and well shaded. The Dutchman from Pennsylvania was in the same hospital. The gangrene got into his wounded leg and very nearly killed him. One poor boy, who had a severe flesh wound in the fore-arm, before he had his arm cleansed suffered the loss of all the muscles and the covering to the *ulna* and *radius*. The gangrene had eaten a cavity of an inch in depth and over eight inches in length,—a severe and horrible looking cavity,—but under the skillful nursing of the surgeon in charge, when I left the hospital the first of November, it had so far healed that he had regained the use of his arm in a measure.

We had one man from a New York regiment who carried a ball in his brain, which he had received at Williamsburg the year before, who was all right apparently, except a slight absent-mindedness. He was walking across the parade-ground one day, when he suddenly fell dead. At the post-mortem examination, at which I was present, the ball was found in the *superior* portion of the brain, just in front of the organ of language, with quite a considerable suppuration.

The days were growing shorter, and we were given all proper liberty. At St. Joseph's Hospital an incident occurred which shows the thoughtlessness of men. Just before the hospital became infected we had, one day, six capital operations. My leg had so far healed that we—that is, James and myself—were put on to help watch and tend the wounded. There were three legs re-amputated, and three arms and heads which had undergone very severe operations. Now, we had in our ward a man from Chenango county, New York, who would persist in eating green apples, which grew very near the balcony on the east side of the hospital. The head steward had noticed his disobedience of orders, and had spoken to Dr. Shrady of Tom's misdeeds. By the way, he was called Tom Hyer, from the fighting-clip of his hair. James had been on from 7 P. M. until 12, when my relief came on. I had just been round to see that all the amputations were free from hemorrhages, and that the bandages were well wet with cold water, when the most dismal groaning shook that part of the ward in which Thomas was supposed to be sound asleep. I hastily wended my way to his cot, and asked him what was the matter. "Oh!" said he, "my stomach! my g—s! Oh, dear, I shall die! Get the doctor! get the doctor!" in tones loud enough to raise the rafters. "Well," says I, "Thomas, I shall go and get Dr. Shrady." Ordinarily the doctors returned to the city before 6 o'clock, leaving one of their number on duty at the hospital. I soon found Dr. Shrady at his room, and not only him, but Gooley and Smith, with some other doctor from the city, and I think they were having a "good time," as men say. I called Dr. Shrady's attention, and reported my case from ward four. Dr. Shrady said, "I'll quiet him," and gave me a prescription and injection for poor Tom, saying, "Watch him sharp." I returned with castor-oil and laudanum (40 drops) and a pint injector, all of which I scrupulously gave Thomas. After he had had it down and up for about one-half hour he grew quiet. At half-past 2 o'clock he commenced to visit the water-closet, and he kept it up all day, and on the third day Thomas left us, never more to return. Whether he went up like a pillar of fire, or surreptitiously stole away, I know not.

As the weather grew crisp and cold there were many men recovering from their wounds who must be sent back to the front. On the 2d day of November, 1863, some one hundred and twenty-five were sent to Bedloe's Island, New York harbor, the writer among the rest. I think the regular boat took us to New York, and we were soon on the island, garrisoned by a squad of regulars. It was very pleasant, but the island was overrun with rats. They would eat everything they could lay their teeth upon, even knaw into the very bed you lay on, and any moonlight night they would run over your feet with the utmost fearlessness. Our rations were good, well cooked, and we had a good chapel and library for reading matter. Dr. Proudfoot of New York City, Dr. Smiley of Jersey City, and other ministers, preached to us regularly every Sunday. Soon we grew robust and healthy, and returned to the regiment.

In the year 1864 there were killed and wounded more men than in any previous year of the war. The overland campaign, rich in horrors, was the slaughter year of the war. When the two armies in Virginia came together in their deadly embrace, the slaughter was terrific. Men were wounded by the thousands, and the dead formed a fearful holocaust to Liberty's shrine. On the night of the 6th of May the wail of the wounded was almost unendurable, that long-drawn pent-up wail which makes even nature cry aloud in anguish.

Previous to this campaign I was in Camp Convalescent, Alexandria, Va., where we had many men from the Seventh Maine Regiment, and others. While in this camp Generals Abercrombie, Heintzelman, Lord Lyons and Secretary Seward visited us. It was a very neat and pleasant camp. Here we had a chapel, in which could be seated four thousand men at one time, and Drs. Foster, Freeman, Dexter and Herring from Maine, and the leading lights of all denominations, with good singing and praying. "Camp-meeting" John Allen held forth here, and many of his subjects were entranced under his manipulations.

The Army of the Potomac suffered almost uninterrupted fighting for four long years, and more than four-fifths of its original three-years' men passed through its field and general hospitals. In conclusion I will say, it always seemed to me sacrilegious to mingle Christianity with bloodshed. He who said if thy brother strike thee, turn to him the other cheek, can hardly look complacently upon the slaughter of His children in war, and therefore I have, as far as possible, kept this history free from religious cant, as I have no faith in any body of religionists who pray for the slaughter of their foes.

These are a few incidents which came personally under my own eyes and are literally true to the best of my knowledge. Therefore, readers, pardon me if I introduce one more incident, or two rather, which came to light upon the battle-field of Antietam. As General Devens' brigade moved forward upon the battle-field of Antietam, it took a course which brought it to the left of Dunker's Church, and through the general field hospital established in a barn upon the field of battle. Before we reached the declivity upon which it was situated, the brigade came very near the ruins of Mumler's house and barn. Right upon the apex of this ridge lay a boy, fair and young, shot through the breast. In his agony he had clutched a handful of grass in either hand, while his feet had worn abrasions in the green-sward by the contant contraction of his limbs as the paroxisms of pain shook his wounded frame. He had long curly hair and a noble brow, stamped with the impress of great intelligence. As we moved slowly by him, his eyes, glazed with approaching dissolution, turned with a beseeching look never to be forgotten. Some home no doubt was desolated, some mother's heart was broken, but what of that if men can manufacture fame from the blood of fellow-mortals?

The other incident was: As we went through the hospital yard, the ground was fairly littered with straw, and in our curiosity we lifted it up. As we did so, we found we were walking on the bodies of the dead, while near the amputating tables lay a heap of arms, legs, feet and hands, over a foot in height. To say that this sight was not sickening would be false. It even at this late day, after twenty-eight years have elapsed, calls up a shudder, and it gave the writer a sudden qualmishness which he never will forget as long as the blood shall pulsate through his veins.

May our fair land never see another war, nor the youth of the land be called upon to pass through the struggles of another war. To the educated masses of the North the war was chastening and educational, but the stay-at-homes, the bankers and many of the money-lenders, it seemed to harden and demoralize, and the great danger of our republican institutions will come from this class who fattened upon the blood of their fellow-citizens, and their posterity, for an aristocracy of wealth has ever been the destruction of republics.

Not those who suffered upon the field of battle, or in field or general hospitals, but from those who took advantage of the necessities of the government in its hour of peril may we look for succeeding dangers.

CHAPTER XXVI.

"HOSPITAL LIFE AS I REMEMBER IT," By Walter S. Goss.—SKETCH OF THE
"HOSPITAL BUMMER."—A TRIBUTE TO THE OLD
ARMY SURGEONS.

THERE are no scenes of the war more vividly remembered by the old soldier than his life in a hospital, after having been stricken down on the field of battle.

After the battle of Chancellorsville, a field hospital of the Sixth Corps was established at Potomac Creek Landing, and the old Seventh Massachusetts was well represented therein. My first experience there was not very exhilarating. The beds were constructed on primitive principles. Running the length of the tents were poles laid on forked stakes. On these were laid in cross-sections small cedar poles on which were ticks of straw. The poles were not secured, and the recumbent victim was at the mercy of their movements. If he dared to move he would feel them crawling apart, and would have the sensation of something dropping to the earth. I remember that I went through the performance several times, and then refused to try it over again until the things were fixed, which they were finally.

Many a wakeful night I passed in that tented home, hanging on to the rugged edge of life. Two inmates of our tent died while we were there. One night a poor sufferer, who lay a few beds from me, commenced to thrash about vigorously, and threw himself from his bed. I called lustily for help, but the man was dead by the time the nurse was awake. Another man, a color-bearer of a New York regiment, I think, one day requested the "nurse" to put on his boots. "Why do you want your boots on?" asked the nurse. "O, never mind why, but put on my boots," persisted the patient. To humor the caprice of the man, his boots were put on. And then he raised himself to a sitting posture, and with uplifted hand as though he was again bearing aloft his regimental banner, he exclaimed, "Now, boys, for the last charge! Forward! Hurrah! they run! Victory! vic—!" and he fell back—dead. His life had floated away to the great unknown. I have seen tragedies real and tragedies simulated, but nothing so thrilling, to me, as the charge of that brave, patriotic spirit, on to the very ramparts of heaven. It may have been delirium; but to me it was more real than the oft-told tale of Thermopylæ or any of the heroics of historic page.

Later on, our field hospital was furnished with iron bedsteads, and the patients were massed by regimental representation. The boys of the Seventh occupied two or three wards. The ward that I was in contained a score or more of us, all but one of whom, I think, pulled through.

I remember that I ate very little, if any, food during the earlier part of my hospital life; but after I had lost sixty pounds of my corporal substance, my appetite became so disproportionate to the rations allowed that the nurse made several excursions to Aqua Creek for my special benefit, and the surgeon, when I complained to him of famine, threatened to send me to clean out the cook-house. All my spare change went for dried beef, fresh shad, and once I was entrapped by a peddling sneak into paying two dollars for two dozen eggs. I had those eggs boiled, but to my sorrow and disgust they were too ancient for a modern stomach, even though it belonged to a hungry soldier.

When the Army of the Potomac left the line of the Rappahannock the hospital patients were transferred to Washington. We went by rail to Aqua Creek, and thence by boat to Washington. I shall never forget the ludicrous scene presented by our battalion of six hundred and fifty cripples as they hobbled from the cars to the boat. Nearly every man of us was on crutches. To a sympathetic looker-on it may have been pathetic, but soldiers did not view things in a pathetic light in those days.

One of our surgeons told me that I could not get through the journey without stimulants. He informed me that he would try to get me some at Aqua Creek, and judging by his tangle-legged appearance afterwards, I should say that he succeeded in finding the article for which he sought, but he became so absorbed in self that he forgot me. After our arrival at the Capital, the red tape of the war department became so strained that we were compelled to lie on the wharf for five long, weary hours. After patience had passed the limits of endurance, we were distributed by ambulance through the different hospitals of Washington. Five of my company managed to keep together and went to the Harwood. Ten days after, there was a general clearing out of the hospitals in Washington, to make room for the victims of an anticipated battle near the Capital, which culminated in the great drama, Gettysburg.

Most of the men of the Seventh were given thirty days' furlough, while I got left on the plea that I was unable to travel. But the little German surgeon of the ward salved my injured feelings with the consoling promise that as soon as I was able to make the journey he would give me a ninety days' furlough, which promise failed to materialize, as I was shortly after transferred to the Satterlee hospital at West Philadelphia.

After the Gettysburg battle this hospital was crowded to repletion, and a field hospital of tents was pitched outside the fence to contain the overflow. I think there is nothing so dreary and monotonous as a hospital life. Every one is talking and longing for home, "so near and yet so far" away. The free and happy-go-lucky life in the field, with all its attendant danger and hardships, is preferable to any but the well-known "hospital bummer." Yes, there were "bummers," but they were not so thick as many would have us believe. I remember one who hailed from Ohio, who had a remarkably crooked leg. He walked, with the aid of a cane, on the end of his toes. He kept in his bed, and only at the call for meals was he the first at the front. But one evil day three surgeons stealthfully crept to his bed-side, when two of them held him down while the other applied a sponge loaded with chloroform to his nose, and in less than three minutes the fellow had the straightest leg in that ward; like Paddy's tree, it was so straight that it leaned the other way. Shortly afterwards he was sent to his regiment, the most ashamed man that ever went to the front.

The thousands of soldiers who made up our army were, as a class, of heroic mould. In field or hospital, they never shrunk nor shirked the trying ordeal which they were called upon to pass through. It took more courage often to withstand the pangs of hospital treatment than it did to face the enemy on the field. I think I have seen more striking examples of heroism and patient devotion in the hospitals than in the field. To-day there is no tie so strong as the fraternal feeling which binds soldiers to one another, even though they be strangers. It is a heartfelt sympathy, a mystic bond that recognizes a comrade who has been tried in the fiery furnace of a war for universal liberty and a common country. For this we fought, for this we suffered in foul prison pens, in hospitals, and on the fields of battle: for this our comrades fell where shot and shell sung their last requiem.

No record of hospital life would be complete without a tribute to our old army surgeons. Their sympathetic devotion, their professional skill, their unselfish, untiring energy, saved many a poor, mangled sufferer from an untimely grave. I owe my life to the kind-hearted, rough and bluff old Dr. Tiff, or Taft, of a New York regiment. The old boys of the Seventh who were in the hospital at Potomac Creek will remember him kindly for his devotion to them. If he is alive, would that some kindly word, a "God-bless-you," might greet him from the boys of the Seventh who were under his care.

I cannot say that I fell in love with the surgeons at Satterlee. The most of them were resident physicians of Philadelphia, who visited the wards but once a day. They were cold and reserved, and they went about their duties as though they had a job and were bound to get through it as easily as possible. I heard a poor, wounded, home-sick boy ask one of these professional dudes for a furlough, and the reply was flung back to him that if he heard any more from him about a furlough he would have him put in a guard-house. It took a strong leverage to get a furlough from that hospital. I got one all the same, but it was at the request of our old war-governor, John A. Andrew. Anything like the name of a governor would make men like those doctors toady to a female cur.

But the days of war and hospital life are over for the boys of the old Seventh, and all that is left for them now to do is to live in the retrospective, and thank God that they were able to do their humble part towards saving our grand old republic from the traitorous foes that assailed it.

ISAAC W. GILES,
2nd Lieutenant Co, "K."

CHAPTER XXVII.

FURTHER INCIDENTS OF HOSPITAL LIFE IN COLUMBIA COLLEGE AND ST. JOSEPH'S HOSPITALS.—GEN. RUSSELL AT FREDERICKSBURG.— FIELD HOSPITALS NEAR WHITE OAK CHURCH.

THE preceding sketch of hospital life, by Walter S. Goss, of Marlboro, Mass., can well be supplemented by a sketch or two of incidents occurring in Columbia College Hospital, Meridian Hill, Washington, D. C. When the Seventh boys had been transferred to that hospital, those who were supposed to be on the road to the river "Styx" were placed in room thirteen, ward four, while opposite, resting in room twelve, were other patients who were carried in to die. While in room thirteen there were thirteen deaths in three weeks, and all of them were seen by the men, who, by their strength of constitution and will, recovered from the disease by which they were attacked, and from which they were expected to die.

One old man of sixty years was brought in after we had been in the room for two or three weeks, who was suffering from congestion of the brain. In his delirium he would rave of the charge of cavalry at Fairfax Court House. Then again he would sing of his country,

"My Country, 'tis of thee, sweet land of liberty."

Then the nurse would try to soothe and comfort him. Anon, and he would be ready to swap horses, and then he would call by endearing names his child at home in Pennsylvania, and would say, "Sarah, bring Flora; I want to kiss her good-bye before I go to the camp, for you know we start for Washington to-morrow." Then he would fall back exhausted. Soon he would rouse up and demand his release, for he must report to the colonel of his regiment, and he did not want to be court-martialed. In the morning he had grown more quiet, but the film of death was stealing over his eyes. When Dr. Abedee, surgeon-in-chief, came in, he passed along between the beds, and as soon as the patient's eye rested upon him, he said, "Say, doctor, do you know how I use a horse when he has the blind staggers?" "No," said Dr. Abedee, with a smile, "how do you?" "Well, I blister and bleed him like d——tion!" "Well, that's all right," says Abedee, who called the nurse to him, and told him to get the man some iced lemonade. Thomas, the nurse, soon procured the mixture and gave it to him, when the poor soldier gave a gasp and was dead. One more for the dead-house! Gone home! One more widow and fatherless child—the curse of war!

In a day or two more there came in a boy from a New York regiment, the Thirty-sixth, who was delirious from the time he came into the room until he died. With oaths and imprecations he declared he would not die. I liked his grit better than I did his language, but he soon succumbed to the great leveller of flesh, the enemy of all mankind,— death. When the body was being prepared for removal, among his effects was found a most beautiful photograph of a lovely child and woman, and on the back was written, "My wife and child."

Among my acquaintances was a soldier from the Adirondack regions of New York, Charles Allen by name. He was fifty-five years old, as straight as a young sapling, and he challenged many a boy to run him a race of an hundred yards.

As nurse-in-chief we had a woman from New York, faithful and true, virtuous and womanly, and as her assistant she had a man from the Fourth or Fifth Pennsylvania cavalry. His name was Ford, and he belonged in Philadelphia. All the boys liked him. Gentle, manly, self-reliant, he was a noble boy. He had a considerable degree of science in the art of manly defence, and to while away the time we would have a bout or two at fisticuffs, all in good feeling and fun.

The First New Jersey cavalry had a man by the name of Simmons in this hospital, and although of more than ordinary intelligence, he could not read or write. He came over to me one day as he saw me draw forth my writing material, and said, "Say, old boy, can you write?" "Why, yes," said I. "Well, I want you to write for me." I said, "Can't you write?" "No." "Who do you wish me to write to?" "Oh, my best girl." "What is her name?" "Susan McIntosh." So I wrote for Ike—that was what we all called him, Isaac being the correct appellation he should be known by. When I told him I had had no experience he said, "Have you got a mother?" "No, she died when I was eleven years old." "Well," said he, "write just as you would write to your mother if she were alive, multiplied by ten in power and affectionate form." So I wrote a warm, affectionate love-letter, and by the answer Isaac got, in two days or more, it seemed to me as if my missive took nicely. I did all of Isaac's writing as long as I remained in the hospital, and he did his courting by proxy of the pen!

The Seventh Maine had a soldier in this hospital by the name of Howard. One of nature's noblemen, over six feet in height, and well-proportioned, he was the acme of manly perfection. He had a very severe attack of erysipelas. When I was removed from room thirteen to room one, on the easterly end of the College, he had been painted with iodine all over the cranium, and a blacker man's head I never saw; but he soon peeled and got well. Many were the hours I whiled away with him playing checkers, at which game he beat me almost every time.

In St. Joseph's Hospital, Central Park, New York, we had a brave Frenchman called Count Remoné, who had lost a leg at Fair Oaks. He had served as orderly on General McClellan's staff, and was a real kind and affable man, well educated and refined, and had the French gift of grace in conversation. After his leg had become healed, he asked Dr. Shrady if he could go to the city. "Well, Remoné, how many glasses of liquor will you drink?" "Oh," said Remie, as we called him, "one — two — three — four." "Ah!" says Dr. Shrady, "you'll get drunk." "No, no," says Remie, "get a little full—that's all; no Frenchman gets drunk." "Well, I guess you had better wait a week." "All right," says Remie. When he did go he came back middling happy no more!

We had an Englishman in our ward, and he was always telling how "old Hingland" used her soldiers, and kept harping on what she would do, and he guessed "the South would whip," until one night the boots and crutches flew in the direction of his bed, so that he had to evacuate it on the double-quick! Dr. Shrady, when he came in, asked where Johnny Englishman was, and they told him. Durkey, who had a leg off just below the knee, and who was of good old Irish stock, said, "We drove him off, and if he comes back insulting us by his English yarns, we'll kill him!" Dr. Shrady laughed, and said, "Well, boys, I guess he won't come back." He didn't feel like being brow-beaten by a Johnny Bull—not after the Trent affair.

One incident occurred at the storming of Mayre's Hill, at Fredericksburg, that will call up tender reminiscences of our old colonel, David A. Russell. As he sat on his horse watching the thin column of blue on the Telegraph Road launched forth to pierce the centre of the rebel position on the heights, and as they met the terrible fire of bullets and shell which checked them for a few minutes, Gen. Russell turned pale, and every feature told of the agony of his soul;

but as the column gathered itself together for the final lunge he exclaimed, "They will carry it now; all hell can't stop them!" It showed how dear to his soldier's heart were the boys of the old Seventh. As his adjutant-general, Dan Packard, of Co. K of the Seventh, rode by his side, he said, "This has been a glorious day for the old Seventh, but a sad one." As he led his brigade out on the Plank road, he passed many of the boys who had been brought to the rear to be operated on, and, as the tears rolled down his cheeks, he said, "You did nobly, boys! You did nobly." And with many a prayer for his safety, from his old comrades in peril, he passed to new fields of honor and usefulness. Lying beside the road were some one hundred and over of the Seventh boys, with many of the gallant Thirty-sixth New York, our support in this column.

After many of the Seventh boys had been carried over the river, into the field hospital of the Sixth Corps, established on Stafford Heights, the brigade-surgeon came around. As I lay beside Lorenzo Williamson, of the regiment, who was very severely wounded, the surgeons examined his wound, which was of the thigh and knee, from bullet and buck-shot. They would run their fingers into the canal made by the bullet, and say, "Well, this is a peculiar wound; the bullet has struck the head of the *femur* and rebounded out of the wound." Poor Williamson would groan, but they very good naturedly kept on probing with their fingers, and Surgeon Leary showed his fingers severely wounded by pieces of bone which the cuticle had struck in his exploration of wounds by the process of fingering rather than by the metallic probe. Well, both of the surgeons were wrong, as that identical bullet was cut out of the leg just above the knee-joint, after fifteen years had elapsed, the surgeons forgetting that lead generally sticketh closer than a brother when introduced into the system.

One other incident: A poor boy of the Sixth Maine,

who charged! upon our left in line of battle, was shot right through the ankle, the ball entering the front of the instep and crashing through the bone, and lodging under the heel. Without any anesthetics applied, they began the operation, and under it the boy never flinched only as nature called up a groan in sympathy with his horrible sufferings. Brave boy, he did not lose his foot, but he suffered untold agony, and was too low to be transferred to Washington when we went.

On May 6th, 1864, as the lines of blue and gray recoiled from the mutual slaughter of the Wilderness, and as darkness and quiet fell upon that gateway to death and glory, the oppressive stillness of the night was broken by the wail of the wounded, and as something would snap or a gun would be discharged, it would sound like a cannon, for it seemed as if all nature was in sympathy with the suffering, and not only suffering, but appalled at the dreadful carnage of the human family. And methinks in nature's realms much of affinity can be found when a slaughter of the human family is enacted upon a mighty sphere. And if the sins of Sodom could call down the condemnation of Jehovah, it may be possible that in a slaughter so immense and brutal as the Wilderness and Spottsylvania, even Nature would weep for her wayward children. I never wish to hear that sound again. So sad, so terrible! It wells up in mind, and seems at this late day to draw forth a shudder and a start as I think of the brave men who went down in honor and glory in the tangled wilds of the Wilderness and Spottsylvania.

The sights of a battle-field are almost unendurable. As we filed into position on the bloody field of Antietam, we passed many a line of blue and gray, cold and silent in death, and that night as we camped down to sleep we lay with many a dead man, and as the men were very tired, we slept soundly, notwithstanding we expected to be launched against the foe in the morning. As Adjt. Dan Packard passed along the lines, he gently shook the boys on the reserve line to awake them. Some of them seemed to waken very slowly and hard, and as he would turn them over to the light of early morning, he would start and shudder as the dead would be relinquished from his grasp. We had lain in among some forty or fifty of the dead during the night.

Early in the morning, as soon as it was light enough to see a few rods in advance of a person, Col. Russell crawled up to the front, took off his hat and peered over the ridge. Soon he came back. "Boys," said he, "the rebels are gone ; they have left us." We were not sorry. Soon we advanced to the sunken road, where the rebel dead lay in tiers three and four deep. One man on the Hagerstown pike lay with his musket by his side, his head entirely gone, as our batteries had smashed a solid shot through the wall in front of him.

That night, as we marched towards Williamsport to drive Stuart's cavalry across the river, it had got to be about eleven o'clock when there was a thundering of hoofs and clatter enough for the charge of a regiment of cavalry. Col. Johns' horse had broken loose from the orderly, and soon he had other horses upon the rampage. Several were severely wounded and the shock was as severe to the nerves of the men as if they had been engaged with the enemy.

The battle of Antietam was appalling in its loss of human life. There seemed to be no concert between corps and divisions, and even the commanding general had only provisional command of the army. It was the most open field-fight of the war, and, with more tenacity and better cohesion of the different parts of the army, Lee should have had a decisive defeat, wherein he only received a severe drubbing and strategical defeat.

At camp near White Oak Church our regimental field hospital had been established early in December, 1862, and from this hospital many of our boys were discharged for disability. Just before Hooker's grand move across the river, I went up to see some of the boys of the regiment who had become endeared to us all by their heroic courage under many and trying circumstances. From this hospital there were discharged Gideon F. White, Frank Martin and Horace S. Swan of Co. A, Joseph Swindles and Frederick Atwood of Co. B, and Harrison A. Wade, musician, of Co. C, with William Powers and William A. Cole of Co. I, and William A. Cook of Co. K, and many others who had wasted away to mere skeletons by chronic diarrhœa, Cook weighing only ninety pounds when he arrived in Scituate, Mass., his place of enlistment. The others were equally as much disabled, the disease seemingly reducing the flesh and blood by fluid evacuations.

While in St. Joseph's Hospital, many of the women of New York came to visit us, and got permission to distribute oranges and lemons, which were very refreshing. The Sisters of the convent were as faithful as they could be, and many a silent prayer has gone up from St. Joseph's Hospital for a blessing upon their holy lives. Sectarianism in the army had a "hard row to hoe," and many a man lost his creed and found his God and Savior in the liberation of his mind and intellect. Indeed, from army life came much of the liberation of the public mind from crude theology.

But hospital life is over. The men of the Seventh are fast passing away. Now, if immortality is a fact, and we meet again in a higher sphere, methinks Fair Oaks, Antietam, Mayre's Heights, Salem Church, Gettysburg, Mine Run, and the Wilderness, will prove a richer theme for the spirit boys to talk of than any creed or religion they swore by while on earth. There we shall meet Russell, Johns and Bullock, Whiting of I, Tillson of K, Grant, Meade and Thomas, Sheridan, Hooker and Burnside, Logan and Canby, Farragut and Foote, and possibly Lee and Jackson, Bragg and Hill; and better than all, as Christian soldiers, our Lord and Savior Jesus Christ, who is the Great Captain of all upon the *Campus Martius* of Eternal Life!

CHAPTER XXVIII.

GENERAL REVIEW OF THE WAR.—THE DEFECTS OF A MILITARY EDUCATION AT WEST POINT.—INFLUENCE OF THE WAR UPON THE PEOPLE, AND THE LESSONS IT TAUGHT THE WORLD.

THE war of the Rebellion taught the people of the United States the power and resources of the nation, and the strength of a democratic form of government when founded upon the suffrages and intelligence of its educated masses. It also taught that a democratic government is weak, in a military view, when depending upon the yoemen as its main support in times of sudden emergencies, and also that one part of the nation can be paralyzed by the machinations of traitors in any other part if they have ample time for preparation, and any section has only to instruct a large and generally enlisted militia to menace the liberties of the nation when the people of that section shall become dissatisfied with the confederation. While education is the mainstay of republican institutions, and State rights are still held inviolable under the constitution, it will, as immigration increases and changes the complexion and nature of the voters in large sections of our country, be necessary to compel education of the masses by compulsory legislation, so that the danger of sudden riots by the excitement of demagogues working upon the minds of the people shall be reduced to the minimum.

The war of Secession was a most costly and cruel war, and it has taught us that no matter how sacred an oath a man may register in heaven, there are some who will break it. West Point, the great military school of the nation, gave us ample evidence of this weakness of human nature; and as it has been said that it was a necessary evil in a democratic government, until nations shall learn war no more, I intend to point out some of its defects as applied to the practical handling of large masses of volunteer troops.

It was a notorious fact, with few exceptions, that no cordial good-will was felt for the able volunteer officer by the graduates of West Point; and if one reads between the lines he can see that the preference was always given to West Point graduates by the regulars in power. And there is one vital weakness in its educational system which seems to promote jealousies and bickerings between its graduates when in the field, as for instance, Sumner, Heintzelmen and Hooker at Williamsburg, and other cases too numerous to mention; the choosing of Howard instead of Logan, the peerless volunteer, to command the Army of the Tennessee when Gen. McPherson was killed before Atlanta, who was the peer of any regular officer graduated at West Point. They seemed to have an idea that if a man graduated at the head of his class he would make a Napoleon, forgetting that adaptation is the leading feature of success. With all their technical knowledge, our Northern officers could not organize a proper staff the first two years of the war, from which inefficiency the Rebellion lasted more than a year longer than it should.

And again, the scholars, using European methods of handling troops, expected the same precision and success in movement and strategy upon our difficult *terrene*, without considering the beautiful roads of the old world upon which to move an army. Also the war of the Rebellion showed very plainly the evils of appointment of officers before they had had experience in the field, and by political influence of the governors of the several states. It also taught the people the greatness of their country, and was most profitable as a means of promoting general intelligence in relation to the different sections, which has been of incalculable benefit to the people. It also taught the military men that the commanding of troops by officers elected by the men to command is detrimental to the best interests of the soldiers. It also taught the North and South the unparalleled stubbornness of the Anglo-Saxon race as fighters. It also taught the nation that there were as many good volunteer officers as regulars, and to cite instances we will mention a few of our noble volunteer generals.

First and foremost as a great general stands Gen. John A. Logan, "Black Jack of the Mingo"; next, Gen. Benjamin F. Butler, of Massachusetts, who, by his words, "contraband of war," cut the gordian-knot for our government in relation to the negro, until Abraham Lincoln issued his Emancipation Proclamation. Next in line, Adelbert Ames, Alfred Terry, Alexander Wadsworth, and also that most excellent soldier, Daniel Sickles, of New York, who won imperishable renown upon many a field of bloody battle.

As second-rate generals we will mention Gen. Nathaniel P. Banks, Gen. Stedman, of Ohio, Prof. Mitchell, the astronomer, Gen. John C. Fremont, Gen. Shields, the hero of Kearnstown, and many others who could amply fill any place unto which they might have been called by the government.

It has been claimed by Gen. Wolsey of the English army that a corps of regular troops would have turned the tide of any battle in which they might have fought. No doubt but the application of twenty-five thousand fresh troops at the critical juncture would have been decisive, so would have been twenty-five thousand of such troops as the Sixth or old First or Fifth Corps of volunteers. At Gaines' Mills a full division of regulars fought and were defeated as readily as any of the volunteers, and they were met by

Southern volunteers, and not the educated kind, either. The last war was fought by regulars principally in places of high command, and General Scott's record as a strategist would not suffer in comparison with either McClellan's or Halleck's. Nobody ever claimed for General Grant, I believe, the qualities of being a great military strategist.

As a counterpart to the long list of able volunteer officers, West Point gave us Generals McClellan, Halleck, Sherman, Buell, Rosecrans, who undoubtedly had only one better strategist as a rival in our army, who could whip Lee and Bragg at their own game in the chances of war. General Grant belonged to a different order of generals, so it is not necessary to recount his exploits. He was a successful general. To that school belonged Gen. George H. Thomas, Gen. Tecumseh Sherman, Gen. Philip H. Sheridan, and Gen. George G. Meade, Grant's great lieutenant. Of the brilliant and sometimes successful generals as leaders and commanders of armies we will name Gen. Geo. B. McClellan, Gen. Joseph Hooker, Gen. Rosecrans, Gen. Buell, Gen. John Pope, of Bull Run fame, and Gen. Ambrose E. Burnside.

Of the successful corps commanders who graduated at West Point we will mention as first, Gen. John Sedgwick, Gen. Schofield, Gen. James B. McPherson, Gen. Darius N. Couch, Gen. Winfield S. Hancock, and Gen. E. V. Sumner, of the Eastern and Western armies. These men were of more than ordinary abilities, and were an ornament to the school from which they graduated.

Of division commanders, Philip Kearney and David A. Russell stood pre-eminently in the armies of the East as remarkable for ability, and would no doubt have risen to the command of corps and armies if they had been spared to their country's service.

The war no doubt was handled in a very wasteful way at first, but as the people learned its needs, and the government learned that it was a revolution instead of an *emeute*, under the circumstances we did as well as could have been expected. The great fault with the government at Washington was the short enlistments of its troops, and the removal of the Army of the Potomac from the James. Otherwise, it did as well as it was possible to do, with the seat of government so near the contending armies, and with the immense political power exerted in favor of corruption in commissary and quartermaster departments, and the promotion of officers by political favor instead of merit won in the field by active service.

The war also showed to the world the incongruity of the Christian church, which exercised in the name of Christ a baleful influence, both North and South, in the previous years,—a voice in favor of the bondage and enslavement of the human race. And only after the printing press of the North and the educational elevation of the masses by the common schools had been felt, was it possible to gain hearers and break them away from the bondage of the church long enough to build up a party to liberate the slave and establish a nationality and a true republican form of government under the Constitution. Therefore it may be said that civil government, as taught in our seminaries of learning, is a better basis for government to rest on than the theocratic ideas of the church. And in the future, as in the past, education of the masses by free schools is a better underpinning than the semi-political creeds issued from the pulpit and the Christian press.

The war also brought to the knowledge of the people the unbounded resources of the nation, the heroic qualities of its people, and the need of time to make us a homogeneous race. It also taught the people, both North and South, that slavery was an incubus upon the nation, and that the quicker it was destroyed the better, for it was blighting both the North and South by its baleful influences upon the

morality of the people. The war also taught that it did
not necessarily contaminate the morals of the men which
the government called forth to battle in its defence, but
rather that it demoralized those who stayed at home, and
who speculated in the necessaries of life at the expense of
those who fought in the field. It also showed to the world
the flexible and intense tenacity of democratic government
when founded upon the intelligence of its people. It
brought to light the almost incomparable skill of its artisans
and mechanics, who constructed bridges and railways,
thereby supporting immense armies by steam transportation
when far from their base of supplies, and who also invented
the best arms of any nation of the world. It revolutionized
the navies of the world, and by the construction of a Merrimac and Monitor made obsolete the wooden walls of old
England, and in one year from the opening of the war the
United States was master of the seas, with over two hundred vessels and eight thousand men on ocean and river
vessels of war.

And lastly, it taught the people of the North and South
proper respect for each other, and that there was no material difference in the make-up or fighting qualities of its
men. And when the red flames of war had ceased and the
blows of death had given way to the clasped hands of friendship, and when the heart-aches had ceased from the land in
a measure, it showed to the world the untold magnanimity
of its people, and the great leader, who said, "Let us have
peace" rather than assassinations and reprisals. And now,
in the short space of a quarter of a century, the scars of war
are healed, and the veterans of the blue and gray fraternize
upon their fields of battle, and swear allegiance to the flag
of their fathers, the emblem of liberty,—the red, white and
blue,—the hope of the oppressed, the signet of equality of
all men before the law.

The war also gave us our national currency, through the

NELSON V. HUTCHINSON,
Corporal Co. "K."

medium of our national banks, one of the greatest improvements in the finances of the people that had ever been made previous to the war. Each State had issued bills of credit as it saw fit, and individual banks, by State law, were established in the several States. A person traveling from one to the other without gold or silver coin had to exchange his bills for a discount, or possibly he could pass his money if the bank had a national reputation. It also gave us the greenback, which should be the great national money, based upon a metallic currency. It also bound together the Eastern States with the far-off States of the Pacific by the great lines of railroad called the Union Pacific and Central Pacific, one of the greatest railroad engineering feats of the century. It also gave to us the Territory of Alaska, rich in all mineral and vegetable matter, with fisheries of unbounded wealth.

And better still, it gave us a place and a name among the empires of the earth, and a credit of unlimited strength in the money markets of the world. It also gave us as a rich legacy to the posterity of the nation, the names of Lincoln, Grant, McClellan, Sheridan, Thomas, Meade, Chase, Seward, Sumner, Stevens and Andrew,—a galaxy of names which will adorn the pages of history as long as noble deeds are sung in prose and poetry.

CHAPTER XXIX.

APPENDIX. — ROSTER OF THE REGIMENT, GIVING AN ACCOUNT OF THE FATALITIES DURING ITS TERM OF SERVICE.

THERE were killed in action of the Seventh Massachusetts Volunteer Infantry, in its three years' service, thirty-two men: died of wounds, fifty-two; died of disease in general hospitals, with no returns to commanding officer of regiment, sixty-eight; prisoners of war, seven; marked as deserters on muster-out rolls, one hundred and sixty; transferred to other organizations, one hundred and forty-eight; mustered out by expiration of service, three hundred and seventy; absent at time of muster-out of regiment, from wounds, ten; mustered out for promotion, thirty-nine.

There were wounded of the non-commissioned officers and privates, on the different battle-fields in which the regiment had engaged the enemy, two hundred and fifty-one men. The mortally wounded were fifty-two, who died upon the field of battle or in hospitals to the rear. The total casualties as given for killed, mortally wounded, taken prisoner, and those who died in field and general hospitals, were six hundred and forty-one men.

Of commissioned officers, there were killed, one captain, three first lieutenants and one second lieutenant; and fifteen other officers wounded. Making in all, six hundred and sixty-one men who were disabled in its different campaigns, after suffering a loss of one hundred and forty-eight transferred to other organizations. The whole number mustered into the regiment, as given in the Adjutant-General's report for the State of Massachusetts, was eleven hundred and forty, from which subtract one hundred and forty-eight transferred to other organizations, leaving nine hundred and ninety-two men who performed service with the regiment until they were disabled or mustered out. From this number subtract six hundred and sixty-one, leaving three hundred and thirty-one as the number who suffered no serious casualty sufficient to disable them from duty,—or from duty by permanent disability. Now subtract three hundred and thirty-one from three hundred and seventy who were mustered out at expiration of term of service, leaving thirty-nine as the number who returned to the regiment from general hospitals, recovered from wounds and disease.

Surely the war for the life of the republic was bloody, and the sacrifices in men and treasure beyond calculation.

ROSTER OF SEVENTH MASSACHUSETTS VOLUNTEER INFANTRY.

Mustered out at Taunton, Massachusetts, June 27, 1864.

NAME AND RANK.	Age	Date of Muster.	Termination of Service and cause thereof.
Darius N. Couch, Col.,	38	June 15, '61	Brig. Gen. U. S. V., Sept. 4, 1861.
Nelson H. Davis, Col.,	—	Sept. 4, '61	Nov. 18, '61, Asst. Ins. Gen. U.S.A.
Joseph Wheelock, Col.,	—	Nov. 20, '61	Jan. 30, 1862, resigned.
David A. Russell, Col.,	—	Jan. 31, '62	Brig Gen U. S. V., Nov. 29, 1862.
Thomas D. Johns, Col.,	37	Feb. 22, '63	June 27, 1864, expiration of service.
Chester W. Greene, Lieut. Col.,	49	June 15, '61	Nov. 22, 1861, resigned.
Charles Raymond, Lieut. Col.,	—	Nov. 23, '61	Oct. 24, 1862, do
Franklin P. Harlow, Lieut. Col.	34	Oct. 25, '62	June 27, 1864, expiration of service.
David E. Holman, Major,	55	June 15, '61	Aug. 1, 1861, resigned.
Franklin P. Harlow, Major,	33	Aug. 1, '61	Lieut. Col. Oct. 25, 1862.
Joseph B. Leonard, Major,	41	Oct. 25, '62	June 27, 1864, expiration of service.
S. Atherton Holman, Surg.,	31	June 15, '61	Surgeon U. S. V., Sept. 9, 1863.
William H. Lincoln, Surg.,	37	Sept. 10, '63	June 27, 1864, expiration of service.
Z. Boylston Adams, Asst. Surg.	31	June 15, '61	May 31, 1862, Surg. 32d Inf.
William H. Lincoln, Asst. Surg.	36	May 27, '62	Surgeon Sept. 10, 1863.
Arthur W. Cowdry, Asst. Surg.	—	Aug. 14, '62	Oct. 26, 1863.
David H. Dyer, Capt.,	27	June 15, '61	Nov. 12, 1861, resigned.
John Cushing, Capt.,	44	15, '61	7, 1861, do
Charles T. Robinson, Capt.,	34	15, '61	Oct. 11, 1861, do
Joseph B. Leonard, Capt.,	40	15, '61	Major, Oct. 25, 1862.
Horace Fox, Capt.,	—	15, '61	Nov. 30, 1861, resigned.
Zeba F. Bliss, Capt.,	36	15, '61	June 27, 1864, expiration of service.
John B. Whitcomb, Capt.,	34	15, '61	27, 1864, do do
Ward L. Foster, Capt.,	37	15, '61	27, 1864, do do
John F. Ashley, Capt.,	33	15, '61	Aug. 1, 1861, resigned.

254   SEVENTH MASSACHUSETTS VOLUNTEER INFANTRY.

NAME AND RANK.	Age	Date of Muster.	Termination of Service and cause thereof.
Franklin P. Harlow, Capt.,	33	June 15, '61	Major Aug. 1, 1861.
Edgar Robinson, Capt.,	25	Aug. 1, '61	Feb. 1, 1863, resigned.
George W. Reed, Capt.,	34	1, '61	Dec. 6, 1862, do
George F. Holman, Capt.,	23	Oct. 11, '61	Sept. 9, 1862, do
Othniel Gilmore, Capt.,	25	Nov. 8, '61	July 17, 1862.
William B. Stall, Capt.,	26	13, '61	Nov. 11, 1862, do
Hiram A. Oakman, Capt.,	35	Dec. 1, '61	Aug. 24, 1863. Recom. Jan. 28, '64.
James R. Matthewson, Capt.,	25	Oct. 25, '62	June 27, 1864, expiration of service.
William H. Gurney, Capt.,	33	Nov. 1, '62	27, 1864, do do
Prentiss M. Whiting, Capt.,	25	22, '62	Died of wounds May 4, 1863.
Dan Packard, Capt.,	32	Dec. 7, '62	June 27, 1864, expiration of service.
Edward F. Hopkins, Capt.,	29	Jan. 17, '63	10, 1863, disability.
David C. Bancroft, Capt.,	26	Feb. 2, '63	27, 1864, expiration of service.
Christopher C. Weston, Capt.,	24	May 5, '63	27, 1864, do do
Wright Bisbee, Capt.,	28	June 11, '63	Feb. 12, 1864, resigned.
William M. Hale, Capt.,	43	April 1, '64	Transf. June 15, 1864, to 37th Inf.
Hiram A. Oakman, Capt.,	37	Jan. 28, '64	Declined. Lieut. Col. U. S. C. T.
William M. Hale, Capt.,	43	April 1, '64	Transf. June 15, 1864, to 37th Inf.
Jesse F. Eddy, 1st Lieut.,	24	June 15, '61	Mar. 4, 1863, resigned.
Jesse D. Bullock, 1st Lieut.,	29	15, '61	Died of wounds June 25, 1862.
Edgar Robinson, 1st Lieut.,	25	15, '61	Captain Aug. 1, 1861.
William B. Stall, 1st Lieut.,	26	15, '61	Captain Nov. 13, 1861.
Hiram A. Oakman, 1st Lieut.,	34	15, '61	Captain Dec. 1, 1861.
James M. Lincoln, 1st Lieut.,	33	15, '61	Dec. 19, 1862, resigned.
John W. Rogers, 1st Lieut.,	21	15, '61	Captain 38th Inf. Aug. 12, 1862.
Augustus W. Lothrop, 1st Lt.,	42	15, '61	July 17, 1862, resigned.
William W. Fisher, 1st Lieut.,	27	15, '61	Aug. 3, 1861, do
George W. Reed, 1st Lieut.,	34	15, '61	Captain, Aug. 1, 1861.
Othniel Gilmore, 1st Lieut.,	25	15, '61	Captain, Nov. 8, 1861.
Daniel Edson, Jr., 1st Lieut.,	34	15, '61	June 27, 1864, expiration of service.
Abijah L. Mayhew, 1st Lieut.,	39	Aug. 1, '61	Sept. 23, 1862, disability.
George F. Holman, 1st Lieut.,	23	1, '61	Captain, Oct. 11, 1861.
Chas. B. Des Jardines, 1st Lieut.	27	Sept. 1, '61	Nov. 12, 1862.
Dan Packard, 1st Lieut.,	30	Oct. 11, '61	Captain, Dec. 7, 1862.
William M. Hale, 1st Lieut.,	40	Nov. 8, '61	Captain, July 23, 1862.
James R Matthewson, 1st Lt.,	24	13, '61	Captain, Oct. 25, 1862.
William W. Carsley, 1st Lieut.,	28	Dec. 1, '61	July 11, 1862, resigned.
William H. Nye, 1st Lieut.,	27	June 26, '62	Dec. 6, 1862, do
William H. Gurney, 1st Lieut.,	33	July 12, '62	Captain, Nov. 1, 1862.
Prentiss M. Whiting, 1st Lieut.	25	21, '62	Captain, Nov. 22, 1862.
John D Burt, 1st Lieut.,	21	23, '62	May 7, 1863, for promotion.
Thomas High, 1st Lieut.,	28	Sept. 3, '62	Apr. 27, 1863, disability.
Edward F. Hopkins, 1st Lieut.,	29	24, '62	Captain, Jan. 17, 1863.
Edward L. Langford, 1st Lieut.	25	Oct. 25, '62	June 27, 1864, expiration of service.
Monroe F. Williams, 1st Lieut.,	31	Nov. 1, '62	Aug. 14, 1863, resigned.
David C. Bancroft, 1st Lieut.,	25	12, '62	Captain, Feb. 2, 1863.
Christopher C Weston, 1st Lt.,	23	22, '62	Captain, May 5, 1863.
Albert A. Tillson, 1st Lieut.,	20	Dec. 7, '62	Killed May 3, 1863, Fred'ksburg,Va.
Edward N. Dean, 1st Lieut.,	22	7, '62	June 27, 1864, expiration of service.
Wright Bisbee, 1st Lieut.,	28	20, '62	Captain, June 11, 1863.
Leonard Hathaway, 1st Lieut.,	39	Jan. 17, '63	June 27, 1864, expiration of service.
George W. Andrews, 1st Lieut.,	29	Feb. 2, '63	17, 1863, resigned.
James H. Langford, 1st Lieut.,	27	Mar. 26, '63	27, 1864, expiration of service.
Anthony Davis, 1st Lieut.,	34	Apr. 28, '63	27, 1864, do do
William H. Wade, 1st Lieut.,	23	May 4, '63	27, 1864, do do
James E. Seaver, 1st Lieut.,	23	5, '63	Nov. 1, 1863, resigned.
Charles T. Lee, 1st Lieut.,	24	8, '63	June 27, 1864, expiration of service.
James W. Thompson, 1st Lieut.	29	June 11, '63	27, 1864, do do
Henry W. Nichols, 1st Lieut.,	28	18, '63	Died of wounds May 12, 1864.

ROSTER OF THE REGIMENT. 255

NAME AND RANK.	Age	Date of Muster.	Termination of Service and cause thereof.
Charles E. Cady, 1st Lieut., -	32	July 18, '63	June 27, 1864, expiration of service.
William H. Nye, 2d Lieut., -	27	June 15, '61	First Lieut., June 26, 1862.
George W. Gifford, 2d Lieut.,	22	15, '61	Aug. 3, 1861, resigned.
George F. Holman, 2d Lieut,	23	15, '61	First Lieut., Aug. 1, 1861.
William M Hale, 2d Lieut., -	40	15, '61	First Lieut., Nov. 8, 1861.
William W Carsley, 2d Lieut.,	28	15, '61	First Lieut., Dec. 1, 1861.
James R. Matthewson, 2d Lieut.	24	15, '61	First Lieut., Nov. 13, 1861.
William F. White, 2d Lieut.,	23	15, '61	Nov. 6, 1861, resigned.
Munroe F. Williams, 2d Lieut.	30	15, '61	First Lieut., Nov. 1, 1862.
C. B. Des Jardines, 2d Lieut.,	27	15, '61	First Lieut., Sept. 1, 1861.
Abijah L. Mayhew, 2d Lieut.,	39	15, '61	First Lieut., Aug. 1, 1861.
William H. Gurney, 2d Lieut.,	32	15, '61	First Lieut., July 12, 1862.
William O'Neil, 2d Lieut., -	28	15, '61	Nov. 6, 1861, resigned.
Josiah M. Eaton, 2d Lieut., -	22	Aug. 4, '61	2, 1861, do
Prentiss M. Whiting, 2d Lieut.,	24	Sept. 10, '61	First Lieut. July 21, 1862.
John B. Burt, 2d Lieut., -	20	Nov. 3, '61	First Lieut., July 23, 1862.
Frank B. Hayden, 2d Lieut., -	22	7, '61	June 16, 1862, resigned.
Thomas High, 2d Lieut., -	27	7, '61	First Lieut., Sept. 3, 1862.
Edward L. Langford, 2d Lieut.,	24	8, '61	First Lieut., Oct. 25, 1862.
Edward F. Hopkins, 2d Lieut.,	28	Nov. 13, '61	First Lieut., Sept. 21, 1862.
David C Bancroft, 2d Lieut.,	24	Dec. 1, '61	First Lieut., Nov. 12, 1862.
Christopher C. Weston, 2d Lt.,	23	June 18, '62	First Lieut., Nov. 22, 1862.
Peleg Mitchell, 2d Lieut., -	29	26, '62	Died Aug. 10, 1862.
Albert A. Tillson, 2d Lieut., -	18	July 12, '62	First Lieut, Dec. 7, 1862.
Wright Bisbee, 2d Lieut., -	27	21, '62	First Lieut., Dec. 7, 1862.
Leonard Hathaway, 2d Lieut.,	38	23, '62	First Lieut., July 17, 1863.
George W. Andrews, 2d Lieut.,	28	Aug. 11, '62	First Lieut., Feb. 2, 1863.
James H. Langford, 2d Lieut.,	26	Sept. 3, '62	First Lieut., Mar. 26, 1863.
Anthony Davis, 2d Lieut., -	33	24, '62	First Lieut., Apr. 28, 1863.
William H. Wade, 2d Lieut., -	22	Oct. 25, '62	First Lieut., May 4, 1863.
Edward N. Dean, 2d Lieut., -	22	Nov. 1, '62	First Lieut., Dec 7, 1862.
John A. Jones, 2d Lieut., -	32	12, '62	June 27, 1864, expiration of service.
James E. Seaver, 2d Lieut., -	22	22, '62	First Lieut., May 5, 1863.
Charles T. Lee, 2d Lieut., -	23	Dec. 7, '62	First Lieut., May 8, 1863.
James W Thompson, 2d Lieut.,	29	7, '62	First Lieut., June 11, 1863.
Henry W. Nichols, 2d Lieut., -	27	20, '62	First Lieut., June 18, 1863.
Charles E. Cady, 2d Lieut., -	31	Jan. 17, '62	First Lieut., June 18, 1863.
George M. Hatch, 2d Lieut., -	22	Feb. 2, '63	June 27, 1864, expiration of service.
John C. Bosworth, 2d Lieut., -	37	Mar. 26, '63	Oct. 23, 1863.
Earl P. Bowen, 2d Lieut., -	30	Apr. 28, '63	June 27, 1864, expiration of service.
William J. Fisher, 2d Lieut.,	30	May 4, '63	Transferred to 37th Inf.
Charles B. Hathaway, 2d Lieut.,	20	4, '63	June 27, 1864, expiration of service.
Isaac F. Giles, 2d Lieut., -	27	8, '63	27, 1864, do do
Luke B. Noyes, 2d Lieut., -	24	June 18, '63	27, 1864, do do

Non-Commissioned Staff.

Dean, Edward N., Sergt. Major,	21	June 15, '61	Second Lieut., Nov. 1, 1862.
Langford, Edward L., Sgt. Maj.	24	15, '61	Second Lieut., Nov. 8, 1861.
Noyes, Luke B., Sergt. Major,	24	15, '61	Second Lieut., June 18, 1863.
Wilkinson, John F., Sergt. Maj.	26	15, '61	June 27, 1864, expiration of service.
Hayden, Frank B, Q. M. Sergt ,	22	15, '61	Second Lieut., Nov. 7, 1861.
Packard, Dan, Q. M. Sergt., -	30	15, '61	First Lieut., Oct. 11, 1861.
McGregor, Simon, Q. M. Sergt.,	22	15, '61	June 27, 1864, expiration of service.
Thompson, J. W., Q. M. Sergt.,	27	15, '61	Second Lieut., Dec. 7, 1862.
Burt, John B., Com. Sergt., -	20	15, '61	Second Lieut., Nov. 3, 1861.
Hill, Isaac F., Com. Sergt., -	27	15, '61	June 27, 1864, expiration of service.
Nichols, Henry W., Com. Sergt.	26	15, '61	Second Lieut., Dec. 20, 1862.
Eldridge, Chas. H., Hos. Stew.,	27	15, '61	June 27, 1864, expiration of service.
Sherman, Horace B., Hos. Stew.	22	15, '61	Aug. 8, 1862, disability.

SEVENTH MASSACHUSETTS VOLUNTEER INFANTRY.

NAME AND RANK.	Age	Date of Muster.	Termination of Service and cause thereof.
Non-Com. Staff—Con.			
Dolan, Thomas, Prin. Mus.,	24	June 15, '61	Feb. 23, 1864, to re-enlist.
Dolan, Thomas, Prin. Mus.,	26	Feb. 24, '64	Transf. June 14, 1864, to 37th Inf.
Sheehan, Robert, Prin. Mus.,	27	June 15, '6	Feb. 25, 1864, to re-enlist
Sheehan, Robert, Prin. Mus.,	29	Feb. 26, '64	Transf. June 14, 1864, to 37th Inf.
Wilkinson, John F., Prin. Mus.,	26	June 15, '61	Appointed Sergt. Major.
Band.			
Thompson, Zadoc, Jr., Leader,	36	June 15, '61	Aug. 11, 1862, order War Dept.
Allen, George H.,	24	15, '61	11, 1862, do do
Bailey, Augustus,	27	15, '61	11, 1862, do do
Bowles, William A.,	27	15, '61	11, 1862, do do
Cushman, Charles F.,	37	15, '61	11, 1862, do do
Hansell, Edward W.,	34	15, '61	11, 1862, do do
Hatton, Francis E.,	23	15, '61	11, 1862, do do
Jackson, William H.,	23	15, '61	11, 1862, do do
Jefferds, Sylvander,	39	15, '61	11, 1862, do do
Knapp, Edward C.,	30	15, '61	Oct. 17, 1861, disability.
Lane, Parker W.,	24	15, '61	Feb. 25, 1862, do
Makinson, John F.,	23	15, '61	Aug. 11, 1862, order War Dept.
Pond, William A.,	21	15, '61	11, 1862, do do
Russell, Warren S.,	21	15, '61	11, 1862, do do
Shepard, Lewis C.,	23	15, '61	11, 1862, do do
Smith, George C.,	29	15, '61	11, 1862, do do
Soule, George	26	15, '61	June 18, 1862, disability.
Stanley, Stephen	19	15, '61	Aug. 11, 1862, order War Dept.
Thompson, Asaph P.,	29	15, '61	11, 1862 do do
Wood, Horatio N.,	38	15, '61	Died Aug. 7, '62, Ft. Monroe, Va.
Company A.			
Durfee, Thomas M., 1st Sergt.,	26	June 15, '61	Transf. Aug. 12, '63, to Sig. Corps.
Langford, Edward L., 1st Sergt.	24	15, '61	Sergt. Major, Aug. 1. 1861.
McEwen, John, 1st Sergt.,	27	15, '61	June 27, 1864, expiration of service.
Bennett, Francis F., Sergt.,	23	15, '61	27, 1864, do do
Bowen, Earl P., Sergt.,	28	15, '61	Second Lieut. May 4, 1863.
Brightman, James L., Sergt.,	24	15, '61	Killed May 3, '63, Salem Hts., Va.
Burgess, Elijah F., Sergt.,	26	15, '61	June 27, 1864, expiration of service.
Canavan, John, Sergt.,	26	15, '61	Deserted Oct. 10, 1862.
Davis, Anthony, Sergt.,	32	15, '61	Second Lieut. Sept. 24, 1862.
Kay, Henry E., Sergt.,	25	15, '61	June 27, 1864, expiration of service.
Langford, James H., Sergt.,	25	15, '61	Second Lieut. Sept. 3, 1862.
Nichols, Henry W., Sergt.,	26	15, '61	Com. Sergt. Jan. 30, 1862.
Palmer, Albert S.,	22	15, '61	June 27, 1864, expiration of service.
Carr, George A., Corp.,	23	15, '61	27, 1864. do do
Clough, James, Corp.,	32	15, '61	Died June 18, '63, Wash'gton, D.C.
Davol, Leander A., Corp.,	33	15, '61	June 27, 1864, expiration of service.
Dunn, William A., Corp.,	29	15, '61	Transf. Aug. 19, '63, to Inv. Cor.
Hayden, Frank B., Corp.,	22	15, '61	Q. M. Sergt. Oct. 11, 1861.
Hill, William, Corp.,	18	15, '61	Died May 7, '64, Wilderness, Va.
Mather, Joseph, Corp.,	25	15, '61	June 27, 1864, expiration of service.
Pickford, Thomas, Corp.,	29	15, '61	27, 1864, do do
White, Gideon Foster, Corp.,	22	15, '61	Feb. 28, 1863, disability.
Brady, Martin, Musician,	19	15, '61	June 27, 1864, expiration of service.
Brown, George A., Musician,	16	Feb. 13, '62	Transf. June 14, '64, to 37th Inf.
Dickerton, William, Musician,	19	June 15, '61	Dec. 23, 1862, disability.
Dyer, Edwin J., Musician,	18	15, '61	Jan. 18, 1862, minority.
Sheehan, Robert, Musician,	27	15, '61	Principal Musician.
Bennett, Henry B., Wagoner,	24	15, '61	Apr. 1, 1862, disability.
Adams, Charles P.,	30	15, '61	Aug. 15, 1861, do
Adams, William,	36	Aug. 11, '62	June 27, 1864, expiration of service.

ROSTER OF THE REGIMENT.

NAME AND RANK.	Age.	Date of Muster.	Termination of Service and cause thereof.
Company A—Con.			
Allen, Charles C.	23	June 15, '61	Apr. 1, 1862, disability.
Allen, Theodore H.	26	15, '61	June 27, 1864, expiration of service.
Anthony, Charles W.	22	15, '61	Feb. 18, 1862, disability.
Baldwin, Amos,	19	15, '61	June 27, 1864, expiration of service.
Barker, Frank,	18	15, '61	Oct. 14, 1862, disability.
Beaumont, Joseph,	19	15, '61	Aug. 5, 1861, do
Benson, James F.	42	Aug. 11, '62	June 27, 1864, expiration of service.
Boomer, Nathan H.	24	June 15, '61	Sept. 12, 1861, to enlist in Navy.
Booth, Richard,	28	Aug. 11, '62	June 27, 1864, expiration of service.
Borden, Arthur R.	25	June 15, '61	July 16, 1861, order Sec. of War.
Bostick, Samuel,	42	Aug. 11, '62	May 14, 1864, disability.
Brayton, Thomas L.	19	June 15, '61	June 27, 1864, expiration of service.
Bramwood, William,	28	15, '61	27, 1864, do do
Buffinton, James	44	15, '61	Aug. 24, 1861, order Sec. of War.
Burgess, Freeman R.	26	15, '61	June 27, 1864, expiration of service.
Burt, John B.	20	15, '61	Com. Sergt. July 1, 1861.
Carroll, Henry,	—	15, '61	Died Nov. 30, 1861.
Carr, William W.	30	15, '61	June 27, 1864, expiration of service.
Chace, Andrew J.	21	15, '61	27, 1864, do do
Chace, Hiram,	19	15, '61	27, 1864, do do
Chace, Philip,	27	15, '61	Nov. 15, 1861, disability.
Cobb, John B.	33	15, '61	Dec. 31, 1862, do
Conley, Lawrence,	21	15, '61	Dropped from rolls Apr. 27, 1864.
Coyle, Thomas F.	20	15, '61	June 27, 1864, expiration of service.
Cunningham, John,	30	15, '61	Deserted Dec. 6, 1862.
Daley, James,	27	Aug. 27, '61	Deserted Jan. 5, 1863.
Desmond, Patrick,	30	June 15, '61	Never joined for service.
Dickenson, John,	30	15, '61	Deserted Dec. 6, 1862.
Downing, Cornelius B.	35	Aug. 11, '62	June 27, 1864, expiration of service.
Dunning, Eben P.	31	June 15, '61	27, 1864, do do
Dunham, Isaac Jr.	19	15, '61	Oct. 28, 1861, disability.
Dwight, Eugene,	18	15, '61	Dropped from rolls April 27, 1864.
Elsbree, Alaunanza S.	26	15, '61	Aug. 1, 1861, disability.
Gerry, Benjamin S.	19	15, '61	June 27, 1864, expiration of service.
Gerry, John W.	25	15, '61	27, 1864, do do in Co. F.
Gerry, Nathaniel S.	26	15, '61	Died May 17, '62, Williamsburg, Va.
Glidden, Benjamin R.	37	Aug. 11, '62	June 27, 1864, expiration of service.
Goss, Walter S.	27	June 15, '61	Transf. Feb. 15, 1864, to V. R. C.
Green, Daniel,	20	15, '61	June 27, 1864, expiration of service.
Green, James E.	28	15, '61	Deserted Oct. 20, 1862.
Greenhalgh, John,	27	15, '61	Nov. 15, 1861, disability.
Gregory, Robert,	19	15, '61	Deserted April 27, 1864.
Hampson, William,	28	15, '61	June 27, 1864, expiration of service.
Hannaford, James	36	Aug. 27, '61	Apr. 1, 1862, disability.
Harding, Christopher,	38	June 15, '61	Dec. 26, 1863, to re-enlist.
Harding, Christopher,	40	Dec. 27, '63	Transf. June 14, 1864, to 37th Inf.
Harding, Lawrence,	42	Aug. 11, '62	Died Jan. 1, '64, Brandy Sta'n, Va.
Herrin, Patrick,	20	June 15, '61	Dropped from rolls April 27, 1864.
Kelley, Michael	19	15, '61	June 27, 1864, expiration of service.
Lang, Richard,	35	15, '61	27, 1864, do do
Lawton, Andrew S.	20	15, '61	Died May 6, 1862, Williamsb'g, Va.
Leonard, William,	21	15, '61	Deserted Dec. 7, 1862.
Lincoln, Willard B.	29	Aug. 27, '61	Nov. 21, 1862, disability.
Lonsdale, Thomas,	27	June 15, '61	Apr. 18, 1862, do
Mahoney, Daniel	24	15, '61	Deserted July 29, 1862.
Malone, Peter,	22	15, '6.	June 27, 1864, expiration of service.
Manchester, William C.	22	15, '61	27, 1864, do do
Marvel, Edward T.	21	15, '61	Nov. 21, 1862, disability.
Martin, Frank,	24	15, '61	Mar. 5, 1863, do

258 SEVENTH MASSACHUSETTS VOLUNTEER INFANTRY.

NAME AND RANK.	Age	Date of Muster.	Termination of Service and cause thereof.
Company A—Con.			
Martin, John C.	34	June 15, '61	July 1, 1861, disability.
McQuillan, Joseph,	19	15, '61	June 27, 1864, expiration of service.
Meadowcraft, William,	29	Aug. 11, '62	27, 1864, do do
Monks, Major,	23	June 15, '61	Died Feb 22,'62, Camp Brightwood.
Murphy, Thomas,	19	15, '61	June 27, 1864, expiration of service.
O'Beirne, James,	36	15, '61	27, 1864, do do
O'Neil, Daniel J.	23	15, '61	Dec. 16, 1863, disability.
O'Neil, James,	21	15, '61	Killed May 3, '63, Marie's Hts., Va.
Peckham, Daniel H.	22	15, '61	Died July 29, '62, Harr. Land'g, Va.
Peckham, John R.	22	15, '61	Dec. 22, 1862, disability.
Randall, Edward E.	18	Jan. 31, '62	Transf. June 14,' 64, to 37th Inf.
Ray, James,	22	June 15, '61	Aug. 17, 1863, disability.
Reed, George H.	25	15, '61	June 27, 1864, expiration of service.
Reed, Thomas A.	21	15, '61	Died July 15,'62, Savage Sta'n, Va.
Roberts, Ebenezer T.	25	Aug. 11, '62	Transf. Nov. 15, 1863, to V. R. C.
Rowe, Zacheus,	29	27, '61	Mar. 14, 1863, disability.
Ryan, Lawrence,	22	June 15, '61	June 27, 1864, expiration of service.
Ryerson, Simeon,	41	Aug. 27, '61	Died Mar. 8, 1863, Falmouth, Va.
Sanderson, William H.	19	June 15, '61	June 27, 1864, expiration of service.
Scott, William,	34	15, '61	27, 1864, do do
Sellers, John,	22	15, '61	Nov. 11, 1863, to enlist in Navy.
Shaw, John,	39	15, '61	July 20, 1862, disability.
Shaw, John, Jr.	18	15, '61	Deserted Oct. 10, 1862.
Swan, Horace S.	18	15, '61	Feb. 28, 1863, disability.
Taylor, John,	35	Aug. 11, '62	June 27, 1864, expiration of service.
Terry, Charles W.	25	11, '62	Died May 7, '64, Wilderness, Va.
Tootles, Edward,	29	June 15, '61	See Company K, 37th Inf.
Turner, Seth F.	21	Aug. 27, '61	Transf. Nov. 15, 1863, to V. R. C.
Uncles, William,	26	June 15, '61	Killed May 3, '63, Salem Hts., Va.
Watson, Wallace R.	—	July 1, '61	Transf. Sept. 1, 1863, to V. R. C.
Whalon, James,	22	June 15, '61	June 27, 1864, expiration of service.
Whalon, John,	19	15, '61	Oct. 20, 1862, disability.
Willis, Charles H.	35	Jan. 31, '62	Died Oct. 10, '62, Ft. Monroe, Va.
Witherell, Eben A.	23	June 15, '61	June 27, 1864, expiration of service.
Wordell, James H.	23	Aug. 11, '62	Killed May 5, '64, Wilderness, Va.
Young, Joseph H.	22	June 15, '61	Oct. 22, 1862, disability.
Company B.			
Davis, Robert F., 1st Sergt.	23	June 15, '61	June 27, 1864, expiration of service.
Eaton, Josiah J., 1st Sergt.	22	15, '61	Second Lieut. Aug. 4, 1861.
Jones, John A., 1st Sergt.	31	15, '61	Second Lieut. Nov. 12, 1862.
Mitchell, Peleg, 1st Sergt.	28	15, '61	Second Lieut. Aug. 12, 1862.
Brown, William A., Sergt.	22	15, '61	June 27, 1864, expiration of service.
Bolger, Joseph, Sergt.	19	15, '61	27, 1864, do do
Calnoon, James F., Sergt.	24	15, '61	27, 1864, do do
Lannagan, John, Sergt.	22	15, '61	27, 1864, do do
Anderson, John, Corp.	28	15, '61	Sept. 10, 1861, disability.
Bullock, Job F., Corp.	18	15, '61	Nov. 21, 1862, disability.
Burrows, Isaac H., Corp.	26	15, '61	Dec. 25, 1863, to re-enlist.
O'Brien, Patrick H., Corp.	30	15, '61	Feb. 27, 1864, to re-enlist.
O'Brien, Patrick H., Corp.	32	Feb. 28, '64	Transf. June 14, 1864, to 37th Inf.
Pierce, Oliver W., Corp.	19	June 15, '61	June 27, 1864, expiration of service.
Regan, David, Corp.	22	15, '61	27, 1864, do do
Rose, Eli V., Corp.	18	15, '61	27, 1864, do do
Ryan, Michael, Corp.	31	15, '61	Killed May 3, '63, Salem Hts., Va.
Smith, Patrick, Corp.	30	15, '61	June 27, 1864, expiration of service.
York, Andrew, Corp.	22	15, '61	Transf. Jan. 15, 1864, to V. R. C.
Birtwell, Thomas E., Musician	18	15, '61	June 27, 1864, expiration of service.
Sullivan, Jeremiah, Musician,	20	15, '61	27, 1864, do do

ROSTER OF THE REGIMENT.

NAME AND RANK.	Age.	Date of Muster.	Termination of Service and cause thereof.
Company B—Con.			
Holmes, Peter A., Wagoner,	39	June 15, '61	June 27, 1864, expiration of service.
Anderson, Andrew,	22	15, '61	Deserted Aug. 4, 1862.
Atwood, Frederick,	21	Mar. 4, '62	Feb. 6, 1863, disability.
Barker, Francis,	30	June 15, '61	June 27, 1864, expiration of service.
Beers, Hiram S.	24	15, '61	Died Sept. 21, '62, Newport News.
Bigelow, Lucius T., Jr.	23	15, '61	Deserted Dec. 18, 1862.
Briggs, Andrew,	33	15, '61	June 27, 1864, expiration of service.
Brightman, Henry W.	22	15, '61	Dropped from rolls Apr. 26, 1864.
Brokaw, Abram,	26	Jan. 20, '62	Dec. 26, 1863, to re-enlist.
Brokaw, Abram,	22	Dec. 27, '63	Transf. June 14, 1864, to 37th Inf.
Brown, Henry E.	22	June 15, '61	June 27, 1864, expiration of service.
Brocklehurst, John,	31	15, '61	27, 1864, do do
Buffinton, Israel, Jr.	22	15, '61	6, 1864, disability.
Burrows, Isaac H.	22	Dec. 26, '63	Transf. June 14, '64, to 37th Inf.
Church, James G.	19	June 15, '61	June 27, 1864, expiration of service.
Costello, Patrick,	18	15, '61	27, 1864, do do
Crompton, George,	31	15, '61	27, 1864, do do
Cunningham, John,	27	Feb. 19, '62	Feb. 27, 1864, to re-enlist.
Cunningham, John,	29	28, '64	Transf. June 14, 1864, to 37th Inf.
Davis, Edward E.	22	June 15, '61	Nov. 16, 1863, order War Dept.
Davis, Otis H.	30	15, '61	Transf. Dec. 15, 1863, to V. R. C.
Doane, Henry,	26	15, '61	June 27, 1864, expiration of service.
Donohue, William,	37	15, '61	Jan. 20, 1864, to re-enlist.
Donohue, William,	39	Jan. 21, '64	Transf. June 14, 1864, to 37th Inf.
Dunham, Ichabod H.	31	June 15, '61	June 27, 1864, expiration of service.
Elsbree, Edwin P.	24	15, '61	Mar. 2, 1862, disability.
Elsbree, Frederick O.	19	15, '61	Deserted May 18, 1863.
Farren, Henry S.	22	15, '61	Deserted Nov. 30, 1862.
Farnsworth, William H.	20	15, '61	Deserted Sept. 1, 1862.
Finneran, John,	25	15, '61	June 27, 1864, expiration of service.
Fish, John R.	26	15, '61	Oct. 11, 1862, disability.
Fleet, James,	30	15, '61	Feb. 18, 1862, do
Fletcher, Phineas D.	20	15, '61	June 27, 1864, expiration of service.
Galligan, Bartley,	25	15, '61	Died Oct 21, 1862, Taunton.
Grimshaw, John,	33	15, '61	Feb. 20, 1862, disability.
Hadfield, Thomas,	19	15, '61	Mar. 9, 1862, do
Hamer, John G.	22	15, '61	Jan. 20, 1864, to re-enlist.
Hamer, John G.	24	Jan. 21, '64	Transf. June 14, 1864, to 37th Inf.
Hambly, John G.	21	June 15, '61	June 27, 1864, expiration of service.
Harrihan, Thomas,	22	15, '61	Mar. 9, 1862.
Haseltine, William,	34	15, '61	Killed May 3, '63, Salem Hts., Va.
Hathaway, Warren,	19	15, '61	June 27, 1864, expiration of service.
Hayes, Stephen,	22	Mar. , '62	Died June 8, 1862, Baltimore, Md.
Hedge, Lemuel M.	21	June 15, '61	Mar. 9, 1863, disability.
Holehouse, James,	22	15, '61	Deserted Nov. 17, 1861.
Holehouse, John	19	15, '61	Deserted Sept. 17, 1862.
Kelley, James,	26	15, '61	Deserted Sept. 5, 1862.
Kelley, Michael C.	24	15, '61	Sept. 15, 1862, disability.
Keenan, John,	18	15, '61	Dec. 10, 1861, minority.
Keenan, Samuel R.	23	15, '61	Mar. 26, 1862, disability.
Lake, Alexander,	22	15, '61	Sept. 10, 1861, do
Lotta, Robert,	22	15, '61	Deserted Dec. 18, 1862.
Mahoney, William,	18	15, '61	Deserted Nov. 28, 1861.
Manley, Edward,	19	15, '61	June 27, 1864, expiration of service.
Manchester, Lorenzo,	22	15, '61	27, 1864, do do
Mather, Thomas,	28	15, '61	27, 1864, do do
McLeod, William	18	15, '61	Deserted Oct. 18, 1861.
Meaney, Patrick,	19	15, '61	Dec. 26, 1863, to re-enlist.
Meaney, Patrick,	21	Dec. 27, '63	Transf. June 14, 1864, to 37th Inf.

Name and Rank.	Age	Date of Muster.	Termination of Service and cause thereof.
Company B—Con.			
Morse, Andrew,	32	June 15, '61	July 10, 1861, disability.
Munroe, John H.	22	15, '61	Deserted Jan. 22, 1862.
Murphy, John,	19	15, '61	Deserted Nov. 17, 1861.
Musson, Thomas,	29	15, '61	June 27, 1864, expiration of service.
Norton, Henry F.	19	15, '61	27, 1864, do do
O'Neil, Robert,	20	15, '61	Deserted Dec. 18, 1862.
Patterson, John,	35	15, '61	Deserted Sept. 5, 1862.
Pierce, Oliver V.	28	15, '61	Mar. 3, 1862, disability.
Potter, James H.	18	15, '61	4, 1862, do
Porter, Alexander,	22	15, '61	Deserted Apr. 26, 1864.
Pucell, William,	32	15, '61	Dec. 26, 1863, to re-enlist.
Pucell, William,	34	Dec. 27, '63	Transf. June 15, 1864, to 37th Inf.
Quinley, Richard H.	34	Mar. 4, '62	Dec. 26, 1863, to re-enlist.
Quinley, Richard H.	36	Dec. 27, '63	Killed May 6, '64, Wilderness, Va.
Reed, Gustavus L.	25	June 15, '61	Deserted Dec. 10, 1862.
Rullerri, Joseph,	25	15, '61	Transf. Mar. 31, 1864, to V. R. C.
Rusby, George,	23	15, '61	July —, 1861, disability.
Shawcross, Bristo,	30	15, '61	Feb. 28, 1863, disability.
Shemn, Frederick A.	20	15, '61	20, 1862, disability.
Smith, John,	26	15, '61	June 27, 1864, expiration of service.
Smithers, Samuel,	20	15, '61	27, 1864, do do
Smythe, Robert,	19	15, '61	Dec. 26, 1863, to re-enlist.
Smythe, Robert,	21	Dec. 27, '63	Transf. June 15, 1864, to 37th Inf.
Sullivan, Michael	22	June 15, '61	Mar. 9, 1863, disability.
Sullivan, Timothy,	19	Aug. 22, '61	Deserted Oct. 1, 1862.
Swindles, Joseph,	22	June 15, '61	Mar. 11, 1863 disability.
Vickery, Augustus,	25	Feb. 12, '62	Dropped from rolls April 26, 1864.
Vocell, James A.	22	June 15, '61	Nov. 19, 1862, disability.
Wallace, Thomas A.	28	15, '61	Died Nov. 17, 1862, Fall River.
Warhurst, William,	21	15, '61	Killed May 5, '64, Wilderness, Va.
Washburn, Arthur,	21	15, '61	June 27, 1864, expiration of service.
West, Edward P.	23	15, '61	Killed May 6, '64, Wilderness, Va.
White, Thomas A.	21	Feb. 26, '62	Deserted Nov. 16, 1862.
Willis, George F.	26	26, '62	Transf. June 15, 1864, to 37th Inf.
Wilbur, Albert B.	22	June 15, '61	June 27, 1864, expiration of service.
Wilbur, Lloyd,	18	15, '61	Dec 26, 1863, to re-enlist.
Wilbur, Lloyd,	20	Dec. 27, '63	Transf. June 15, 1864, to 37th Inf.
Winslow, Abiel W.	26	June 15, '61	June 27, 1864, expiration of service.
Withington, Henry,	31	Feb. 7, '62	Transf. June 15, 1864, to 37th Inf.
Wordell, Ephraim,	29	June 15, '61	Deserted Sept. 5, 1862.
Wright, John G.	34	Feb. 11, '62	Died July 8, '62, Ports'h Grove, R.I.
Company C.			
Benton, Henry S., 1st Sergt.	18	June 15, '61	Dec. 26, 1863, to re-enlist.
Benton, Henry S., 1st Sergt.	20	Dec. 27, '63	Died of wds. July 10, '64, Alex'a, Va.
Dunham, William M., 1st Sergt.	22	June 15, '61	Killed May 3, '63, Salem Hts., Va.
O'Neil, William, 1st Sergt.	28	15, '61	Second Lieut. Aug. 1, 1861.
Weston, Christopher C., 1st Sgt.	22	15, '61	Second Lieut. June 18, 1862.
Dunham, George L., Sergt.	29	15, '61	Died Feb 6, '63, gunboat Cincinnati
Hathaway, Leonard, Sergt.	37	15, '61	Second Lieut. July 23, 1862.
Nichols, John, Sergt.	28	15, '61	Deserted Jan. 20, 1863.
Paine, Levi R., Sergt.	27	15, '61	June 27, 1864, expiration of service.
Robinson, Henry H., Sergt.	21	15, '61	July 1, 1861, order War Dept.
Rogers, Hiram, Sergt.	36	15, '61	Dec. 26, 1863, to re-enlist.
Rogers, Hiram, Sergt.	38	Dec. 27, '63	Transf. June 14, 1864, to 37th Inf.
Staples, Edward C., Sergt.	22	June 15, '61	Jan. 20, 1864, to re-enlist.
Staples, Edward C., Sergt.	24	Jan. 21, '64	Transf. June 14, '64, to 37th Inf.
Andrews, Daniel D., Corp.	22	June 15, '61	June 27, 1864, expiration of service.
Cahoon, William C., Corp.	18	15, '61	Jan. 21, 1864, to re-enlist.

ROSTER OF THE REGIMENT. 261

NAME AND RANK.	Age	Date of Muster.	Termination of Service and cause thereof.
Company C—Con			
Cahoon, William C., Corp.	20	Jan. 24, '62	Transf. June 15,' 64, to 37th Inf.
Dennis, Alex. J., Corp.	28	June 15, '61	Aug. 27, 1862, disability.
Haseltine, Hiram R., Corp.	24	15, '61	June 27, 1864, expiration of service.
Hathaway, William E., Corp.	23	15, '61	Jan. 20, 1864, to re-enlist.
Hathaway, William E., Corp.	25	Jan. 21, '64	Transf. June 15, 1864, to 37th Inf.
Hamilton, John L., Corp.	18	June 15, '61	Jan. 20, 1864, to re-enlist.
Hamilton, John L., Corp.	20	Jan. 21, '64	Killed May 6, '64, Wilderness, Va.
Perkins, Salmon W., Corp.	26	June 15, '61	Sept. 4, 1862, disability.
Pitts, John H., Corp.	22	15, '61	Jan. 20, 1864, to re-enlist.
Pitts, John H., Corp.	24	Jan. 21, '64	Killed June 3,'64, Bethesda Ch., Va.
Ross, David, Corp.	19	June 15, '61	June 27, 1864, expiration of service.
Seklean, Charles, Corp.	30	15, '61	Deserted Jan. 20, 1863.
Staples, Charles E., Corp.	24	15, '61	Jan. 20, 1864, to re-enlist.
Staples, Charles E., Corp.	26	Jan. 21, '64	Transf. June 14, 1864, to 37th Inf.
Dolan, Thomas, Musician,	24	June 15, '61	Principal Musician.
Marrs, George M., Musician,	19	15, '61	June 27, 1864, expiration of service.
Wade, Harrison A., Musician,	15	15, '61	Jan. 3, 1863, disability.
Guthrie, Roger C., Wagoner,	28	15, '61	June 27, 1864, expiration of service.
Adams, Westley F.	19	15, '61	27, 1864, do do
Andros, Charles E.	26	15, '61	27, 1864, do do
Ariel, Isaac,	22	15, '61	Transferred to 37th Inf.
Briggs, Roland W.	21	15, '61	June 27, 1864, expiration of service.
Burns, Alexander,	21	15, '61	Deserted Jan. 2, 1863.
Carey, Michael,	20	15, '61	Died Oct. 4, '61, Brightwood, D.C.
Caswell, Lambert O.	24	15, '61	Mar. 21, 1863, disability.
Casey, Michael D.	25	15, '61	June 27, 1864, expiration of service.
Chace, Baylies R.	18	15, '61	Sept. 11, 1861, disability.
Chace, Joseph A.	21	15, '61	Deserted Jan. 20, 1863.
Chace, Joseph H.	25	15, '61	June 8, 1862, disability.
Cole, George N.	27	15, '61	Dec. 26, 1863, to re-enlist.
Cole, George N.	29	Dec. 27, '63	Transf. June 15, 1864, to 37th Inf.
Conlin, Owen,	23	June 15, '61	Jan. 21, 1863, disability
Coogan, Patrick,	32	15, '61	May 5, 1862, disability.
Corcoran, Daniel,	30	15, '61	Deserted Dec. 11, 1862.
Corrigan, William,	23	15, '61	- - -
Cronan, Andrew,	34	15, '61	Feb. 2, 1863, disability.
Cummings, Robert,	28	15, '61	Deserted Jan. 20, 1863.
Cushing, Henry J.	18	Feb. 19, '62	Transf. Mar. 7, 1864, to V. R. C.
Dean, John Q. A.	17	June 15, '61	Transf. Aug. 1, 1863, to V. R. C.
Drake, Samuel W.	35	15, '61	Aug. 8, 1862, disability.
Dyer, Peter,	37	15, '61	June 27, 1864, expiration of service.
Eagan, John,	19	15, '61	Deserted Sept. 1, 1862.
Ellis, Warren,	21	15, '61	Deserted Jan. 20, 1863.
Fisher, Gustavus,	23	15, '61	June 27, 1864, expiration of service.
Foley, James,	21	15, '61	Died May 3, '63, Salem Hts., Va.
Fox, John,	37	15, '61	Died of wds. May 19,'64,Fred'ksb'g.
Fuller, George W.	18	15, '61	June 27, 1864, expiration of service.
Gilchrist, Patrick,	36	15, '61	27, 1864, expiration of service.
Grinnell, David,	25	15, '61	Deserted Sept. 8, 1862.
Hand, Michael,	28	15, '61	Deserted Jan. 20, 1863.
Hauprick, William,	28	15, '61	June 27, 1864, expiration of service.
Hart, John,	33	15, '61	Killed May 6, '64, Wilderness,Va.
Hathaway, Henry E.	23	15, '61	June 12, 1865, Pres. proclamation.
Hickey, Patrick,	26	15, '61	Deserted Jan. 20, 1863.
Hinds, James H.	40	15, '61	Nov. 13, 1862, disability.
Hinds, John B.	21	15, '61	June 27, 1864, expiration of service.
Holland, Patrick,	43	15, '61	27, 1864, do do
Kelley, James,	22	15, '61	27, 1864, do do
Kelley, James,	30	15, '61	May 19, 1862, disability.

NAME AND RANK.	Age	Date of Muster.	Termination of Service and cause thereof.
Company C—Con.			
Kelley, Morty,	22	June 15, '61	Deserted Jan. 20, 1863.
Leddy, John,	35	15, '61	Transf. Dec. 15, 1863, to V. R. C.
Lee, Joseph,	18	15, '61	Deserted Jan. 2, 1863.
Littleton, Michael,	22	15, '61	June 27, 1864, expiration of service.
Martin, Elbridge,	20	15, '61	Deserted Jan. 20, 1863.
Marshall, Frank,	26	15, '61	May 15, 1865, Pres. proclamation.
Martin, Kinsley,	20	15, '61	Deserted July 3, 1863.
McGuire, Andrew,	35	15, '61	Dec. 25, 1862, disability.
McManus, Andrew,	43	15, '61	May 29, 1863, do
McMann, John,	28	15, '61	Sept. 22, 1862, do
Medbury, Theophilus H.	24	15, '61	Deserted Jan. 29, 1862.
Mellville, Dean,	21	15, '61	Apr. 30, 1862, disability.
Monaghan, Patrick,	19	15, '61	Deserted Jan. 20, 1863.
Moore, Robert,	35	15, '61	Deserted June 3, 1863.
Morse, Ezra,	23	15, '61	June 27, 1864, expiration of service.
Murray, Patrick,	24	15, '61	27, 1864, do do
Nixon, James,	20	15, '61	27, 1864, do do
O'Neil, George,	38	15, '61	27, 1864, do do
Orcutt, Alpheus S.	22	15, '61	27, 1864, do do
Phillips, Henry,	20	15, '61	27, 1864, do do
Pierce, Isaac O.	35	15, '61	Mar. 26, 1862, disability.
Powers, Cornelius,	23	15, '61	Deserted Dec. 11, 1862.
Powers, John,	20	15, '61	Feb. 18, 1863, disability.
Powers, William,	19	15, '61	18, 1863, do
Rawson, James E.	29	15, '61	June 27, 1864, expiration of service.
Sanders, Lewis T.	18	15, '61	Oct. 22, 1862, disability.
Scandling, James,	20	15, '61	Died Sept. 7, 1862, Newport News.
Smith, James E.	22	15, '61	
Smith, James,	19	15, '61	June 27, 1864, expiration of service.
Smith, Thomas J.	19	15, '61	27, 1864, do do
Talbot, Henry C.	23	15, '61	Deserted Aug. 16, 1862.
Tracy, Thomas A.	21	15, '61	Deserted Jan. 20, 1863.
Warren, George A.	23	15, '61	Killed May 5, '64, Wilderness, Va.
Welch, Thomas A.	28	15, '61	Deserted Jan. 20, 1863.
Whittemore, George,	30	15, '61	Feb. 25, 1862, disability.
Williams, Silas C.	18	15, '61	June 27, 1864, expiration of service.
Company D.			
Hatch, George M., 1st Sergt.	20	June 15, '61	Second Lieut. Feb. 2, 1863.
Pierce, Abner J., 1st Sergt.	19	15, '61	June 27, 1864, expiration of service.
Seaver, James E., 1st Sergt.	21	15, '61	Second Lieut. Nov. 22, 1862.
Babbitt, Rollin H., Sergt.	20	15, '61	June 27, 1864, expiration of service.
Blake, Samuel O., Sergt.	22	15, '61	27, 1864, do do
Corey, Ebenezer, Sergt.	23	15, '61	Deserted Dec. 2, 1862.
Long, James, Sergt.	28	15, '61	June 27, 1864, expiration of service.
Macomber, James H., Sergt.	23	15, '61	Dec. 26, 1863, to re-enlist.
Macomber, James H., Sergt.	25	Dec. 27, '63	Transf. Apr. 8, 1864, to Navy.
Allen, James B., Corp.	20	June 15, '61	Died of wounds May —, 1864.
Bliss, Matthew, Corp.	20	15, '61	Jan. 5, 1864, disability.
Luther, James H., Corp.	20	15, '61	June 27, 1864, expiration of service.
Peck, George G., Corp.	30	15, '61	Transf. Sept. 30, 1863, to V. R. C.
Williams, Benjamin F., Corp.	33	15, '61	Died of wds. May–, '64, Wilderness.
Wilbur, Charles L., Corp.	21	15, '61	Died May 3, 1863, Fred'ksburg, Va.
Chamberlain, Edward W., Mus.	25	15, '61	Aug —, 1861, disability.
Neal, John, Musician,	16	15, '61	June 17, 1863, disability.
Mason, N. Everett, Wagoner,	30	15, '61	27, 1864, expiration of service.
Barton, Lewis B.	18	15, '61	Transf. Feb. 12, 1864, to U. S. A.
Barrows, William J.	21	15, '61	Sept. 14, 1861, disability.
Beach, Henry H.	21	15, '61	Died Jan. 22, 1864.

ROSTER OF THE REGIMENT.

NAME AND RANK.	Age.	Date of Muster.	Termination of Service and cause thereof.
Company D—Con.			
Besse, Christopher C.	20	June 15, '61	Dec. 26, 1863, to re-enlist.
Besse, Christopher C.	22	Dec. 27, '63	Transf. June 14, 1864, to 37th Inf.
Bidwell, Cyrus B.	18	June 15, '61	Sept. 4, 1861, disability.
Bliss, Andrew,	24	15, '61	Deserted Feb. 20, 1863.
Boston, George W.	22	15, '61	Died of wds. May 6,'64, Wilderness.
Braman, William O.	20	15, '61	June 27, 1864, expiration of service.
Briggs, George T.	21	Jan. 6, '62	Jan. 20, 1864, to re-enlist.
Briggs, George T.	23	21, '64	Transf. June 14, 1864, to 37th Inf.
Briggs, Joel,	26	June 15, '61	Dec. 26, 1863, to re-enlist.
Briggs, Joel,	28	Dec. 27, '63	Transf. June 14, 1864, to 37th Inf.
Brown, William O.	25	Feb. 19, '62	Transf. June 14, 1864, to 37th Inf.
Bubser, Mark W.	20	June 15, '61	Deserted April 27, 1864.
Burt, Charles,	19	15, '61	Died June 15,'62, Wh. House L'd'g.
Carpenter, William H.	21	15, '61	June 27, 1864, expiration of service.
Caswell, George E.	18	15, '61	Feb. 28, 1863, disability.
Chace, Orville S.	18	15, '61	Died Feb 18,'62, Camp Brightwood.
Chace, Reuben,	21	Jan. 6, '62	Dec. 26, 1863, to re-enlist.
Chace, Reuben,	23	Dec. 27, '63	Transf. June 14, 1864, to 37th Inf.
Codding, Henry H.	21	Aug. 28, '61	Transf. June 14, 1864, to 37th Inf.
Conlin, James,	19	June 15, '61	Died June 4, 1863.
Carnes, James,	33	15, '61	Deserted Feb. 20, 1863.
Craig, William H.	32	Aug. 13, '62	Died Nov. 14,'62, Hagerstown, Md.
Dary, Nelson,	18	June 15, '61	Nov. 2, 1862, disability.
Davis, Thomas	21	15, '61	Died of wounds May —, 1864.
Dean, James A.	21	15, '61	June 27, 1864, expiration of service.
Dean, James T.	24	15, '61	Sept. 3, 1862, disability.
Dewsnap, John	24	15, '61	Died Aug. 11,'62, on Gov. transport
Dorgan, Jeremiah,	25	15, '61	Died of wounds May —, 1864.
Eddy, John F.	18	15, '61	Feb. 2, 1863, disability.
Eldredge, Jeremiah,	28	15, '61	Jan. 20, 1864, to re-enlist.
Eldredge, Jeremiah,	30	Jan. 21, '64	Transf. June 14, 1864, to 37th Inf.
Farrell, Benjamin,	21	June 15, '61	Died July 28, '62, Harr. Land'g, Va.
Fenen, Edward,	20	15, '61	Deserted.
Frazier, Benjamin V.	28	15, '61	June 27, 1864, expiration of service.
Fuller, Noel B.	20	15, '61	27, 1864, do do
Galligan, Michael,	21	15, '61	Deserted Dec. 20, 1862.
Gammons, Augustus F.	19	15, '61	Jan. 10, 1863, disability.
Gammons, Edward,	—	15, '61	Deserted Sept. 1, 1862.
Gay, Charles,	40	15, '61	July 10, 1861, disability.
Gay, James L.	19	15, '61	Died Aug. 29,'62, Newp't News, Va.
Gibbs, Ralph,	39	15, '61	Aug. 6, 1861, disability.
Gilmore, James W.	25	15, '61	June 27, 1864, expiration of service.
Goodwin, James,	22	15, '61	Dec. 26, 1863, to re-enlist.
Goodwin, James,	24	Dec. 27, '63	Killed May 6, '64, Wilderness, Va.
Guild, Alonzo M.	19	June 15, '61	Nov. 19, 1862, disability.
Hamilton, Naman D.	22	15, '61	Sept. 26, 1862, do
Hathaway, Edward B.	23	15, '61	May 15, 1865, Pres. proclamation.
Hathaway, Isaac F.	18	Jan. 6, '62	Jan. 20, 1864, to re-enlist.
Hathaway, Isaac F.	20	21, '64	Transf. June 14, 1864, to 37th Inf.
Hathaway, Royal,	36	June 15, '61	Died Dec. 24, 1862, Swanzey.
Hathaway, William,	20	15, '61	June 27, 1864, expiration of service.
Hewett, Richard L.	18	15, '61	27, 1864, do do
Hickey, Eugene,	18	15, '61	Sept. 14, 1861, disability.
Hudson, Horatio,	22	15, '61	Dec. 26, 1863, to re-enlist.
Hudson, Horatio,	24	Dec. 27, '63	Died of wounds May —, 1864.
Ingells, George R.	18	June 15, '61	Dec. 26, 1862, disability.
Irving, Alexander,	19	15, '61	June 27, 1864, expiration of service.
Jones, Henry H.	21	Jan. 6, '62	Died Oct. 21, '62, Washington, D.C.
Leach, Horatio,	25	June 15, '61	Nov. 14, 1862, disability.

Name and Rank.	Age	Date of Muster.	Termination of Service and cause thereof.
Company D—Con.			
Lee, George T.	18	June 15, '61	Died May 4, '63, Fred'ksburg, Va.
Leddy, Patrick,	19	15, '61	Deserted Sept. 1, 1862.
Leonard, Andrew	24	15, '61	Died Aug. 11,'62, Newp't News,Va.
Lockwood, John J.	18	15, '61	Deserted Sept. 1, 1862.
Macomber, Enoch,	23	15, '61	Dec. 26, 1863, to re-enlist.
Macomber, Enoch,	25	Dec. 27, '63	Transf. Apr. 8, 1864, to Navy.
McCarty, Jeremiah,	20	June 15, '61	Oct. 4, 1862, disability.
McGee, John,	20	15, '61	June 27, 1864, expiration of service.
McLean, George L.	20	15, '61	Deserted Sept. 1, 1862.
McMahon, James,	23	Aug. 29, '61	Nov. 18, 1861, disability.
Milan, Patrick,	20	June 15, '61	Deserted Dec. 20, 1863.
Mitchell, Charles H.	23	15, '61	Deserted Dec. 23, 1862.
Mitchell, James D.	20	15, '61	Died Apr —, 1862, Taunton.
Mulligan, James,	24	15, '61	Deserted Sept. 17, 1863.
Murphy, Philip,	21	15, '61	Died 1864, Andersonville, Ga.
Packer, William,	26	15, '61	Died May 6, '63, Fred'ksburg, Va.
Paull, Albert M.	18	15, '61	June 27, 1864, expiration of service.
Peck, Marcus R.	22	Nov. 10, '61	Deserted Dec. 20, 1862.
Perry, George N.	18	June 15, '61	Deserted June —, 1863.
Peyton, Charles A.	23	15, '61	Died Sept. 23, '62, Newport News.
Pierce, Charles B.	24	Aug. 16, '62	June 27, 1864, expiration of service.
Pratt, Phineas M.	23	June 15, '61	Aug. 6, 1861, disability.
Raymond, Rufus,	44	Aug. 13, '62	July 23, 1863, disability.
Raymond, Levi S.	32	13, '62	Jan. 2, 1864, disability.
Reed, Henry E.	18	June 15, '61	Transf. Feb. 15, 1864, to V. R. C.
Rothwell, John,	18	15, '61	Deserted Dec. 20, 1862.
Ryan, James,	21	15, '61	Deserted Sept. 2, 1862.
Sanford, Joseph E.	21	15, '61	Dec. 26, 1863, to re-enlist.
Sanford, Joseph E.	23	Dec. 27, '63	Died of wds., June 16,'64,Taunton.
Shaw, Frederick W.	28	June 15, '61	July 10, 1861.
Sherman, Charles H.	20	15, '61	June 27, 1864, expiration of service.
Sherman, James L.	22	15, '61	Aug. 6, 1861, disability.
Simmons, James N.	22	15, '61	June 27, 1864, expiration of service.
Smith, Henry B.	21	15, '61	Died Sept. 27, 1862, Taunton.
Smith, John B.	22	15, '61	Deserted Apr. 1, 1864.
Smith, William N.	18	15, '61	Aug. 14, 1861, disability.
Staples, Barzilla F.	27	Aug. 12, '62	Oct. 13, 1863, disability.
Staples, John P.	20	June 15, '61	June 27, 1864, expiration of service.
Telford John,	28	15, '61	Deserted Sept 14, 1862.
Tratton, George R.	19	Jan. 6, '62	Transf. June 15, 1864, to 37th Inf.
Walker, William E.	18	6, '62	Jan. 20, 1864, to re-enlist.
Walker, William E.	20	21, '64	Transf. June 14, 1864, to 37th Inf.
Whelan, Thomas J.	19	June 15, '61	June 27, 1864, expiration of service.
Wilbar, Darius M.	26	15, '61	Deserted Dec. 20, 1862.
Williams, Bildad,	36	15, '61	June 27, 1864, expiration of service.
Williams, Israel,	28	15, '61	27, 1864, do do
Wilson, Isaac S.	26	15, '61	Deserted Dec. 20, 1862.
Willey, William,	25	15, '61	Deserted Sept. 19, 1862.
Company E.			
Cook, John, 1st Sergt.	31	June 15, '61	June 27, 1864, expiration of service.
Fisher, William J., 1st Sergt.	28	15, '61	Second Lieut. May 4, 1863.
Hopkins, Edward F., 1st Sergt.	28	15, '61	Second Lieut. Sept. 24, 1862.
Bonney, Henry B., Sergt.	33	15, '61	Dec. 26, 1863, to re-enlist.
Bonney, Henry B., Sergt.	35	Dec. 27, '63	Transf. June 14, 1864, to 37th Inf.
Hetherston, Martin C., Sergt.	20	June 15, '61	Dec. 26, 1863, to re-enlist.
Hetherston, Martin C., Sergt.	22	Dec. 27, '63	Transf. June 14, 1864, to 37th Inf.
Kirbey, Patrick T., Sergt.	25	June 15, '61	Deserted Jan. 3, 1862.
Kittredge, Henry G. W., Sergt.	18	15, '61	Dec. 26, 1863, to re-enlist.

Company E—Con.

Name and Rank.	Age	Date of Muster.	Termination of Service and cause thereof.
Kittredge, Henry G. W., Sergt.	20	Dec. 27, '63	Transf. June 14, 1864, to 37th Inf.
Packard, Albert S., Sergt.	27	June 15, '61	Apr. 8, 1863, disability.
Ruggles, Frank S., Sergt.	25	15, '61	26, 1864, do
Crowell, Josiah C., Corp.	35	15, '61	June 27, 1864, expiration of service.
Ewell, Job L., Corp.	29	15, '61	Dec. 26, 1863, to re-enlist.
Ewell, Job L., Corp.	31	Dec. 27, '63	Died of wounds June 5, 1864.
Fais, Cleophas, Corp.	22	June 15, '61	Jan. 19, 1864, disability.
Hopkins, Nathan F., Corp.	25	15, '61	June 27, 1864, expiration of service.
Lord, James F., Corp.	20	15, '61	Dec. 26, 1863, to re-enlist.
Lord, James F., Corp.	22	Dec. 27, '63	Transf. June 14, 1864, to 37th Inf.
Needham, Henry S., Corp.	40	June 15, '61	June 27, 1864, expiration of service.
Spiller, James F., Corp.	18	15, '61	Feb. 12, 1863, disability.
Thayer, George, Corp.	28	15, '61	June 27, 1864, expiration of service.
Wright, Allen, Corp.	18	Feb. 12, '62	Dec. 26, 1863, to re-enlist.
Wright, Allen, Corp.	20	Dec. 27, '63	Transf. June 14, 1864, to 37th Inf.
Harding, James, Musician,	18	June 15, '61	Deserted Feb. 3, 1862.
Schwinn, Charles F., Musician,	20	15, '61	June 27, 1864, expiration of service.
French, Charles E., Wagoner,	34	15, '61	27, 1864, do do
Bailey, Caleb E.	26	15, '61	27, 1864, do do
Barry, George H.	24	15, '61	Jan. 20, 1864, to re-enlist.
Barry, George H.	26	Jan. 21, '64	Transf. June 14, 1864, to 37th Inf.
Bent, George,	23	June 15, '61	Died Mar. 9, '62, Brightwood, D.C.
Blake, Charles,	20	15, '61	Nov. 8, 1862, disability.
Blake, Walter,	19	15, '61	June 27, 1864, expiration of service.
Bole, William,	20	15, '61	Died of wounds May —, 1863.
Boston, John,	24	15, '61	June 27, 1864, exp. of serv. in Co. A.
Brown, David,	21	15, '61	Killed May 3, '63, Marie's Hts., Va.
Broad, Horace S.	21	15, '61	Sept. 15, 1863, disability.
Buker, Edward K.	29	Aug. 1, '61	Transf. June 14, 1864, to 37th Inf.
Burgess, Albina H.	20	June 15, '61	Mar. 23, 1863, disability.
Burrows, Henry H.	20	15, '61	Transf. Sept. 30, 1863, to V. R. C.
Cahoon, David H.	32	15, '61	June 27, 1864, expiration of service.
Casey, Dennis,	29	15, '61	Deserted Jan. 28, 1863.
Chandler, George S.	42	15, '61	June 27, 1864, expiration of service.
Chamberlain, James,	19	15, '61	27, 1864, do do
Church, David,	27	15, '61	Dec. 26, 1863, to re-enlist.
Church, David,	29	Dec. 27, '63	Killed May 6, '64, Wilderness, Va.
Clarke, George,	20	June 15, '61	June 27, 1864, expiration of service.
Clarke, James,	33	15, '61	Mar. 22, 1863, disability.
Cook, Peter,	40	15, '61	June 27, 1864, expiration of service.
Crossley, Edmund,	27	15, '61	27, 1864, do do
Crossley, George E.	28	15, '61	Dec. 26, 1863, to re-enlist.
Crossley, George E.	30	Dec. 27, '63	Transf. June 14, 1864, to 37th Inf.
Darby, William,	22	June 15, '61	June 27, 1864, expiration of service.
Douglass, William,	19	15, '61	Deserted July 3, 1861.
Dunn, Charles,	22	15, '61	Deserted Sept. 1, 1862, from Co. B.
Dunphy, James,	29	15, '61	June 27, 1864, expiration of service.
Ewell, Samuel,	25	15, '61	Died Oct 4, '61, Washington, D.C.
Ewell, Thatcher,	25	15, '61	Transf. Mar. 15, 1864, to V. R. C.
Fais, Andrew,	21	15, '61	Died Mar. 9, 1863, Falmouth, Va.
Feenan, Hugh,	20	15, '61	Transf. Nov. 15, 1863, to V. R. C.
Fisher, Herman,	21	15, '61	Transf. 1863, to V. R. C.
Flaherty, John,	30	15, '61	Jan. 20, 1864, to re-enlist.
Flaherty, John,	32	Jan. 21, '64	Transf. June 14, 1864, to 37th Inf.
Ford, John M.	18	Feb. 12, '62	Transf. June 14, 1864, to 37th Inf.
Goward, Albert V.	18	June 15, '61	Jan. 24, 1865, expiration of service.
Griggs, George H.	33	15, '61	June 27, 1864, do do
Grover, John M.	34	15, '61	Oct. 15, 1862, disability.
Haggerty, John	21	15, '61	Deserted Dec. 11, 1862.

SEVENTH MASSACHUSETTS VOLUNTEER INFANTRY.

NAME AND RANK.	Age	Date of Muster.	Termination of Service and cause thereof.
Company E—Con.			
Hatch, Ezra W.	24	June 15, '61	May 15, 1865, Pres. proclamation.
Hickey, Hugh,	23	15, '61	Dec. 26, 1863, to re-enlist.
Hickey, Hugh,	25	Dec. 27, '63	Transf. June 14, 1864, to 37th Inf.
Hill, John O.	30	June 15, '61	Acc'y shot Sep.21,'62,W'msp't,Md.
Hollis, Nathan S.	22	15, '61	June 27, 1864, expiration of service.
Houghton, William J.	27	15, '61	27, 1864, do do
Ingles, Thomas,	36	Dec. 29, '63	Transf. June 14, '64, to 37th Inf.
Joyce, Joseph,	25	June 15, '61	Sept. 8, 1862, disability.
Keegan, Stephen J.	22	15, '61	June 27, 1864, expiration of service.
Lacey, Thomas J.	23	15, '61	Mar. 17, 1862, disability.
Lewis, Jesse L.	40	15, '61	June 27, 1864, expiration of service.
Lord, George F.	19	15, '61	Oct. 12, 1863, disability.
Lycett, James,	19	15, '61	June 27, 1864, expiration of service.
Mahoney, Thomas,	21	15, '61	27, 1864, do do
Malloy, James,	27	15, '61	Deserted Jan. 28, 1863.
Manchester, William W.	23	15, '61	Killed May 6, '64, Wilderness, Va.
Marsden, Thomas,	23	15, '61	Deserted Aug. 21, 1862.
Mason, William A.	39	15, '61	Nov. 12, 1861, disability.
McElroy, George,	21	15, '61	Died May 10,'63,Washington, D.C.
McGovern, Charles,	23	15, '61	Deserted July 3, 1861.
McIntosh, George,	29	15, '61	Aug. 17, 1863, disability.
Merrill, Thomas,	18	15, '61	Nov. 22, 1862, disability.
Morrow, Henry,	18	15, '61	22, 1862, do
Murphy, Dennis,	31	15, '61	June 27, 1864, expiration of service.
Nightingale, James H.	21	15, '61	27, 1864, do do
Nightingale, William H.	46	15, '61	14, 1862, disability.
O'Connor, Patrick,	21	15, '61	Dec. 26, 1863, to re-enlist.
O'Connor, Patrick,	23	Dec. 27, '63	Transf. June 14, 1864, to 37th Inf.
Piper, Elijah,	19	June 15, '61	June 27, 1864, expiration of service.
Randall, Ethan A.	37	15, '61	Dec. 26, 1863, to re-enlist.
Randall, Ethan A.	39	Dec. 27, '63	Transf. June 17, 1864, to 37th Inf.
Rockwood, William O. V.	22	June 15, '61	Died Mar. 3, '62, Brightwood, D.C.
Sampson, Japhet,	27	15, '61	Sept. 19, 1862, disability.
Scaverns, Alfred A.	24	15, '61	Transf. Nov. 6, 1863, to V. R. C.
Scaff, John,	21	15, '61	Died Oct. 19, '62, Washington, D.C.
Schwinn, Lewis C.	22	15, '61	June 27, 1864, expiration of service.
Sherman, Nathan, Jr.	37	15, '61	Oct. 29, 1862, disability.
Sias, Sylvester,	18	15, '61	June 27, 1864, expiration of service.
Stevens, Charles,	19	15, '61	27, 1864, do do
Sulasky, Joseph,	21	15, '61	Deserted June 28, 1861.
Thayer, Frederick,	21	15, '61	Deserted Aug. 21, 1862.
Thayer, Josiah C.	28	15, '61	June 27, 1864, expiration of service.
Tisdale, William E.	29	Aug. 27, '61	Mar. 11, 1862, disability.
Tolman, Henry,	40	June 15, '61	Dec. 26, 1863, to re-enlist.
Tolman, Henry,	42	Dec. 27, '63	Transf. Apr. 8, 1864, to Navy.
Tolman, William H.	19	Feb. 12, '62	Nov. 8, 1862, disability.
Weather, Charles,	29	June 15, '61	Died at Andersonville, Ga.
Weeman, Orin,	20	15, '61	Aug. 5, 1861, disability.
Wheeler, George W.	20	15, '61	Deserted Dec. 10, 1862.
Wheeler, Sylvester, Jr.	25	15, '61	Died Sept. 5, 1862, Annapolis, Md.
Whitney, Jacob,	21	15, '61	Apr. 8, 1863, disability.
Wild, Warren T.	19	15, '61	June 27, 1864, expiration of service.
Williams, Enos L.	18	Aug. 28, '61	14, 1862, disability.
Williamson, Seth,	35	Feb. 12, '62	14, 1862, do
Company F.			
Bancroft, David C., 1st Sergt.	24	June 15, '61	Second Lieut. Dec. 2, 1861.
Byram, Joseph W., 1st Sergt.	24	15, '61	June 27, 1864, expiration of service.
Dean, Charles F., 1st Sergt.	26	15, '61	Killed May 3, '63, Marie's Hts., Va.

ROSTER OF THE REGIMENT. 267

NAME AND RANK.	Age	Date of Muster.	Termination of Service and cause thereof.
Company F—Con.			
Lee, Charles T., 1st Sergt.	22	June 15, '61	Second Lieut. Dec. 7, 1862.
Aldrich, Theodore N., Sergt.	20	15, '61	June 27, 1864, expiration of service.
Calehan, Joseph D., Sergt.	24	15, '61	Feb. 19, 1864, to re-enlist.
Calehan, Joseph D., Sergt.	26	Feb. 20, '64	Transf. June 14, 1864, to 37th Inf.
Cushman, Harrie A., Sergt.	16	June 15, '61	Dec. 26, 1863, to re-enlist.
Cushman, Harrie A., Sergt.	18	Dec. 27, '63	Transf. June 14, 1864, to 37th Inf.
Elliott, Joseph, Sergt.	23	June 15, '61	Jan. 20, 1864, to re-enlist.
Elliott, Joseph, Sergt.	25	Jan. 21, '64	Died of wds. May 24,'64,Fred'ksb'g.
Hathaway, Charles B., Sergt.	18	June 15, '61	Second Lieut. May 4, 1863.
Howarth, John, Sergt.	22	15, '61	June 27, 1864, expiration of service.
Morton, Gideon E., Sergt.	21	15, '61	Killed May 3, '63, Marie's Hts.,Va.
Walker, John H., Sergt.	24	15, '61	Dec. 1, 1862, disability.
Boyle, James, Corp.	22	15, '61	Deserted Sept. 18, 1862.
Burt, George B., Corp.	30	15, '61	June 27, 1864, expiration of service.
Cunningham, Benj. F., Corp.	27	15, '61	Aug. 8, 1863, disability.
Davis, Francis E., Corp.	24	15, '61	Sept. 10, 1861, do
Dean, David H., Corp.	22	15, '61	Transf. Sept. 12, 1863, to V. R. C.
Estes, William H., Corp.	21	15, '61	June 27, 1864, expiration of service.
Hall, John W., Corp.	21	15, '61	27, 1864, expiration of service.
Harmon, William H., Corp.	23	15, '61	Killed May 3, '63, Marie's Hts.,Va.
Maxham, Lowell M., Corp.	19	15, '61	Aug 16, 1863, disability.
Park, William, Corp.	21	15, '61	June 27, 1864, expiration of service.
Wordell, Webster, Corp.	25	15, '61	Died Sep. 10,'62, David's Is'l'd,N.Y.
Bassett, Greenleaf, Musician,	25	15, '61	Sept. 10, 1861, disability.
Coe, Jerome W., Musician,	19	15, '61	June 27, 1864, expiration of service.
Dickens, James E., Musician,	24	15, '61	27, 1864, do do
Moulton, Henry D., Wagoner,	23	15, '61	27, 1864, do do
Adshed, Levi A.	19	15, '61	Deserted Dec. 27, 1862.
Angier, Samuel A.	38	15, '61	Transf. Feb. 15, 1864, to V. R. C.
Barton, James N.	24	15, '61	June 27, 1864, expiration of service.
Bartlett, John W.	19	15, '61	27, 1864, do do
Black, Alexander,	45	Aug. 18, '61	Mar. 22, 1862, disability.
Bridges, Wesley,	24	June 15, '61	Died of wds. May,'63, Potomac Ck.
Brown, John,	34	15, '61	Killed May 3, '63, Marie's Hts.,Va.
Buckley, John,	24	15, '61	Died Oct. 10, '62, Ft. Monroe, Va.
Burns, James,	25	15, '61	Feb. 19, 1864, to re-enlist.
Burns, James,	27	Feb. 20, '64	Transf. June 14, 1864, to 37th Inf.
Caswell, Abraham H.	21	June 15, '61	Sept. 8, 1863, disability.
Cash, Alvin,	20	15, '61	June 27, 1864, expiration of service.
Chandler, Jacob,	22	15, '61	Dec. 28, 1863, disability.
Chace, John C.	18	15, '61	June 27, 1864, expiration of service.
Cooper, James,	22	15, '61	27, 1864, do do
Corbett, Charles H.	33	Feb. 26, '62	Died Aug. 5, '62, Harr. Land'g, Va.
Cornish, Edmund,	22	June 15, '61	Deserted Feb. 8, 1863.
Dean, Barney T.	21	15, '61	Aug. 15, 1861, disability.
Douglass, Edwin E.	23	15, '61	June 27, 1864, expiration of service.
Eames, Louis D	28	15, '61	July 20, 1862, disability.
Eddy, William L.	18	15, '61	Aug. 15, 1861, disability.
Elliott, Duncan S.	20	15, '61	Transf. Sept. 12, 1863, to V. R. C.
Field, Albert,	21	15, '61	June 27, 1864, expiration of service.
Foskett, George W.	22	15, '61	27, 1864, do do
Foulds, William H.	18	15, '61	Sept. 10, 1861, disability.
Francis, Henry W.	23	15, '61	June 27, 1864, expiration of service.
Francis, Leonard A.	27	15, '61	Died Nov. 6, 1862, Philadelp'a, Pa.
Francis, Lucian E.	21	15, '61	July 20, 1862, disability.
Gardner, Joseph M.	23	15, '61	June 27, 1864, expiration of service.
Gibson, Seth,	24	15, '61	Killed May 3, '63, Marie's Hts.,Va.
Gifford, Henry T.	22	15, '61	Aug. 6, 1862, disability.
Godfrey, Elijah A.	19	15, '61	Deserted Nov. 1, 1862.

Name and Rank.	Age	Date of Muster.	Termination of Service and cause thereof.
Company F — Con.			
Godfrey, John F.	21	June 15, '61	Nov. 30, 1862, disability.
Gregory, Joseph G.	24	15, '61	Aug. 29, 1862, do
Groves, James,	41	15, '61	D'd of wds. June 10, '63, Po.Cr.Hos.
Hall, Edward W.	23	Feb. 27, '62	Died Oct. 31, '62, Philadelphia, Pa.
Hall, Frederick,	23	June 15, '61	June 27, 1864, expiration of service.
Hancock, Joseph F.	19	15, '61	27, 1864, do do
Hannon, James,	39	Aug. 26, '62	Mar. 9, 1864, disability.
Hardy, Charles A.	21	June 15, '61	June 27, 1864, expiration of service.
Haskins, Albert M.	19	15, '61	Sept. 10, 1861, disability.
Hathaway, John F.	21	15, '61	Aug. 10, 1862, disability.
Holden, James,	26	15, '61	June 27, 1864, expiration of service.
Holt, John,	21	15, '61	Jan. 16, 1863, disability.
Hunt, Thomas,	29	15, '61	Deserted Nov. 4, 1862.
Knowles, Edward T.	26	15, '61	June 27, 1864, expiration of service.
McAvoy, William H.	22	15, '61	Sept. 1, 1862, disability.
McCormick, James,	22	Feb. 27, '62	Killed May 6, '64, Wilderness, Va.
Miller, Charles F.	19	June 15, '61	June 27, 1864, expiration of service.
Mullen, Thomas,	37	Aug. 25, '62	Dec. 4, 1863, disability.
Osborne, Levi,	22	June 15, '61	Deserted May 1, 1862.
Packer, William A.	19	15, '61	Transf. Sept. 1, 1863, to V. R. C.
Paine, Charles B.	23	15, '61	June 27, 1864, expiration of service.
Park, George H.	23	15, '61	Jan. 16, 1863, disability.
Peck, Charles H.	18	15, '61	Dec. 26, 1863, to re-enlist.
Peck, Charles H.	20	Dec. 27, '63	Transf. June 14, 1864, to 37th Inf.
Percival, Charles L.	23	June 15, '61	June 27, 1864, expiration of service.
Perry, Nathaniel,	18	15, '61	27, 1864, do do
Pierce, Edward A.	20	15, '61	27, 1864, do do
Pray, Evander,	18	15, '61	27, 1864, do do
Pratt, Lloyd W.	21	15, '61	Killed May 3, '63, Marie's Hts., Va.
Richmond, Samuel W.	25	15, '61	Aug. 15, 1861, disability.
Seymour, Edward D.	26	15, '61	Mar. 26, 1862, disability.
Shaw, Everett,	23	15, '61	June 27, 1864, expiration of service.
Shaw, William,	28	15, '61	May 15, 1865, Pres. proclamation.
Smith, Luther H.	21	15, '61	Died Nov. 28, '62, Philadelp'a, Pa.
Smith, William E.	21	15, '61	Jan. 16, 1863, disability.
Stevens, Hiram H.	26	Jan. 27, '62	Transf. Jan. 14, 1864, to V. R. C.
Stowell, John W.	19	Nov. 27, '63	Tr. June 14, '64, to 37th Inf. fr. Co. D.
Stowell, William O.	20	June 15, '61	June 27, 1864, expiration of service.
Studley, George,	24	15, '61	Transf. Sept. 12, 1863, to V. R. C.
Thayer, Edwin S.	25	Jan. 29, '62	Transf. June 14, '64, to 37th Inf.
Thrasher, Henry,	23	June 15, '61	Nov. 15, 1861, disability.
Trickey, Edwin H.	23	15, '61	June 27, 1864, expiration of service.
Ward, James,	23	15, '61	Deserted Sept. 18, 1862.
Washburn, Everett,	22	Oct. 24, '61	Deserted July 1, 1863.
Westcott, Charles S.	26	June 15, '61	Aug. 6, 1862, disability.
White, John,	21	15, '61	Killed June 25, '62, Fair Oaks, Va.
Whitcomb, William J.	18	15, '61	Died Mar. 20, '62, Washington, D.C.
Williams, Edward,	24	15, '61	June 27, 1864, expiration of service.
Williams, Erastus F.	18	15, '61	Nov. 15, 1861, disability.
Williams, Samuel K.	21	Aug. 28, '61	June 27, 1864, expiration of service.
Wilbur, Philo B.	21	June 15, '61	Died Mar. 18, '62, Wash'gton, D. C.
Wordell, Seth,	21	15, '61	Dec. 26, 1863, to re-enlist.
Wordell, Seth,	23	Dec. 27, '63	Transf. Mar. —, 1864, to Navy.
Company G.			
Andrews, George W., 1st Sergt.	27	June 15, '61	Second Lieut. Aug. 11, 1862.
Fecto, Philander W., 1st Sergt.	31	15, '61	June 27, 1864, expiration of service.
Bouldry, William W. C., Sergt.	20	15, '61	27, 1864, do do
McGregor, Simon, Sergt.	22	15, '61	Q. M. Sergt. Apr. 24, 1863.

ROSTER OF THE REGIMENT.

NAME AND RANK.	Age	Date of Muster.	Termination of Service and cause thereof.
Company G—Con.			
Newman, James S., Sergt.	23	June 15, '61	June 27, 1864, expiration of service.
Wells, Freeman E., Sergt.	20	15, '61	27, 1864, do do
Wilbur, Edwin F., Sergt.	26	15, '61	27, 1864, do do
Healey, Frederick E., Corp.	30	15, '61	15, 1864, do do
Howard, Samuel F., Corp.	22	15, '61	Transf. Mar. 15, 1864, to V. R. C.
McCullough, James, Corp.	24	15, '61	Died of wds., May 15,'64, Fred'ksb'g.
Roach, Jacob, Corp.	21	15, '61	Killed May 6, '64, Wilderness, Va.
Wallace, Martin R., Corp.	24	Aug. 28, '61	Transf. Nov. 15, 1863, to V. R. C.
Humphrey, James A., Musician,	20	June 15, '61	Died Sept. 30, '62, Alexandria, Va.
Packard, Francis S., Musician,	33	15, '61	Deserted July 18, 1861.
Sager, George, Musician,	16	Nov. 14, '61	Feb. 18, 1864, to re-enlist.
Sager, George, Musician,	18	Feb. 19, '64	Transf. June 14, 1864, to 37th Inf.
Wells, James, Wagoner,	43	June 15, '61	Jan. 3, 1863, disability.
Birmingham, Michael,	21	15, '61	June 27, 1864, expiration of service.
Bowen, George,	26	15, '61	Nov. 16, 1863, order War Dept.
Burt, Eustis E.,	20	15, '61	June 27, 1864, expiration of service.
Carnes, Paul,	25	15, '61	27, 1864, do do
Cassidy, Thomas,	22	15, '61	Jan. 12, 1862, disability.
Clark, Horace M.	31	15, '61	Aug. 6, 1861, disability.
Cooks, Joseph,	23	15, '61	Died Apr. 23, 1864, Andersonville.
Dallery, George,	44	Aug. 26, '61	Mar. 18, 1862, disability.
Dean, John B.	22	June 15, '61	June 27, 1864, expiration of service.
Dollard, Garrett,	32	15, '61	27, 1864, do do
Donovan, Daniel,	21	15, '61	Killed May 6, '64, Wilderness, Va.
Dunbar, Norman L.	17	Sept. 4, '61	Nov. 14, 1863, disability.
Dunbar, Seth T.	40	June 15, '61	Killed June 12,'64, Cold Harbor,Va.
Eldredge, Charles H.	27	15, '61	Hospital Steward, Mar. 1, 1863.
Eldredge, Jason F.	32	15, '61	Died Aug. 27, 1862.
Fadden, James,	30	15, '61	Jan. 16, 1863, disability.
Fay, Philip,	23	15, '61	Deserted June 20, 1861.
Field, Shepherd,	29	15, '61	Deserted Jan. 17, 1863.
Fisher, Billings,	43	15, '61	June 27, 1864, expiration of service.
Flaherty, Matthew T.	19	15, '61	Feb. 19, 1862, disability.
Freeman, Cyrus A.	17	15, '61	June 27, 1864, expiration of service.
Gallagher, James P.	31	15, '61	Jan. 16, 1863, disability.
George, Charles W.	26	15, '61	June 27, 1864, expiration of service.
Gilmore, Samuel H.	20	15, '61	Died Jan. 4, 1863, Easton.
Griffin, John,	21	15, '61	June 27, 1864, expiration of service.
Griffin, Thomas,	38	15, '61	Jan. 3, 1863, disability.
Hall, Lorenzo,	42	July 8, '61	June 27, 1864, expiration of service.
Hamilton, Alonzo,	18	June 15, '61	Deserted Sept. 1, 1862.
Hevers, Thomas,	33	15, '61	Aug. 6, 1864, disability.
Higgins, Russell S.	34	15, '61	Deserted Apr. 25, 1863.
Holbrook, Caleb R.	22	15, '61	Deserted May 1, 1864.
Horr, George L.	31	15, '61	June 27, 1864, expiration of service.
Horton, Oliver J.	25	Aug. 28, '61	Deserted Dec. 11, 1862.
Hudson, Edward,	19	June 15, '61	Died Jan. 24, '62, Brightwood, D.C.
Hudson, Samuel,	18	15, '61	June 27, 1864, expiration of service.
Hunt, Albert C.	34	15, '61	25, 1864, disability.
Johnson, John,	37	Jan. 4, '61	Transf. June 14, 1864, to 37th Inf.
Jones, Morgan,	38	June 15, '61	Mar. 26, 1862, disability.
Keenan, James H.	19	15, '61	June 27, 1864, expiration of service.
Lane, William H.	22	15, '61	Deserted Dec. 11, 1862.
Leach, Edward B.	21	15, '61	Deserted Nov. 20, 1863.
LeBarron, Otis D.	20	July 11, '61	Died Sept. 17,'62, Philadelphia, Pa.
Leddingham, George A.	44	Aug. 24, '61	Apr. 25, 1863, disability
Lester, Henry M.	22	June 15, '61	June 27, 1864, expiration of service.
Lincoln, Albert A.	23	15, '61	Deserted Dec. 11, 1862.
Locke, Parmenas,	32	15, '61	June 27, 1864, expiration of service.

NAME AND RANK.	Age	Date of Muster.	Termination of Service and cause thereof.
Company G—Con.			
Loftes, Nicholas,	39	June 15, '61	Feb. 18, 1864, to re-enlist.
Loftes, Nicholas,	41	Feb. 19, '64	Transf. June 14, 1864, to 37th Inf.
Lothrop, Charles F.	33	June 15, '61	June 27, 1864, expiration of service.
Lowe, John W.	29	15, '61	27, 1864, do do
Madigan, Michael,	20	15, '61	27, 1864, do do
McCue, Michael,	22	15, '61	27, 1864, do do
McDonald, John,	27	15, '61	Dec. 30, 1862, disability.
McKenney, Francis,	19	15, '61	June 27, 1864, expiration of service.
McKeegan, John,	32	15, '61	27, 1864, do do
McMullen, Terrence,	20	15, '61	27, 1864, do do
McNamara, Thomas,	25	15, '61	Deserted June 25, 1861.
Middleton, James P.	26	15, '61	June 27, 1864, expiration of service.
Miller, Charles E.	18	15, '61	Deserted May 4, 1864.
Murphy, George M.	18	15, '61	June 27, 1864, expiration of service.
Murphy, James,	43	15, '61	Transf. Sept. 1, 1863, to V. R. C.
Murphy, James H.,	19	15, '61	Deserted May 5, 1864.
O'Brien, Charles,	21	15, '61	Nov. 16, 1863, order War Dept.
O'Rourke, William,	21	15, '61	Deserted June 25, 1861.
Packard, Elijah B.	40	15, '61	Aug. 25, 1863, disability.
Packard, William H.	32	Aug. 28, '61	Deserted Oct. 10, 1862.
Packard, William W.	18	June 15, '61	Deserted Dec. 11, 1862.
Park, Charles E.	29	15, '61	June 27, 1864, expiration of service.
Peck, Henry W.	45	15, '61	Jan. 3, 1863, disability.
Phillips, Asaph W.	22	15, '61	June 27, 1864, expiration of service.
Phillips, Howard W.	25	15, '61	Jan. 20, 1864, to re-enlist.
Phillips, Howard W.	27	Jan. 21, '64	Transf. June 14, 1864, to 37th Inf.
Quinn, Charles,	21	June 15, '61	Deserted Dec. 3, 1862.
Quinn, Thomas,	22	15, '61	Sept. 22, 1861, disability.
Quinlan, Daniel,	38	15, '61	June 27, 1864, expiration of service.
Randall, Nathan P.	19	15, '61	Mar. 17, 1864, to re-enlist.
Randall, Nathan P.	21	Mar. 18, '64	Deserted June 3, 1864.
Reynolds, Joseph,	36	June 15, '61	Deserted July 3, 1863.
Rooney, Michael,	21	15, '61	Deserted Oct. 10, 1862.
Ruby, Daniel,	20	15, '61	Deserted Sept. 5, 1862.
Ryan, Bryant,	19	15, '61	Deserted Dec. 3, 1862.
Shaw, Charles,	18	15, '61	Aug. 6, 1861, disability.
Sheehan, James,	26	15, '61	June 27, 1864, expiration of service.
Smeddy, Morris,	27	Jan. 18, '64	Transf. June 14, 1864, to 37th Inf.
Smiddy, Thomas,	22	June 15, '61	June 27, 1864, expiration of service.
Stanley, George R.	24	July 1, '61	Sept. 22, 1862, disability.
Staples, William H.	19	11, '61	June 27, 1864, expiration of service.
Sulkooki, Charles,	19	June 15, '61	Deserted June 25, 1861.
Sullivan, Patrick,	22	15, '61	June 27, 1864, expiration of service.
Sweet, Alanson E.	20	15, '61	Transf. Sept. 30, 1863, to V. R. C.
Thompson, David,	22	15, '61	June 27, 1864, expiration of service.
Tilden, Alfred H.	19	15, '61	27, 1864, do do
Torrey, Charles S.	31	15, '61	Died Aug. 17, 1864, Andersonville.
Tucker, William B.	18	15, '61	Nov. 20, 1862, disability.
White, Samuel R.	19	15, '61	June 27, 1864, expiration of service.
Williams, Charles E.	26	15, '61	Deserted June 20, 1861.
Woodward, Henry B.	18	15, '61	Died June 14, 1862, Baltimore, Md.
Young, William,	28	15, '61	Jan. 20, 1864, to re-enlist.
Young, William,	30	Jan. 21, '64	Transf. Apr. 15, 1864, to Navy.
Company H.			
Cady, Charles E., 1st Sergt.	30	June 15, '61	Second Lieut. Jan. 17, 1863.
High, Thomas, 1st Sergt.	27	15, '61	Second Lieut. Nov. 7, 1861.
Smith, William H., 1st Sergt.	25	15, '61	June 27, 1864, expiration of service.
Drake, Francis, Sergt.	32	15, '61	Feb. 19, 1863, disability.

NAME AND RANK.	Age	Date of Muster.	Termination of Service and cause thereof.
Company H—Con.			
Hill, Mason A., Sergt.	31	June 15, '61	Killed May 8, '64, Spottsylv'a, Va.
Knowles, Charles W., Sergt.	33	15, '61	June 27, 1864, expiration of service.
Thompson, William J., Sergt.	23	15, '61	27, 1864, do do
Tillson, Albert A., Sergt.	18	15, '61	Second Lieut. July 12, 1862.
Wood, Simeon S., Sergt.	22	15, '61	June 27, 1864, expiration of service.
Wright, Henry B., Sergt.	22	15, '61	27, 1864, do do
Austin, Sanford B., Corp.	22	15, '61	27, 1864, do do
Grover, Vernon F., Corp.	20	15, '61	27, 1864, do do
Hull, John G., Corp.	22	15, '61	27, 1864, do do
Kerr, William, Corp.	23	15, '61	27, 1864, do do
Kittrell, Albert S., Corp.	25	15, '61	Nov. 27, 1862, disability.
Kittrell, James P., Corp.	26	15, '61	Apr. 7, 1863, do
Lawton, Horatio M., Corp.	20	15, '61	Sept. 29, 1863, do
Shepard, George H., Corp.	20	15, '61	Transf. Mar. 23, 1864, to V. R. C.
Stearns, Henry W., Corp.	20	15, '61	June 27, 1864, expiration of service.
Vallett, Alexander F., Corp.	19	15, '61	27, 1864, do do
Williams, Josiah, Corp.	33	15, '61	Mar. 18, 1862, disability.
Frazier, William F., Musician,	25	15, '61	Transf. Sept. 1, 1863, to V. R. C.
Cabot, Frederick H., Wagoner,	27	15, '61	Deserted Apr. 26, 1864.
Adams, William F.	24	15, '61	Nov. 12, 1861, disability.
Atwood, William H.	33	15, '61	Aug. 27, 1862, do
Belcher, Charles W.	30	15, '61	Dec. 23, 1862, do
Biggs, John,	20	15, '61	Deserted Feb. 27, 1863.
Birchard, Isaac R.	30	15, '61	Nov. 21, 1862, disability.
Blanchard, James,	30	15, '61	June 27, 1864, expiration of service.
Blanchard, John,	32	15, '61	Died of wds. May 25,'63, Wash'gton.
Brown, Levi,	38	15, '61	June 27, 1864, expiration of service.
Chadwick, John A.	21	15, '61	27, 1864, do do
Cobb, Alanson W.	20	15, '61	27, 1864, do do
Cobb, William A. M.	26	15, '61	Died Dec 31,'63, Washington, D.C.
Colby, John S.	25	15, '61	Transf. Jan. 27, '63, to V. R. C.
Coleman, William,	22	15, '61	June 27, 1864, expiration of service.
Cook, George S.	22	15, '61	27, 1864, do do
Downing, John,	20	15, '61	Sept. 24, 1862, disability.
Eagan, Michael,	25	15, '61	June 27, 1864, expiration of service.
Fisher, John W.	24	15, '61	27, 1864, do do
Foster, William B.	18	15, '61	Transf. Sept. 30, 1863, to V. R. C.
Fox, John,	36	15, '61	June 27, 1864, expiration of service.
Gallagher, Edward,	36	15, '61	Transf. Jan. 15, 1864, to V. R. C.
Gammons, Sanford B.	19	15, '61	June 27, 1864, expiration of service.
George, Thomas M., Jr.	32	15, '61	27, 1864, do do
Gerrish, Daniel B.	22	Feb. 17, '62	Oct. 7, 1863, disability.
Gerrish, John B.	25	Aug. 13, '62	June 27, 1864, expiration of service.
Goff, Joseph B.	20	June 15, '61	Deserted July 1, 1861.
Gooch, Samuel H.	25	15, '61	June 27, 1864, expiration of service.
Gorman, John,	23	15, '61	Feb. 18, 1862, disability.
Gray, William,	23	15, '61	June 27, 1864, expiration of service.
Hall, Edward F.	22	15, '61	Transf. Sept. 25, 1863, to V. R. C.
Hayward, Albert M.	22	Aug. 30, '62	June 27, 1864, expiration of service.
Hodges, Frank H.	21	June 15, '61	20, 1861, disability.
Holmes, Alonzo P.	24	15, '61	Oct. 1, 1862, disability.
Howard, Everett F.	31	Mar. 4, '62	Transf. June 14, 1864, to 37th Inf.
Hunt, George C.	22	June 15, '61	June 27, 1864, expiration of service.
Hunnewell, Theodore H.	18	15, '61	27, 1864, do do
Ide, George H.	29	15, '61	Deserted Dec. 12, 1862.
Ingalls, Elhanan,	26	15, '61	Deserted Dec. 12, 1862.
Keenan, Alanson C.	34	15, '61	June 27, 1864, expiration of service.
King, Richard H.	21	15, '61	Nov. 12, 1861, disability.
Lamb, Henry,	24	15, '61	Deserted Dec. 8, 1862.

NAME AND RANK.	Age	Date of Muster.	Termination of Service and cause thereof.

Company H—Con.

Lord, Frost,	24	June 15, '61	Mar. 30, 1862, disability.
Martin, Hiram L.	18	15, '61	Dropped from rolls April 26, 1864.
Martin, John W.	19	15, '61	July 20, 1862, disability.
Martin, William,	21	15, '61	June 27, 1864, expiration of service.
McCausland, William,	19	15, '61	27, 1864, do do
McCourt, Barney,	33	15, '61	27, 1864, do do
McDonald, Edward,	31	15, '61	15, 1862, disability.
McGee, Andrew,	34	15, '61	Died Oct. 30, 1862, Taunton.
McGinnis, Patrick,	37	Aug. 26, '62	June 27, 1864, expiration of service.
Melvin, Henry D.	22	June 15, '61	Deserted Feb. 17, 1863.
Morse, Charles A.	20	15, '61	Died Apr. 18, '63, Falmouth, Va.
Morse, Stillman F.	24	15, '61	Died Mar. 10, '63, Foxborough.
O'Malley, Owen,	36	15, '61	Killed May 3, '63, Marie's Hts.,Va.
Palmer, James S.	22	15, '61	June 27, 1864, expiration of service.
Patten, William H.	21	15, '61	Dec. 15, 1862, disability.
Pike, Chandler J.	24	15, '61	June 27, 1864, expiration of service.
Prime, James,	22	15, '61	Dec. 3, 1862, disability.
Reed, Hiram B.	22	15, '61	June 27, 1864, expiration of service.
Reeves, John,	33	Feb. 22, '62	15, 1862, disability.
Richardson, Charles D.	18	June 15, '61	Jan. 17, 1863, disability.
Robinson, Charles A.	30	15, '61	Dec. 5, 1862, disability.
Rose, Francis,	26	15, '61	Deserted Dec. 12, 1862.
Rounds, Enon H.	22	15, '61	Oct. 2, 1862, disability.
Seagraves, Charles,	26	15, '61	June 27, 1864, expiration of service.
Shaw, Nathan M.	20	15, '61	27, 1864, do do
Shepardson, Erastus,	18	15, '61	27, 1864, do do
Shields, Timothy,	29	15, '61	Mar. 18, 1862, disability.
Slattery, Dennis,	18	15, '61	June 25, 1861, disability.
Smith, Adolphus P.	24	15, '61	Deserted Apr. 26, 1864.
Smith, Jesse W.	17	15, '61	Dec. 5, 1862, disability.
Smith, Philip,	18	15, '61	Deserted Feb. 7, 1863.
Stephenson, Joseph,	27	15, '61	Feb. 21, 1863, disability.
Sweet, Benjamin F.	18	15, '61	Deserted Oct. 8, 1863.
Sweet, George L.	18	15, '61	Sept. —, 1862, disability.
Tobit, John L.	19	15, '61	Jan. 4, 1863, do
Wiggins, James F.	22	15, '61	June 27, 1864, expiration of service.
Willard, Eber,	20	15, '61	Killed May 3, '63, Marie's Hts.,Va.
Williams, Albert,	22	15, '61	Mar. 5, 1863, disability.
Williams, Charles F.	18	Aug. 8, '62	June 27, 1864, expiration of service.
Williams, Otis,	23	June 15, '61	Mar. 16, 1863, disability.
Wink, Frank,	20	15, '61	Deserted Feb. 7, 1863.
Wink, Frederick,	26	15, '61	Deserted Oct. 1, 1862.
Wetherell, Sumner H.	21	15, '61	June 27, 1864, expiration of service.
Wood, Benjamin F.	19	15, '61	27, 1864, do do

Company I.

Giles, Isaac F., 1st Sergt.	25	June 15, '61	Second Lieut. May 8, 1863.
Hall, John N., 1st Sergt.	25	15, '61	June 27, 1864, expiration of service.
Hill, William H., 1st Sergt.	22	15, '61	Died of wds. May 7,'64, Wilderness.
Savery, Abraham B., 1st Sergt.	25	15, '61	Died Dec. 16, '63, Brandy Sta'n,Va.
Wade, William H., 1st Sergt.	21	15, '61	Second Lieut. Oct. 25, 1862.
Whiting, Prentiss M., 1st Sergt.	24	15, '61	Second Lieut. Sept. 2, 1861.
Bliss, Harlan P., Sergt.	21	15, '61	June 27, 1864, expiration of service.
Faas, Charles, Sergt.	34	15, '61	Sept. 28, 1862, disability.
Gay, Samuel F., Sergt.	19	15, '61	June 27, 1864, expiration of service.
Richards, Baylies B., Sergt.	21	15, '61	Died Oct. 1, '62, David's Is'd, N.Y.
Snell, Charles W., Sergt.	33	15, '61	June 27, 1864, expiration of service.
Swett, Thomas C., Sergt.	33	15, '61	27, 1864, do do
Wilkinson, John F., Sergt.	26	15, '61	Principal Musician, Jan. 18, 1863.

www.ingramcontent.com/pod-product-compliance
Lightning Source LLC
Chambersburg PA
CBHW030318240426
43673CB00040B/1208